HOW THE GOOD NEWS BEGAN

HOW THE GOOD NEWS BEGAN

Study Guide to Mark's Gospel

by

FRANCIS FOULKES, M.A., B.D., M.SC.

St John's College, Auckland, New Zealand, and formerly
Principal of the Vining College,
Akure, Nigeria

AFRICA CHRISTIAN PRESS

First edition 1986

ISBN 9964 87 515 0

The Bible text in this publication is from the Revised Standard
Version of the Bible, copyrighted in 1946 and 1952 by the
Division of Christian Education, National Council of Churches of
Christ in the U.S.A.

Trade orders to:
Nigeria: Challenge Bookshops, P.M.B. 12256, Lagos, and
Fellent Ltd., P.O. Box 5923, Lagos
Zambia: P.O. Box 21689, Kitwe
Kenya: Keswick Bookshop, P.O. Box 10242, Nairobi
S. Africa: A.C.L.A., P.O. Box 332, Roodepoort 1725, Transvaal
Zimbabwe: Word of Life Bookshops, P.O. Box 3700, Harare
Australia: Bookhouse, P.O. Box 115, Flemington Markets,
N.S.W. 2129
U.K.: A.C.P., 49 Thornbury Road, Isleworth,
Middlesex TW7 4LE

All other orders to:
A.C.P., P.O. Box 30, Achimota, Ghana, W. Africa

Designed and printed for
AFRICA CHRISTIAN PRESS
by Nuprint Services Ltd, Harpenden, Herts AL5 4SE.

PREFACE

MARK'S GOSPEL, like the rest of the Bible, has been translated into hundreds of the world's languages. There are in fact many languages in which there is as yet no other part of Scripture except this Gospel. In some languages, like English, countless books have been written *about* Mark's Gospel. Some set out to explain in detail what the Gospel says, chapter by chapter, verse by verse. Others try to apply what it says to our life today. Others again help the readers to study the Gospel more deeply for themselves. This Study Guide tries to combine different purposes. It sets out to show some of the things on which the Gospel places great emphasis as it tells of the life and death and resurrection of our Lord Jesus Christ, and in doing this to explain things that need explaining. Yet its plan is not just to feed the mind with knowledge. Each study ends with a prayer or a suggestion for meditation, because the reading of the Bible should always lead us to the response of repentance, faith, and obedience, that we express first in prayer and then in action in our daily lives. So that it may be used for daily readings, the book has been divided into passages that are not too long for daily study and meditation. Finally, because there is a depth of truth and breadth of application that such a Study Guide can only begin to reach, suggestions are made in each section for further study.

The Revised Standard Version is the translation printed in each section because it is a version widely used and one that sets out to keep as closely as possible to what was written in the original languages of the Bible.

THE GOSPEL
ACCORDING TO MARK

SUCH IS the heading of this book in our Bible, 'The Gospel according to Mark'. Thus it is called a 'Gospel' and it is said to be by 'Mark'. Nowhere in the book itself is Mark's name mentioned. It was important to the writer to write about Jesus and not about himself. It is from the 2nd Century, two generations after the Gospel was written, that we have Christian writers telling us that Mark wrote the Gospel and that Mark was 'the interpreter' and the 'disciple' of Peter. There are no strong reasons why we should doubt what these early writers say. From other New Testament books we know that this man Mark (sometimes called John Mark), had his home in Jerusalem and the early Christians met there for fellowship and prayer (Acts 12:12). Paul and Barnabas took him to work with them when they set out from Antioch for their first great missionary journey (Acts 13:1–4). Mark was the cousin of Barnabas (Colossians 4:10). Unfortunately, when the way was hard and the work difficult, Mark turned back (Acts 13:13), and so Paul was unwilling to take him with him when he set out from Antioch on a second missionary journey (see Acts 15:36–41). One failure, however, did not mean the end of Mark's usefulness. Barnabas took him to work with him, and in the end Paul also could speak of him as 'very useful' as a fellow-worker (2 Timothy 4:11).

The link of Mark with the apostle Peter is shown to us in 1 Peter 5:13, and we can think of him as learning much from Peter about the earthly life and ministry of Jesus. He would have learnt how Peter and the other preachers of the Gospel used the stories of what Jesus did to show who He is and what He came to do. He would have learnt how they applied the teaching of Jesus to the lives of Christians, showing what it meant to be disciples. Many of the things told in this Gospel show the weaknesses of Peter and the others who from the first were disciples of Jesus, and we can imagine how Mark heard Peter telling these things to show how, although he and the other disciples failed often and did not at first understand the ways of their Master, Jesus was patient with them and led them on to know Him better and to serve Him more truly.

The Christian writers who say that Mark wrote this Gospel tell us that he wrote it in Rome after Peter and Paul had died. Although other suggestions have been made, we are likely to be correct if we say that this Gospel was written in Rome about 65 AD or a little later. Since both Matthew and Luke were written with a knowledge of Mark, this Gospel could not have been written very much later. If it were written a few years earlier or if it were written from somewhere else than Rome, it would make little difference to our understanding of what it says.

Purposes in writing

1. He wanted to tell *how the good news of Jesus began*. He says this in the first verse. When he uses the word 'gospel', he is not speaking of a book but of the good news that was preached (see 1:14–15, 8:35, 10:29, 13:10 and 14:9). He passed on the things that Peter and the other early apostles and evangelists told about Jesus. The outline of the Gospel is like the outline of the Christian preaching that we read of in the Acts of the Apostles (in such passages as Acts 2:22–24, 10:36–41 and 13:23–31), beginning with

John the Baptist, telling of the mighty works of Jesus, how 'he went about doing good and healing...', then, most important of all, telling of His death and resurrection. Mark also shows that the right response to the good news should be repentance and faith and discipleship.

2. In one way the good news could be said to be preached by Jesus. In another way the good news was the good news about Jesus and so the Gospel had to *tell who this Jesus is*. Mark speaks of Him as 'Son of man', as the 'Christ' (though that title had to be used in the right way), as 'Son of God'. It was not enough, however, to give Him the right titles. *The work that He did* had to be made plain, and right through the Gospel we see Him constantly teaching and preaching, and meeting the deepest needs of the people around Him. That work of Jesus was to be carried on by His followers for whom Mark wrote – teaching, preaching, caring, showing in life what 'the kingdom of God', the rule of God, means, of which Jesus spoke so often.

3. Those who preached the good news of Jesus had to tell – and indeed were determined to tell – how He died on a Roman cross. They felt they must tell *why He died such a death*. From one point of view the reason could be given in terms of the opposition of the Jews and the part played by the Roman authorities. There was, however, a deeper reason. Mark tells us that Jesus spoke of it before it happened, and showed that it was in the purpose of the Father (8:31, 9:31, 10:33). It was the greatest part of the work that He had to do, 'to give His life as a ransom for many' (10:45), and by His blood shed in His death to make a new covenant between sinful men and women and God (14:22–24).

4. Mark tells us a good deal in his book about three groups of people. There were those who opposed Jesus. There were also the crowds whom Jesus taught, to whom He preached the good news and for whom He cared. He did His miracles to meet their needs. Mark further tells us of men and women called to be disciples, and of the *life-*

style that discipleship meant. As Jesus faced opposition and suffering, so His disciples had to be willing to face such opposition and suffering. This has emphasis in Mark's writing. He wrote at a time when Roman authorities were persecuting Christians and perhaps the great apostles Peter and Paul had been recently put to death for their faith.

5. One of Mark's purposes in writing was to show that *the good news was for Gentiles* (non-Jews) as well as for Jews. The laws and customs which kept Jews separate from others were no longer to be such a barrier (7:14–23). The Jews were not to think of themselves alone as God's people and possessors of His inheritance (12:1–9). The good news of Jesus was for the 'whole world' (14:9), to be 'preached to all nations' (13:10).

Arrangement of the Gospel

The way that the Gospel is arranged helps us to see some of these purposes and emphases which Mark had in mind as he wrote. There is a careful arrangement, sometimes to bring out clearly the work that Jesus came to do, sometimes to show the reasons why people were against Him, and to show the things that led to His death – and also to the resurrection. We may divide the Gospel into sections as follows:

Mark 1:1–13
INTRODUCTION

1:1	Title
1:2–8	John the Baptist
1:9–11	Baptism of Jesus
1:12–13	His temptation

Mark 1:14–45
BEGINNING OF JESUS' MINISTRY

1:14–15	Preaching the good news of God's kingdom
1:16–20	Calling His first disciples

Mark 4:35—5:43
FOUR MIGHTY ACTS OF JESUS

Mark 6:1—8:30
WIDER MINISTRY, FAITH AND UNBELIEF,
THE TRAINING OF DISCIPLES

Mark 8:31—11:11
JOURNEY TO JERUSALEM

Mark 11:12—12:44
MINISTRY IN JERUSALEM

Mark 13:1–37
TEACHING ABOUT THE FUTURE

Mark 16:9–20
WAY THE GOSPEL ENDS

These last verses, printed in some Bible translations but not in others, are not in most of the earliest copies of the Gospel that we have. It is possible that the Gospel originally ended at verse 8 and that later it was felt that more should be told, especially of the way the risen Lord Jesus came to

His disciples. Or it may be that the original ending was lost and verses 9–20 were added. More will be said about this in the final study.

BOOKS RECOMMENDED

The following are specially recommended for further study of the Gospel:
R. A. Cole, *The Gospel According to Mark* (Tyndale Commentary), IVP
John Hargreaves, *A Guide to St Mark's Gospel* (TEF Study Guides), SPCK
A. M. Hunter, *The Gospel According to St Mark* (Torch Commentary), SCM
C. F. D. Moule, *The Gospel According to Mark* (Cambridge Bible), CUP
W. L. Lane, *The Gospel According to Mark* (New International Commentary), Eerdmans (a very fine more detailed commentary)

MARK
INTRODUCTION
Mark 1:1–13

The four Gospels begin in very different ways. Matthew, the most Jewish of the Gospels, begins with the 'family tree' of Jesus going back to Abraham, the great ancestor of the Hebrew people. Luke begins with the story of the birth of John the Baptist who prepared the way for Jesus and then he gives the record of Jesus' birth. John begins by speaking of Jesus as the Word of God, the Son who was 'in the beginning with God' and who came and lived a truly human life amongst us.

Mark begins by telling who Jesus is and then he shows how what John the Baptist did fulfilled the Old Testament Scriptures. He goes on, much more briefly than Matthew or Luke, to tell of the baptism of Jesus and His temptation. So here we have:

1:1	Title
1:2–8	John the Baptist
1:9–11	Baptism of Jesus
1:12–13	His temptation

Study 1: HOW THE CHRISTIAN GOOD NEWS BEGAN

The beginning of the gospel of Jesus Christ, the Son of God (1:1).

As far as we know, for the first hundred years of the Church the word 'gospel' was not used for the New Testament books which we call the four Gospels. The word meant simply the good news about Jesus. So when Mark heads his Gospel as he does in this first verse, he is saying that what he writes is telling how the good news began. It is good news, the best news ever told, because it is centred in a Person and that One the greatest who has ever lived our human life in this world. The whole of Mark's work tells who He is. In this very first verse Mark gives us the three names which describe Him and the work that He came to do.

a. He is Jesus

According to Luke 1:31 and Matthew 1:21 this name was given before He was born. Many other Jewish people had had this name before, a name meaning 'The Lord saves'. It was the ordinary human name by which He was most often called, and is used nearly 100 times in Mark's Gospel. But it had a special importance. The good news is in this name and its meaning. Matthew 1:21 gives the words spoken to Joseph: 'You shall call his name Jesus, for he will save his people from their sins.' Many of the incidents that Mark has written down for us show His work as Saviour from sin and from evil. (See, for example, 2:1–12, 13–17 and 5:1–20.) The name Jesus is good news indeed because the name describes the Person and the work He does.

b. He is the Christ

Often in the New Testament we read of Jesus Christ or Christ Jesus, and we might think of 'Christ' as just another name given to Jesus. It is much more than that. 'Christ' means 'anointed', and is the Greek form of the Hebrew word 'Messiah'. From the time of King David onwards (see 2 Samuel 7:8–16) the Hebrew people had had the hope of a special King, an 'anointed' one who would come to them. The prophets, as God's messengers, put this hope in different ways. He would be a King greater than David. He would bring deliverance to the people from their enemies. He would rule in justice and bring peace (see, for example, Isaiah 9:1–7, 11:1–9 and Jeremiah 23:5–6). This was the hope of the Messiah, the Christ.

The Christian believes that Jesus came as the Christ of God, fulfilling all the hopes and prophecies that God had given to Israel by His messengers in earlier generations. Mark goes on to tell us the *kind* of Messiah Jesus came to be. He tells us how the disciples were led to believe in Him as Christ (8:27–30). The Jewish leaders did not accept Him as their Christ (14:61–62). They crucified Him, but the resurrection proved them wrong and, as the apostles came to preach it, 'God has made him both Lord and Christ, this Jesus whom you crucified' (Acts 2:36). This is good news indeed, that Jesus is the Christ.

c. Jesus is the Son of God

This is the greatest name possible, the greatest claim that could be made for any person who has lived our human life. Not *a* son of God, but *the* Son of God. All our four Gospels and many of the other New Testament books make this claim clearly. There have been many messengers, many men and women of God but, Christians believe, only One who could bear this name, 'the Son of God'. So Hebrews 1:1–2 (Good News Bible) puts it, 'In the past God spoke to our ancestors many times and in many ways through the prophets, but in these last days he has spoken to us through his Son.' He lived our human life in great humility, but He taught as no other person has ever taught and He did things that no other person has ever done.

Mark, along with all the earliest Christians, was convinced

that Jesus is the Son of God. He claimed to be this, even though His claim meant His crucifixion (14:61–62). He was declared this from heaven (1:11 and 9:7). Even the demons recognized Him to be the Son of God (3:11). So the disciples came to believe that. Jesus is the Son of God. The well-known words of John 3:16 sum it up: 'God so loved the world that he gave his only Son, that whoever believes in Him should not perish but have eternal life.'

Prayer   *'Thanks be to God for his inexpressible gift'* (2 Corinthians 9:15).

For further thought and study   1. Look up the ways the four Gospels begin and compare them.
   What is special about each of these introductions?
   2. In what ways do the names of Jesus express the good news about Him? Do we tell the story of Jesus and live by it as *good news* for the world?

Notes   1. Because we may mean two different things when we use the word 'gospel', we will use 'gospel' (with a small 'g') in this book when we mean the good news of Jesus, and 'Gospel' (with a capital 'G') when we mean this book written by Mark or any of the other three Gospels.
   2. Jesus is spoken of as 'Son of God' in all the Gospels (see Matthew 14:33, 16:16, Luke 1:35, 4:41, John 1:14, 5:19–23, 20:31), in Acts (9:20, 13:33) and in the Epistles (e.g. Romans 1:3–4, 8:29, Galatians 4:4, 1 John 4:15).

———————

Study 2: PREPARING THE WAY OF THE LORD

²As it is written in Isaiah the prophet,
   'Behold, I send my messenger before thy face
   who shall prepare thy way;
   ³the voice of one crying in the wilderness:

> Prepare the way of the Lord,
>   make his paths straight –'

⁴John the baptizer appeared in the wilderness, preaching a baptism of repentance for the forgiveness of sins. ⁵And there went out to him all the country of Judea, and all the people of Jerusalem; and they were baptized by him in the river Jordan, confessing their sins. ⁶Now John was clothed with camel's hair, and had a leather girdle around his waist, and ate locusts and wild honey. ⁷And he preached, saying, 'After me comes he who is mightier than I, the thong of whose sandals I am not worthy to stoop down and untie. ⁸I have baptized you with water; but he will baptize you with the Holy Spirit'   (1:2-8).

In our first study we saw what it meant that Jesus could be called the Christ, the fulfilment of the hopes and prophecies of the Old Testament. Whenever the early Christians preached the good news to the Jews they spoke of this fulfilment of the Old Testament. All four Gospels do the same.

We have noticed that Mark does not begin the story of Jesus with His birth, as do Matthew and Luke. He begins by telling of the one who was sent to prepare the way for Jesus, John the Baptist, or really, we should say, 'John the Baptizer' (verse 4). It is clear from John 1:23 that John the Baptizer saw his life-work well described in the Old Testament words of Isaiah 40:3. He was sent to be 'the voice of one crying in the wilderness: Prepare the way of the Lord, make His paths straight' (verse 3). Malachi 3:1 also fitted his ministry, as John was the messenger sent before Jesus to prepare the way (verse 2).

Notice three things that these verses tell us of John.

a. How he prepared the way

As John preached he told people simply and clearly that the one way to prepare for the Lord was the way of repentance (verse 4). God can only work in the lives of those who turn from things that they know are wrong in His sight. Only by such repentance do we come to a right relationship with God and live the life He intends us to live. From the beginning of the Bible to the end, in the whole story of God's dealing with men and women, we see that He expects of us repentance and faith – turning from wrong, turning to Him, ready to obey and to serve.

John preached 'a baptism of repentance'. That meant that he asked people to show by an outward action that they had turned from their sin and wanted God's cleansing and forgiveness. The Jews knew that non-Jewish converts were asked to be baptized, to show their faith and their desire for the purifying of their lives. But John called on Jewish people – even the religious Pharisees and Sadducees (Matthew 3:7) – to accept this 'baptism of repentance'. They, as much as anyone else, needed to prepare the way for the Lord in their lives.

b. How he lived

Because it mattered to John more than anything else that he should be the messenger of the Lord, he lived very simply. He did not live in the city with its comforts and luxuries, but in the wilderness (Luke 1:80). He ate the food that could be found then, 'locusts and wild honey', and dressed simply in cloth made of 'camel's hair', with a 'leather girdle around his waist' (verse 6). Perhaps he dressed like this because this was the dress of a prophet (see what is said of the prophet's clothing in the Old Testament in 2 Kings 1:8 and Zechariah 13:4). The people had not seen or heard a true prophet in Israel for generations. Certainly the way John lived and the way he preached the word of God made people feel that God had again sent them a prophet.

c. How he spoke of Jesus

John the Baptizer was a great man. Jesus later said that before him there had been no greater person born (Luke 7:28). But he did not want people to think him important.

He was a 'voice crying in the wilderness'. The One who mattered was the One who was coming. 'Mightier than I He will be,' John said. 'I am not good enough even to be His slave to take off His sandals.' 'I have baptized you with water,' John said – the baptism of repentance, repentance that makes possible cleansing and pardon of sin. 'He will baptize you with the Holy Spirit' – in other words, He will bring new life by the Spirit of God coming into the hearts and lives of men and women.

When we consider how John preached, how he lived, and how humbly he bore witness to Jesus, we are not surprised that the whole nation was stirred and 'there went out to him all the country of Judea and all the people of Jerusalem' (verse 5).

Meditation   *How do I prepare the way for the Lord to enter fully into my life and into the lives of others?*

For further thought and study   1. The contrast between water baptism and baptism with the Holy Spirit (verse 8) is mentioned also in Matthew 3:11, Luke 3:16. John 1:26 and 33, Acts 1:5 and 11:16. Look up these passages and consider what the work of Jesus and His sending to us His Holy Spirit should mean to us.

2. In what ways is John an example to all who would be preachers of Christ and witnesses to Him today? Look also at John 1:19–23 and 3:25–30.

Note   1. The first of the two quotations in verses 2 and 3 comes from Malachi. The words 'as it is written in Isaiah the prophet' apply to the second quotation. Perhaps the Malachi quotation was added later, or in collecting the Old Testament texts it could have been put in between the heading and the quotation of Isaiah 40:3.

2. We have seen that 'the wilderness' was a fitting place for John to be brought up and to be prepared to be God's messenger. It was also fitting for people to have to come from city life to the wilderness, away from the city's distracting influences, to hear God's message. In the history of Israel the time in the wilderness after

their Exodus from Egypt was a time of meeting with God. The prophet Hosea (2:14–23) said how God would again lead them out into the wilderness and there turn their hearts back to Him and give them new hope.

3. We have a fuller record of the work and preaching of John the Baptist in the other Gospels. See Matthew 3:1–12, Luke 3:1–17 and John 1:6–8, 19–37.

Study 3: JESUS' BAPTISM AND TEMPTATION

[9]In those days Jesus came from Nazareth of Galilee and was baptized by John in the Jordan. [10]And when he came up out of the water, immediately he saw the heavens opened and the Spirit descending upon him like a dove; [11]and a voice came from heaven, 'Thou art my beloved Son; with thee I am well pleased.'

[12]The Spirit immediately drove him out into the wilderness. [13]And he was in the wilderness forty days, tempted by Satan; and he was with the wild beasts; and the angels ministered to him   (1:9–13).

Matthew (2:23) and Luke (2:39, 51) tell us that most of the early life of Jesus was spent in Nazareth in Galilee (see map). Of these early years we know only what Luke (2:42–51) tells us, and that is very little. Luke (3:23) also tells us that Jesus 'began his ministry' when He was 'about thirty years of age'. The preaching of John the Baptist, preparing the way of the Lord (verse 3), seems to have been the sign for Jesus to come from His home in Nazareth to begin His public work. This is where Mark's account of Jesus begins. He was baptized; He was tempted; then His public work began.

a. Jesus' baptism

Verse 4 tells us that John's baptism was 'a baptism of

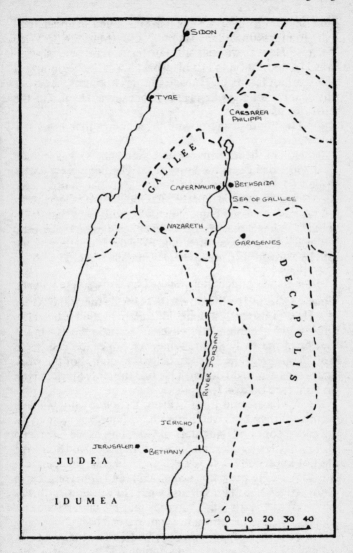

repentance for the forgiveness of sins'. We can understand why John was unwilling to baptize Jesus (Matthew 3:13–15) because He was without sin. For Jesus, however, baptism was His dedication to His life work; it was the beginning of the work of taking on Himself the sins of others, the work that was completed when He bore our sins as He died on the cross for us.

At His baptism there were three things that Jesus saw and heard.

1. 'He saw the heavens opened.' Sometimes it has seemed that God has been far away from His people on earth. Isaiah 64:1 (Basic English Bible) says what people have sometimes thought and prayed to God, 'Oh, let the heavens be broken open and come down.' Verse 10 says that this is what God has done. We need never again think that God is far away. He has come to us and lived our life in the coming of His Son, Jesus Christ. He is 'Emmanuel', 'God with us' (Matthew 1:23).

2. 'He saw...the Spirit descending upon Him like a dove.' Jesus in His life on earth was truly the Son of God; but He was also truly human, like one of us. So He lived His life – as we are intended to live our Christian lives – in the power of the Holy Spirit. Whatever work God calls us to do, He gives us His Spirit to help us to do it. For the work that Jesus was to do on earth He had the Holy Spirit in Him to do it (see Luke 4:1, 14, 18).

3. 'A voice came from heaven, "Thou art my beloved Son; with thee I am well pleased."' In one way we may all be called sons and daughters of God, but, as we have seen in verse 1, Jesus is *the* Son of God, God's 'beloved Son'. We do not know fully *how* Jesus, human like us, 'increased in wisdom' as He grew up (Luke 2:52), and *how* He grew in knowledge about Himself and what His work on earth was to be. What Mark tells us here is that He understood this clearly by this voice from heaven. We can best understand verse 11 if we keep in mind two Old Testament verses. In Psalm 2:7 it was said to God's anointed King, 'You are my

son, today I have begotten you.' In Isaiah 42:1 it is said to the one who would serve God and suffer for Him and for the sins of others, 'Behold my servant...my chosen in whom my soul delights. I have put my Spirit upon him.' Jesus could go into His work, knowing that the Spirit of God was on Him, knowing that He was the anointed Son, the Christ, and knowing that He had to be the suffering Servant of His Father. The Gospel later shows us much more of what this meant.

b. Jesus' temptation

We have seen that at the time of His baptism, if not before, Jesus knew who He was and what His work was to be. Satan was determined now to turn Him away from that. Matthew (4:1–11) and Luke (4:1–13) give us more details of the temptations. Mark gives us just a few words, but they tell us some important facts.

'The Spirit immediately drove him out into the wilderness.' The Spirit led Him out to the loneliness of the wilderness to prepare Him for His work. Yet preparation meant testing, temptation. The Spirit allows us to be tested as Jesus was. But in times of testing, Satan comes to tempt us (even as He came to tempt Jesus), to try to persuade us to turn aside from the will of God.

Jesus was 'in the wilderness forty days, tempted by Satan'. The people of Israel were forty years in the wilderness. For them that was a time of testing and temptation. They failed and gave in to temptation. Where they failed, Jesus was victorious. There was no human help, only 'the wild beasts' around Him. Help came from heaven – as it does to all who turn to God in the hour of temptation – as 'the angels ministered to him'.

Meditation *Consider what Hebrews 4:14–16 says about the temptations of Jesus and about our temptations.*

For further thought and study 1. The Greek word translated in the words the heavens 'opened' in verse 10, is only used again by Mark in 15:38 when he says the curtain in the Temple was 'torn' in two when Jesus died on the cross. Do you think there is a connection between what happened at the baptism of Jesus and what happened when He died on the cross?

2. Read the account of Jesus' three temptations in Matthew 4:1–11. In what ways can you see them as temptations to Jesus to turn aside from His life work? Are there similar ways in which we are tempted?

Note We have noted above the record of Jesus' temptations in Matthew and Luke. Matthew 3:13–17 and Luke 3:21–22 tell of His baptism.

BEGINNING OF JESUS' MINISTRY

Mark 1:14–45

In the Introduction, telling how the good news of Jesus began, Jesus has been introduced to us as the Christ, the Son of God. From His baptism and His temptation He goes out to His work. This next part of Mark's Gospel shows in seven ways what that work was:

1:14–15	Preaching the good news of God's kingdom
1:16–20	Calling His first disciples
1:21–22	Teaching with authority
1:23–28	Driving out demons
1:29–34	Healing the sick
1:35–39	Praying and preaching
1:40–45	Cleansing the leper

Study 4: PREACHING AND CALLING DISCIPLES

[14]Now after John was arrested, Jesus came into Galilee, preaching the gospel of God, [15]and saying, 'The time is fulfilled, and the kingdom of God is at hand; repent, and believe in the gospel.'

[16]And passing along by the Sea of Galilee, he saw Simon

and Andrew the brother of Simon casting a net into the sea; for they were fishermen. [17]And Jesus said to them, 'Follow me and I will make you become fishers of men.' [18]And immediately they left their nets and followed him. [19]And going on a little further, he saw James the son of Zebedee and John his brother, who were in their boat mending the nets. [20]And immediately he called them; and they left their father Zebedee in the boat with the hired servants, and followed him (1:14-20).

Two events stand out in this first part of Mark's description of Jesus' public work and ministry. Jesus preached the good news of God's kingdom, and He called people to be His disciples.

a. His preaching

The work of John the Baptist was done. He would soon be arrested and put in prison (see 6:17-29). John had spoken of the One mightier than he who was coming. Now this One had come. The prophets had spoken of a coming day when God would bless His people in a new and wonderful way. That day had dawned. Psalmists and prophets in the Old Testament had spoken of God's kingdom, God's rule. In one way God is always King, ruling over His people (Isaiah 43:15) and ruling over the whole world (Jeremiah 10:7). In another way He promised that a time was coming when His rule in the world would be seen and realized more than it had ever been realized before. That time had come. Jesus could say, 'The time is fulfilled, and the kingdom of God is at hand.' Those who heard this preaching of Jesus were challenged to do two things. First, to 'repent', which meant to turn away from all those ways in which they did not allow God to rule as King in their lives. Second, to 'believe in the gospel', the good news of what God would do in the lives of those who turned to Him.

b. His calling of disciples

Jesus preached to all who would listen to His words. He also called those who would share His work and be the beginning of a new community, a community of disciples. In verses 16–20 there are three important things to notice.

1. *The kind of people whom Jesus called.* These first four disciples were ordinary working men, fishermen. Jesus did not choose those whom the world thinks the most important, the most educated, or the most influential people. If He had, some of us might have said, 'He does not want people like me.' How thankful we can be that from the beginning He chose ordinary men and women to be His disciples and to share His work! How thankful we can be for the humble birth and simple life of Jesus Himself! None of us can say, 'I am too poor or unimportant for Him to accept a person like me.' It is interesting also to see that Jesus chose two pairs of brothers. Sometimes Christian discipleship causes division in families (see 13:12–13), but the Lord wants families to be united in serving Him.

2. *What they were called to do.* The one thing that Simon and Andrew, James and John, were called to do was to 'follow' Jesus. Jewish people knew what it was to follow a teacher or rabbi. Usually they chose to do this. Here it was a case of Jesus calling them. It might seem strange that Jesus came to them at their work on the lake and called them. If, however, we read John 1:35–42, we see that they had been with John the Baptist and had had the opportunity of coming to know a good deal about Jesus. They were not called to follow blindly; but they knew that for them to follow meant to leave home and work to be with Jesus. Not all were called in the same way, but the call of Jesus to be His disciple always means putting Jesus first and doing what He wants us to do.

3. *What they were called to become.* Jesus said to them, 'Follow me and I will make you become fishers of men' (verse 17). Notice how Jesus always spoke to people in ways that they could best understand. To the Samaritan

woman who came to the well to draw water He spoke about the water of life (John 4:7–14). To a rich young man He spoke about the way to have 'treasure in heaven' (Mark 10:17–22). These fishermen He called to become 'fishers of men'. In whatever way we put it, we can say that if we are disciples of Jesus, we have good news to share, and we are to try with His help to bring others to know Him and to follow Him.

Prayer   *'In simple trust like theirs who heard*
  Beside the Syrian sea
The gracious calling of the Lord
  Let us, like them, without a word
Rise up and follow Thee.'
                                          J. G. Whittier

For further thought and study   In what ways do you think that the kingdom of God (or the rule of God) came into human life with the coming of Jesus? See what is said about God's kingdom in this Gospel in 4:11, 26–32, 9:1, 47, 10:14–15, 23–25, 12:28–34. Is there a difference between preaching the gospel and preaching the kingdom of God?

Notes   1. When we read John 1:35–42 and 3:22–30 we see that John the Baptist was still working for a while after Jesus had begun His ministry. Perhaps the early part of Jesus' ministry was in Judea. The main point of verse 14 is that John's work came first; his work was really done when Jesus began His.
    2. Matthew 4:12–22 is parallel to these verses, adding that Jesus' ministry in Galilee fulfilled the prophecy of Isaiah 9:1–2. Luke 4:14–15 tells how Jesus' ministry began in Galilee; Luke 5:1–11 has a different story of Jesus with Simon and Andrew, James and John with their fishing boats on Lake Galilee.

Study 5: AUTHORITY – IN WORD AND ACTION

²¹And they went into Capernaum; and immediately on the sabbath he entered the synagogue and taught. ²²And they were astonished at his teaching, for he taught them as one who had authority, and not as the scribes. ²³And immediately there was in their synagogue a man with an unclean spirit; ²⁴and he cried out, 'What have you to do with us, Jesus of Nazareth? Have you come to destroy us? I know who you are, the Holy One of God.' ²⁵But Jesus rebuked him, saying, 'Be silent, and come out of him!' ²⁶And the unclean spirit, convulsing him and crying with a loud voice, came out of him. ²⁷And they were all amazed, so that they questioned among themselves, saying, 'What is this? A new teaching! With authority he commands even the unclean spirits, and they obey him.' ²⁸And at once his fame spread everywhere throughout all the surrounding region of Galilee   (1:21–28).

'Authority' is the key word in these verses. People were more surprised at the authority and power of Jesus than at anything else. In two ways His authority was seen. 'They were astonished at his *teaching*, for he taught them as one who had *authority*, and not as the scribes' (verse 22). 'They were all amazed...saying... "With *authority* he commands even the *unclean spirits*, and they obey him"' (verse 27).

a. His teaching

For hundreds of years – perhaps from the time when the Jewish people had been exiles in Babylon – they had had synagogues where the Scriptures were taught and where the people met each sabbath to worship. Jesus would have worshipped in the synagogue from His boyhood and He continued to do so (see Luke 4:16). For hundreds of years also there had been scribes who taught the Law (in Nehemiah 8:1 Ezra is spoken of as a 'scribe'). But the scribes in the time of Jesus did not always make plain the way of God for people's lives. They quoted the different sayings of the great rabbis, but often they did not help people very much to know and to choose the right way.

The way that Jesus taught was different – it was 'not as the scribes'. He taught the truth of God simply, clearly and strongly. When we read the record of His teaching in the Sermon on the Mount (in Matthew chapters 5–7), we see this. He set aside teaching which had twisted God's law. 'You have heard that it was said, "You shall love your neighbour and hate your enemy", but I say to you, Love your enemies and pray for those who persecute you' (Matthew 5:43–44). He made the demands of the Law reach not just to people's words and actions, but also to their thoughts. He dealt in this way with the commandments against murder and adultery (Matthew 5:21–28). He gave the people a principle which they could apply to every part of their life: 'Seek first (God's) kingdom and his righteousness and everything else that you need will be added to you' (Matthew 6:33). We can understand why the crowds of ordinary people wanted to listen to His teaching. They could see that He taught with 'authority' and was very different from the scribes. (See also Matthew 7:28–29.)

b. His authority over evil spirits

Mark goes on to tell us that when Jesus was teaching in the synagogue there was a man who had 'an unclean spirit'. He was demon-possessed. The Gospels often tell us of such people possessed by demons, and of the way that the demons in them recognized the power of Jesus over them. They saw Him as 'the Holy One of God' (verse 24). They knew him (verse 34), and sometimes called Him the 'Son of the Most High God' (5:7). Matthew 12:28 and Luke 11:20 say that the power of Jesus over demons was one of the ways in which it was clear that the kingdom of God, the rule of God, had come into human life with the coming of Jesus. No longer did people need to be bound by the powers of evil or be terrified by them. Jesus rebuked the demon and said, 'Be silent, and come out of him!' And 'he came out of him' (verses 25–26). All the people were amazed at His authority and power.

The two signs of the authority of Jesus were still true for the Christians for whom Mark wrote his gospel – and still are important for the Church today. The simple, clear authoritative teaching of Jesus is the way for us to follow. He brings God's word to us and (as John 1:1–18 puts it) He is the living Word of God to the world. Moreover, He came (as 1 John 3:8 says) 'to destroy the works of the devil'. He still delivers men and women from every power of evil – from demons, from sin, from fear, from failure and frustration, from pride and selfishness. He sets us free to serve God and to love our fellowmen and women.

Prayer   *Lord Jesus, Saviour and Master, help us to know Your way and Your will and to accept Your authority over our lives.* AMEN.

For further thought and study   1. Many times in Mark's Gospel it says that people were 'amazed' or 'astonished' at the things that Jesus said or did or that happened in His ministry. See verses 22 and 27 in this passage and look up the following verses and find out from them the reasons why people were so 'amazed': 2:12; 5:20, 42; 6:2, 51; 7:37; 9:15; 10:24, 26, 32; 11:18; 12:17; 15:5, 44 and 16:5–6.

2. We read here of the authority of Jesus and again in 3:15 and 6:7 and in Matthew 28:18–20 of His disciples being sent out with His authority. What does this mean for us today? But is it possible for us to have a wrong sense of authority in what we say or do?

Notes   1. There is a parallel to this passage in Luke 4:31–37 but not in Matthew's Gospel.

2. There are three different attitudes that people today take to the thought of demonic possession. (a) Some people, especially in western countries, say that demons and evil spirits do not exist, but that this is the way people in biblical times or in other countries describe what they cannot explain, especially in relation to illness

of body or mind. Against this we should note that Jesus accepted the reality of demons and often exorcised them. It is hard to explain the power of evil in human lives today if we do not admit that forces of evil exist and can control people's minds and bodies. (b) Some people live in constant fear of demons and of the harm that others may do to them by spiritual means. But there is no need for anyone who knows the power of God in Jesus Christ to fear any power of evil. (c) The New Testament guides us to recognize the reality of Satan, the ways he tempts us, and also the ways that the powers of evil may harm and destroy human life. But the Scriptures also show us the way of victory and deliverance through Christ as the conqueror of evil and of Satan.

Study 6: PLACES OF MINISTRY

[29] And immediately he left the synagogue, and entered the house of Simon and Andrew, with James and John. [30] Now Simon's mother-in-law lay sick with a fever, and immediately they told him of her. [31] And he came and took her by the hand and lifted her up, and the fever left her; and she served them.

[32] That evening, at sundown, they brought to him all who were sick or possessed with demons. [33] And the whole city was gathered together about the door. [34] And he healed many who were sick with various diseases, and cast out many demons; and he would not permit the demons to speak, because they knew him.

[35] And in the morning, a great while before day, he rose and went out to a lonely place, and there he prayed. [36] And Simon and those who were with him pursued him, [37] and they found him and said to him, 'Every one is searching for you.' [38] And he said to them, 'Let us go on to the next towns, that I may preach there also; for that is why I came out.' [39] And he went throughout all Galilee, preaching in their synagogues and casting out demons (1:29–39).

Mark may intend us to see the whole of verses 21–39 in this chapter as a day in the ministry of Jesus, a typical day which shows us the kind of things that He was doing as He went about His work. Another way in which we could study these verses is to see the places where He worked. Verses 21–28 have told what he did in the synagogue. Verses 29–39 tell what He did in the home, then with the crowds, and then in a 'lonely place'.

a. In the home

In very many places in the Bible we see the importance, in the eyes of God, of the home and the family. We see how family relationships mattered to Jesus and how He loved to be welcomed into the homes of those who invited Him. We have seen how He called two pairs of brothers to be His disciples (verses 16–20). Now He went into the home of the brothers, Simon and Andrew, and we soon see the blessing of His presence there. There was anxiety in the home because one member of the family was sick 'with a high fever' (Luke 4:38). There follows a beautifully simple description of prayer. 'They told him of her', trusting His power and willingness to help. He responded. 'He came and took her by the hand and lifted her up, and the fever left her.' Her gratitude and love were then expressed in practical ways as, healed and strengthened, 'she served them'.

b. With the crowds

It was the sabbath when Jesus was in the synagogue (verses 21–28) and when He healed Peter's mother-in-law (verses 29–31). The Jewish sabbath lasted from sunset on Friday until sunset on Saturday. Jewish regulations said how far one could travel on the sabbath, and also that a sick person could not be taken anywhere to seek healing unless in danger of death. The people of Capernaum, therefore, were not free to bring their sick and troubled people to Jesus till sunset. Then they did – and they brought people with all kinds of troubles: 'they brought to him all who were sick or possessed with demons.' It seemed that the whole city had come to the door of Simon and Andrew's house. 'And he healed many...and cast out many demons'.

Mark says that Jesus 'would not permit the demons to speak, because they knew him' (verse 34). We have seen already (in verse 24) that the demons recognized Jesus as the One who had power to conquer them and drive them from the lives of people. They cried out and called Him 'the Holy One of God', 'the Son of God' (3:11), 'Son of the Most High God' (5:7). Jesus silenced these cries because He wanted belief and trust in Him to come not by what others said or by what the demons shouted, but by people coming to accept Him for themselves. This Gospel shows us that only slowly and step by step were Peter and the other disciples led to that faith and to confess Jesus as 'the Christ' (8:29).

c. The lonely place

The days of Jesus' ministry were full. People with their deep needs pressed on Him constantly. He healed and exorcised. He gave much time to preaching and teaching. Because He was truly human, He needed time to be alone with His Father to renew His strength. So 'in the morning, a great while before day, he rose up and went out to a lonely place, and there he prayed' (verse 35). All who work in ministry to others in the name of Christ can learn from this. We need to come aside from the world with all its pressures to be alone with God, to hear His word, to tell Him about our situation, to be renewed, guided, strengthened, and filled afresh with His love. Withdrawal from the world for prayer, return to the world for service – this is the rhythm of the Christian life.

We can understand how Simon and the others would be excited to tell Jesus that everyone in Capernaum was searching for Him. Yet the One who cared for the sick and troubled people in Capernaum knew that there were needy people 'in the next towns' also. 'Let us go on to them,' He said – and this has always been the challenge to Christians, to reach those who have not yet been reached with His love and power, with the good news of His truth and His salvation.

Meditation *Prayer is opening our hearts to God, telling Him all that concerns us in our lives and in the lives of others, trusting Him in His power and love and wisdom to do all that He wishes to do.*

For further thought and study 1. What lessons can we learn for our own praying from the verses of this section?

2. What other passages in the Gospels show that Jesus did not want people to keep the good news for themselves or their own town, but to share it with others? See, for example, Matthew 9:35–38, 10:1–8, 28:18–20. What should this mean for us personally and in the life of our church fellowship?

Note We have parallel passages to these verses in Matthew 8:14–17 and Luke 4:38–44.

Study 7: JESUS AND THE LEPER

[40]And a leper came to him beseeching him, and kneeling said to him, 'If you will, you can make me clean.' [41]Moved with pity, he stretched out his hand and touched him, and said to him, 'I will; be clean.' [42]And immediately the leprosy left him and he was made clean. [43]And he sternly charged him, and sent him away at once, [44]and said to him, 'See that you say nothing to any one; but go, show yourself to the priest, and offer for your cleansing what Moses commanded, for a proof to the people.' [45]But he went out and began to talk freely about it, and to spread the news, so that Jesus could no longer openly enter a town, but was out in the country;

and people came to him from every quarter   (1:40–45).

Mark has just told us of that memorable sabbath day in Capernaum and of the morning after (verses 21–39). He has made clear to us a number of things that were important in the whole ministry of Jesus – teaching with authority, casting out demons, healing the sick, spending time alone in prayer. Now Mark adds one further work of Jesus – the cleansing of a leper – before he goes on to the next main section of his Gospel (2:1—3:6).

Why does he do this? Probably because in some ways people saw leprosy as different from other diseases and sicknesses. It could cause the death of the flesh of a person's body (perhaps fingers or toes, nose or ears). It was contagious, and so the person who had leprosy had to live away from other people and cry 'Unclean, unclean', when anyone came near (see Leviticus 13:45–46). The leper, therefore, needed not only to be healed, but to be 'cleansed' and declared to be clean before he was able to return to his people. Although many different skin diseases went under the name of leprosy, what we today call 'leprosy' had no human cure until recently. The Jewish rabbis said that the cleansing of a leper was 'as difficult as raising the dead'. So we can see the importance of Mark's telling of this miracle here. When the work of Jesus' ministry is told to John in prison, this was one disease specially mentioned: 'the blind receive their sight, the lame walk, lepers are cleansed, and the deaf hear and the dead are raised up, the poor have good news preached to them' (Luke 7:22).

The attitude of Jesus to this leper was very different from the attitude of other people to lepers. We can learn much from it and also from the attitude of the leper to Jesus.

a. Attitude of Jesus

Few people cared for lepers in those days. Rather they wished that they did not exist. They would rather not think of them. But, as with others who were sick or troubled, or demon-possessed, or in other ways cut off from their own people, Jesus was 'moved with pity' for the leper. Others would avoid lepers and keep them at a great distance. Jesus 'stretched out his hand and touched' this leper. He acted in power and healed him.

Notice the two things that Jesus said to the man when he was healed.

1. He told him to do what the Law of Moses required. The priests (who in this work were like health officers) had to see and declare that a leper was free from the disease, and the person had to make a sacrificial offering in thanksgiving (see Leviticus 14:1–32). In the light of what the Gospel goes on to tell of the opposition of the Jewish religious leaders to Jesus, it is important to see here the respect He showed for the Old Testament law.

2. Jesus also said to the man, 'See that you say nothing to anyone.' Jesus did His miracles of healing out of pity and compassion and to show the power and blessing of God's kingdom, but He did not just want to be known as a miracle-worker. Above all things He wanted people to pay attention to the teaching of the kingdom of God and His preaching of the good news. (See also 5:43 and 7:36.)

b. Attitude of the leper

There are several things that we can learn from this leper's attitude to Jesus. He came humbly, 'kneeling' down to Him. He came earnestly, 'beseeching him'. Because he had heard of the things that Jesus had done, he came believing in the power of Jesus to help him: 'If you will, you can make me clean.' He need not have had doubts about the willingness of Jesus. He had the answer of Jesus without delay: 'I will; be clean.' 'And immediately the leprosy left him and he was made clean.'

We then read that Jesus told him to 'say nothing to anyone', but 'he went out and began to talk freely about it, and to spread the news'. In one way we must blame him for doing what was against the word of Jesus to him. But we can understand how he could not be silent. His whole life was changed. He must tell others what Jesus had done for him. Would that we Christian people today were as keen to tell what great things the Lord has done for us!

Prayer *Pray today for all who suffer from leprosy and for all who, because of sickness of mind or body, are cut off from their own people.*

For further thought and study 1. Compare this passage with what is described in Luke 17:11–19 of the cleansing of ten lepers. What similar points and what differences do you find?

2. Who for us today are in a position like that of the lepers in the time of Jesus' ministry? Are there those from whom we would choose to keep far away? What does the attitude of Jesus teach us?

Notes 1. We have parallels to this passage in both Matthew 8:2–4 and Luke 5:12–16.

2. The words of verse 44, 'for a proof to the people' or 'as a testimony to them' (New International Version) have been understood in several different ways. It could be that what the Law required and what the priests had to do was 'to prove to everyone' that a leper was cured (Good News Bible). It could be that the leper's report was to be a 'testimony' to the priests of what Jesus was doing, or perhaps a witness to the fact that Jesus respected and obeyed the Law.

3. There are forms of leprosy that are not contagious. Thanks to God's gifts to us through medical science, leprosy can often be completely cured. Then it is perfectly safe for those who have suffered from leprosy to return to their own communities.

OPPOSITION TO HIS MINISTRY

Mark 2:1—3:6

In this next main part of the Gospel we have five sections that clearly belong together because they all show us reasons why the Jewish religious leaders opposed Jesus. They opposed Him because He claimed the power to forgive sins, because He made Himself the friend of 'tax-collectors and sinners', because He did not train His disciples to fast as they did, and because of the way that He regarded the sabbath day. For all these reasons their opposition to Jesus steadily increased and at the end of this part of the Gospel we read that 'the Pharisees...held counsel with the Herodians against him, how to destroy him' (3:6).

These sections also show us what Jesus came to do: to bring the sinner back to God, to give new life, to help men and women to rejoice in His law and to bring healing and blessing. The five sections are:

2:1–12   Healing and forgiveness for a paralysed
           man
2:13–17   Call of the tax-collector, Levi, and the
           feast in his home
2:18–22   Jesus' attitude to fasting
2:23–28   Purpose of the sabbath
3:1–6   Healing on the sabbath

Study 8: AUTHORITY TO FORGIVE SINS

[1]And when he returned to Capernaum after some days, it was reported that he was at home. [2]And many were gathered together, so that there was no longer room for them, not even about the door; and he was preaching the word to them. [3]And when they could not get near to him because of the crowd, they removed the roof above him; and when they had made an opening, they let down the pallet on which the paralytic lay. [5]And when Jesus saw their faith, he said to the paralytic, 'My son, your sins are forgiven.' Now some of the scribes were sitting there, questioning in their hearts, 'Why does this man speak thus? It is blasphemy! Who can forgive sins but God alone?'[8]And immediately Jesus, perceiving in his spirit that they thus questioned within themselves, said to them, 'Why do you question thus in your hearts? [9]Which is easier, to say to the paralytic, "Your sins are forgiven," or to say, "Rise, take up your pallet and walk"? [10]But that you may know that the Son of man has authority on earth to forgive sins' – he said to the paralytic – [11]'I say to you, rise, take up your pallet and go home.' [12]And he rose, and immediately took up the pallet and went out before them all; so that they were all amazed and glorified God, saying, 'We never saw anything like this!' (2:1–12).

In 1:14–45 we have read of the beginning of the ministry of Jesus and the things that He did, teaching and preaching, calling disciples, healing the sick, cleansing the leper, casting out demons. Crowds of people came to Him constantly as we have read in chapter 1, verses 33, 37 and 45. We have seen that people were amazed at His authority – His authority in teaching (1:22), and His authority in casting out demons (1:27). Now we read of the crowds coming again to Jesus and of His authority shown in another way.

This incident took place in Capernaum, and perhaps 'home' for Jesus (verse 1) was the house of Simon and Andrew (1:29). Crowds came 'so that there was no longer room for them, not even about the door' (verse 2). 'He was

preaching the word to them', but our attention is turned to
one man and his needs, and the way that Jesus met his
needs.

a. The man's needs

The man was paralysed and unable to walk. He had to be
carried on his mat ('pallet') by his four friends. They were
determined to take their friend to Jesus, but the crowds
made it impossible for them to get near to the door. A
Palestinian house had a flat roof and stairs up to the roof.
'The roof consisted of flat beams laid across from wall to
wall, perhaps three feet apart. The space in between the
beams was fitted with brushwood packed tight with clay....
It was the easiest thing in the world to dig out the filling
between two of the beams; it did not even damage the
house very much, and it was easy to repair the breach again'
(Barclay). Thus they lowered their friend so that he lay in
front of Jesus.

Jesus had stretched out His hand to the leper (1:41) and
had healed him. He had healed many sick people (1:34).
But the first words of Jesus to this man said nothing about
the healing of his body. To the great surprise of all who
were listening, He said to him, 'My son, your sins are
forgiven.' Why speak of his sin and not his paralysis? Why
speak of forgiveness and not of healing? Jesus saw sin as a
cause of sickness. Sin is not always, of course, the *direct*
cause of a person's illness. Jesus made that clear in His own
teaching (see John 9:1–3). But there are cases where
suffering *is* directly caused by a person's sin. That was the
situation here, and Jesus offered to the man first what he
needed most.

b. The claim to forgive

Everyone would have been surprised at the words of
Jesus to the paralysed man. The scribes were not only
surprised; they were offended. They were 'questioning in
their hearts, "Why does this man speak thus? It is blas-

phemy! Who can forgive sins but God alone?"' Jesus answered their unspoken question with a question of His own to them: 'Which is easier, to say to the paralytic, "Your sins are forgiven", or to say, "Rise, take up your pallet and walk"?' Clearly people could see if a paralysed man were made to walk; they could not see if his sins were forgiven. Jesus' purpose was not only to show that the man's greatest need was the need for forgiveness, but to demonstrate that 'the Son of man has authority on earth to forgive sins'. It was good news for the paralysed man. Sadly, this claim of Jesus was a reason why the scribes opposed Him. For those who first read Mark's Gospel and for us today it is good news, and we can glorify God as people did then (verse 12) because 'Christ Jesus came into the world to save sinners' (1 Timothy 1:15).'

The four friends who helped this man to come to Jesus and to find forgiveness and healing were determined to overcome every difficulty in their way. Verse 5 says that 'Jesus saw their faith' and so brought the help that the man needed. How thankful we should be for all of those who have wanted to bring us to Jesus! We can have no greater privilege than that of bringing others – by prayer and in other practical ways – to find Jesus and to receive His love, forgiveness and healing.

Meditation *Consider what James 5:19–20 says about what it means to bring another person to know the forgiveness and saving power of God.*

For further thought and study   1. In what ways does sin lead directly to physical suffering? On the other hand, why do we need to be careful not to suggest that all people are suffering because of their own wrong-doing?

2. What does it mean to say that God was 'glorified' because of what happened? With verse 12 consider also Matthew 9:8, 15:31 and Luke 5:25–26, 7:16 and 18:43.

Notes This incident is told also in Matthew 9:1–8 and Luke 5:17–26. As is often the case, Mark's account has more detail than Matthew's and Luke's. This is one of the reasons why it is thought that Matthew and Luke have used Mark's Gospel as a source for their own writing and have shortened Mark's fuller record.

2. In verse 10 for the first time in this Gospel Jesus is spoken of as 'the Son of man'. In Matthew Jesus is called 'the Son of man' 31 times, in Mark 14 times, in Luke 26 times and in John 12 times and in most cases Jesus Himself uses the words. He could not openly call Himself 'Christ' because so often people wrongly understood that word. The words 'Son of man' could mean just 'man' (see Psalm 8:4, 144:3 and Ezekiel 2:1). At the same time for those who were willing to consider it, 'Son of man' could mean much more, because Daniel 7:13–14 spoke of 'one like a son of man' coming 'with the clouds of heaven' and 'to him was given dominion and glory and kingdom, that all peoples, nations and languages should serve him'. (See also pages 135 and 206.)

Study 9: THE FRIEND OF SINNERS

[13]**He went out again beside the sea; and all the crowd gathered about him, and he taught them.** [14]**And as he passed on, he saw Levi the son of Alphaeus sitting at the tax office, and he said to him, 'Follow me.' And he rose and followed him.**

[15]**And as he sat at the table in his house, many tax collectors and sinners were sitting with Jesus and his disciples; for there were many who followed him.** [16]**And the scribes of the Pharisees, when they saw that he was eating with sinners and tax collectors, said to his disciples, 'Why does he eat with tax collectors and sinners?'** [17]**And when Jesus heard it, he said to them, 'Those who are well have no need of a physician, but those who are sick; I came not to call the righteous, but sinners** (2:13–17).

We have seen that the first reason why the Jewish

teachers of the law opposed Jesus was His claim to offer people God's forgiveness. Here we see a second reason: He offered God's forgiveness to those whom the scribes thought of as the worst of sinners. They were amazed that Jesus would think of calling such people to be His disciples.

a. Call

Again we read that there were crowds who came to listen to Jesus and again we read how He taught them (verse 13). We see that He called those who were to be His special disciples, as it says in the next chapter (3:14), 'to be with him and to be sent out to preach.' We have read of the call of the fishermen, Simon and Andrew, James and John (1:16–20). Now He calls Levi from the 'tax office'. Tax-collectors are never the most popular people in any country! No one enjoys paying taxes. There were two particular reasons, however, why most Jewish people at that time hated them. Though they may have collected taxes for the local ruler, Herod Antipas, the taxes went to the Roman colonial authorities, who ruled over Palestine. Second, the tax-collectors would take as much as they could from the people; some of the money they would pass to the authorities, but they would keep the rest for themselves. Levi, whom Jesus called, was a tax-collector, although his name showed he was from the priestly tribe of Israel.

b. Criticism

The Jewish religious leaders not only hated the tax-collectors, but they spoke of them as the worst of people. 'Tax-collectors and sinners' – they put the words naturally together (see Matthew 11:19 and Luke 15:1). Sometimes they would speak of 'tax-collectors and harlots' (Matthew 21:31–32). Although the religious leaders, as shepherds of Israel, should have healed the sick, brought back the straying and sought the lost (Ezekiel 34:4), they thought there was no possibility of the tax-collectors having a place in the kingdom of God. They had no desire to see them turn to

God, and so they rejected them.

Levi rejoiced in Jesus' acceptance of him and therefore 'made him a great feast in his house' (Luke 5:29) so that his fellow tax-collectors and other friends could meet Jesus. But the scribes criticized. They did not address their criticism to Jesus Himself but to His disciples, wanting to make them realize what kind of Master they were following: 'Why does he eat with tax collectors and sinners?' Eating together is for most people a sign of friendship and fellowship. It certainly was for the Jews. But religious Jews would never eat with a Gentile, or with those whom they thought of as 'sinners' – the 'tax-collectors' among them. How could Jesus be a true teacher of the truth of God if He ate with such people?

c. Answer

Jesus answered the criticism of the scribes in the words of a proverb: 'People who are well do not need a doctor, but only those who are sick.' What is the use of a Saviour if He does not help the sinner? In the words and actions of Jesus and in the words and attitudes of the scribes, we see two different kinds of religion. The religion of the scribes was the religion of the law. They tried to keep the law; they thought that they pleased God in keeping it. They despised those who did not try to keep it. But they failed to see their own weaknesses and sins, and they felt no pity for others who had gone astray.

The religion of Jesus was the religion of grace. He wanted people to keep God's law, but He saw how all people (including the self-righteous) had failed. He began by turning people back to God, offering them His forgiveness, so that they would love to serve and obey Him. He came, He said, not to call the righteous or those who thought themselves righteous, but sinners to repentance.

Prayer *Lord God, help us to see and admit our great need of Your forgiveness, and then in love and thankfulness may* *we show the way of forgiveness and life to others, through Jesus Christ our saviour.* AMEN.

For further thought and study   1. Consider other passages in the Gospels where we see this difference between the attitude of Jesus and the attitude of the scribes to 'tax-collectors' and 'sinners' (such as Matthew 11:16–19 and Luke 7:36–50). Note the answer of Jesus to the criticism of Him in Luke 15:1–2, that He received sinners and ate with them.

2. What changes does Paul speak of in Philippians 3:1–11 in his own turning from the kind of religion that he had as a Pharisee to that which he found in Jesus?

Notes   1. Matthew 9:9–13 and Luke 5:27–32 are the parallels to this incident.

2. Verse 16 speaks of 'the scribes of the Pharisees'. Most scribes were of the party of the Pharisees, but there were also scribes who belonged to the Sadducees' party (for the Sadducees see Study 46).

3. The parallel to this passage in Matthew 9:9–13 has the name 'Matthew' instead of 'Levi'. Matthew is named in all the lists of the 12 disciples (and not Levi). There is also a 'James the son of Alphaeus' in the list in 3:18. Perhaps James and Matthew were another pair of brothers. Some old manuscripts here in Mark read the name 'James' instead of 'Levi'.

Study 10: NEWNESS OF LIFE

[18]**Now John's disciples and the Pharisees were fasting; and people came and said to him, 'Why do John's disciples and the disciples of the Pharisees fast, but your disciples do not fast?'** [19]**And Jesus said to them, 'Can the wedding guests fast while the bridegroom is with them? As long as they have the bridegroom with them, they cannot fast.** [20]**The days will**

come, when the bridegroom is taken away from them, and then they will fast in that day. ²¹No one sews a piece of unshrunk cloth on an old garment; if he does, the patch tears away from it, the new from the old, and a worse tear is made. ²²And no one puts new wine into old wineskins; if he does, the wine will burst the skins, and the wine is lost, and so are the skins; but new wine is for fresh skins' (2:18–22).

A third difference between Jesus and the Jewish religious leaders arose about fasting. The Old Testament law did not require fasting, but the Pharisees said that people should fast two days each week. John's disciples may have kept these fast days too, or perhaps they were fasting at this time because of the death of John the Baptist (see 6:17–29). People thought that Jesus was discouraging His disciples from fasting. So the question was put to Him, 'Why do John's disciples and the disciples of the Pharisees fast, but your disciples do not fast?' It is clear from Matthew 6:16 that Jesus was not against fasting. He said, 'When you fast...' and spoke of what people's attitude should be in fasting. Notice three points in the answer that Jesus gave to the people's question.

a. A time for joy
There are times for joy and times for sorrow, times for feasting and times for fasting (compare Ecclesiastes 3:1–5). No one wants to fast when there is a wedding. The coming of Jesus, and the breaking of the kingdom of God into human life, was a time for joy and celebration. It was like the joy of a wedding, and the world needed to see and know it. John the Baptist had prepared people for the Coming One with the serious preaching of repentance. Now the Coming One had come. Hopes and prophecies were being fulfilled. He was teaching, preaching, healing and delivering people from the power of evil. This was a time for rejoicing. 'Can the wedding guests fast while the bridegroom is with them?' The invitation to be members of

God's kingdom through following Jesus is like the invitation to a wedding (see Matthew 22:1–10); and He is the Bridegroom (see also John 3:25–30).

b. A time for sorrow

Jesus had to go on to say, however, that after this time of joy there would be, for a while, a time of sorrow. John's disciples grieved when their master was 'taken away' from them (6:29). This would happen to Jesus. He would be taken away by force and put to death, and it would be like 'the bridegroom' 'taken away' from the wedding guests (verse 20). Now the crowds were rejoicing in all that Jesus was doing. But the shadow of the cross hung over His ministry. Even now the Jewish leaders were increasing their opposition to Him. He knew that the path ahead for Him led to His suffering and dying for others (see Study 32).

c. New ways for old

The third part of Jesus' answer was in two short parables. In the first He said that if an old, worn-out garment is mended with a new, strong piece of cloth, the old will soon tear away again from the new. In the second He said it was not wise to put new wine into old, dry skins. Fermentation would take place, the skins would crack and the wine would be lost.

With Jesus the new had come – new life and a new way of living. He came not to patch up the old, but to bring in the new. The kingdom of God was like new wine. It could not be put into the old wine skins of the religious life of the Pharisees. As we saw in the last study, the religion of Jesus was not a religion of laws and rules, when to fast, when not to fast, what to eat and what not to eat, or details of what to do and what not to do on the sabbath. A Christian life is life lived with Jesus, making Him King, loving, serving and obeying Him.

Meditation   *'The kingdom of God is not food and drink* *but righteousness and peace and joy in the Holy Spirit; he who thus serves Christ is acceptable to God and approved by men'* (Romans 14:17–18).

For further thought and study   1. What can we learn from what is said about fasting in Matthew 6:16–18, Acts 13:1–3 and 14:23? What is important about the link of prayer with fasting? Do you think that what Paul says in 1 Corinthians 9:24–27 about his life as an apostle helps us to see a right Christian attitude to fasting? Note also in Isaiah 58:1–9 what an Old Testament prophet says is more important than fasting.

2. Consider with this passage the emphasis on joy in the Christian life in such passages as Romans 5:1–3, 15:13, 2 Corinthians 6:10, Galatians 5:22, Philippians 4:4, 1 Thessalonians 1:6 and 1 Peter 1:3–8.

Note   Matthew 9:14–17 and Luke 5:33–38 tell of this same incident and also place it following the record of the call of Levi (Matthew) and the Pharisees' criticism of Jesus for eating with 'tax-collectors and sinners'.

Study 11: THE PURPOSE OF THE SABBATH

23One sabbath he was going through the grainfields; and as they made their way his disciples began to pluck heads of grain. 24And the Pharisees said to him, 'Look, why are they doing what is not lawful on the sabbath?' 25And he said to them, 'Have you never read what David did, when he was in need and was hungry, he and those who were with him: 26how he entered the house of God, when Abiathar was high priest, and ate the bread of the Presence, which it is not lawful for any but the priests to eat, and also gave it to those who were with him?' 27And he said to them, 'The sabbath

was made for man, not man for the sabbath; [28]**so the Son of man is lord even of the sabbath'** (2:23–28).

We have seen in the last three sections of the Gospel three ways in which the attitudes of Jesus were different from the attitudes of the Jewish religious leaders, and how they opposed Him in these things. Another great difference and great cause of opposition to Him was His attitude to the sabbath.

a. The Old Testament and the sabbath

The fourth commandment said that people should keep the seventh day of the week as a day of rest, as a day specially set apart for God, to remember and praise God for His work in creation (Exodus 20:8–11) and in setting His people free from slavery (Deuteronomy 5:12–15). It was a day intended for the worship of God, a day when all could enjoy rest and leisure, young and old, employers and employees, even the cattle used for work on the farm (Exodus 23:12). Even when work was very demanding at planting time or harvest time, people should rest and be refreshed (Exodus 34:21). The Old Testament also said that the keeping of the sabbath would be a sign that the people loved and served God and wanted to honour and obey Him in their lives (Exodus 31:12–17 and Ezekiel 20:12–20). The sabbath was intended to be kept joyfully and not to be a burden (Isaiah 58:13–14).

b. Pharisees and the sabbath

The Pharisees in New Testament times made the law of the sabbath seem very different. To be sure that they and other people kept the sabbath and did no work on it, they added many rules and regulations. They listed thirty-nine different kinds of work which must not be done on the sabbath. The Old Testament Law said that if you were walking through someone else's farm you could pluck a few heads of grain and eat them (Deuteronomy 23:25). But to the Pharisees that was work. So when Jesus' disciples did this on the sabbath the Pharisees accused them of reaping and preparing food! They said to Jesus, 'Look, why are they doing what is not lawful on the sabbath?'

c. Jesus and the sabbath

Jesus answered the Pharisees from the Old Testament. He said, as the scribes often said, 'Have you never read...?' He took them back to the life of David, their greatest king. In David's life-time, before the Jerusalem temple was built, there was a sanctuary at Nob, near Jerusalem. Ahimelech and then his son, Abiathar, were priests there. One of the customs of the sanctuary (we read of it in Leviticus 24:5–9) was to put special bread in the sanctuary every sabbath. It was called 'the bread of the Presence' (in older translations, 'shewbread'). After a week new bread was put there, and the priests, but only the priests, could eat the loaves taken from the sanctuary. David and his men, escaping from Saul, came to Nob tired and desperately in need of food. The only food was 'the bread of the Presence'. The priest gave this to them. Their need was of greater importance than the rule of the sanctuary (see 1 Samuel 21:1–6).

The same principle could apply to sabbath law. The sabbath was meant to be a blessing to the people. The Pharisees made it into a burden. Verse 27 says so: 'The sabbath was made for man, not man for the sabbath.' All God's laws are made for our benefit and not to restrict us. In His teaching concerning the sabbath we are wise to follow Jesus. 'The Son of man is lord even of the sabbath.' He is our Guide showing us how we should think about all laws (see Matthew 5:17–48).

Meditation *Consider Matthew 22:35–40 and how Jesus there sums up all the teaching of the law and the prophets.*

For further thought and study 1. Read carefully the Old Testament passages mentioned above that relate to the

sabbath and see what you think were the purposes of sabbath law.

2. Are there ways in which we (or the church) may make
detailed rules for Christians which can lead us to miss the
most important principles of Christian living?

Notes 1. Matthew 12:1–8 and Luke 6:1–5 are the parallel passages to this. Matthew puts this incident after the words of Jesus,
'my yoke is easy, and my burden is light' – comparing the Lord's
way with the burdens that 'the scribes and the Pharisees' put on
people with their many rules (Matthew 23:1–4).

2. It seems clear that the early Church changed from keeping
the sabbath of the seventh day and made the first day of the week,
the day of Jesus' resurrection, 'the Lord's day', their special day of
worship (see 1 Corinthians 16:2 and Revelation 1:10). We, therefore, should take the guiding principles of the sabbath law and
apply them as well as we can to the keeping of Sunday.

3. 1 Samuel 21 speaks of Ahimelech, not Abiathar, as the priest
at Nob when David and his men went there. Ahimelech's father
and one of his sons were called Abiathar (see 1 Samuel 22:20–23
and 2 Samuel 8:17). Several reasons have been suggested to explain
why Abiathar is mentioned here, but the difference is unimportant
for the meaning of the passage.

Study 12: HEALING ON THE SABBATH

[1]Again he entered the synagogue, and a man was there who
had a withered hand. [2]And they watched him, to see whether
he would heal him on the sabbath, so that they might accuse
him. [3]And he said to the man who had the withered hand,
'Come here.' [4]And he said to them, 'Is it lawful on the
sabbath to do good or to do harm, to save life or to kill?' But
they were silent. [5]And he looked around at them with anger,
grieved at their hardness of heart, and said to the man,
'Stretch out your hand.' He stretched it out, and his hand

was restored. ⁶The Pharisees went out, and immediately held counsel with the Herodians against him, how to destroy him (3:1–6).

The end of chapter 2 and the beginning of chapter 3 belong closely together. Our last section (2:23–28) dealt with the Pharisees' criticism of Jesus' disciples for what they thought was working on the sabbath day. Now they criticize Jesus for healing on the sabbath. We see again the great difference between two attitudes.

We see Jesus full of love and concern for any person in need, wanting to do all in His power to help. We see the Pharisees so concerned for their own rules, their own position as teachers of the law, that they came and 'watched' Jesus, 'that they might accuse him' if He dared to heal on the sabbath (verse 2). Notice in particular what these verses say about the attitude, the words and the action of Jesus.

a. Attitude of Jesus

Jesus 'looked around... with anger' at those who wanted to stop His healing work because it was the sabbath. Many kinds of anger do harm, but there is a righteous anger. The Bible often speaks of the righteous anger (or 'wrath') of God against human sin. God sees what sin does to our own lives, to our relationship with Him and to our relationships with other people. Sometimes we see anger in Jesus – usually when people want to stop good being done. So He was angry here. Later He acted in anger when He cleared the temple court of the money-changers and traders, because they prevented the temple from being 'a house of prayer for all the nations' and 'made it a den of robbers' (see 11:15–17).

Jesus was not only angry, he was 'grieved at their hardness of heart'; 'deeply distressed at their stubborn hearts' is the way that the New International Version puts it. We may say that what grieves the heart of God most is when our minds are closed to His truth and our hearts are closed to

His love, so that we do not want to do or to let others do what is just and right and good.

b. The words of Jesus

The Pharisees thought they were putting Jesus on trial. Now He put them on trial by asking them a direct question. It was an appeal to them to think about what they were doing, to see the reasons for what He intended to do, and to see how wrong their own attitude was. He called the man with the withered hand to come out and stand in front of them all. Then He put the question, 'Is it lawful on the sabbath to do good or to do harm, to save life or to kill?' The law in the Old Testament did not allow work on the sabbath, but, as we have seen, the purpose of the law was to bring blessing and fulness of life to people. Jesus had the opportunity and the power to help this man back to fulness of life and health. The words of James 4:17 apply, 'Whoever knows what is right to do and fails to do it, for him it is sin.' Which is right, to do the good that one is able to do or to refuse to do it?

Mark adds that when Jesus had asked His question, the Pharisees 'were silent'. They had no answer. Whatever they thought in their hearts, they were unwilling to admit that He was right and they were wrong.

c. The action of Jesus

Jesus had spoken and the Pharisees gave no answer. He would not let them stop Him doing good. So He said to the man, 'Stretch out your hand.' He was able immediately to stretch it out 'and his hand was restored'. Jesus never held back from doing the right action for fear of what people would say or do. The path He chose would make Him enemies. It would lead to the cross. Yet He never turned away from it. All the different actions of Jesus we have read of from the beginning of chapter 2 have led the Jewish religious leaders to oppose Him. Now after all these things, 'the Pharisees went out, and immediately held counsel with the Herodians against him how to destroy him' (verse 6). The Pharisees were so determined to silence the voice that spoke against them, and to stop the work of One who acted in love and compassion, that they were willing to team up with their enemies the Herodians (see Note below) to 'destroy Him'. When we read this, the question of Jesus stands out even more strongly. Which should a person do, good or harm, save life or kill?

Meditation *Which do we choose? A religion of rules and regulations or a religion of love – love for God and concern to help people in need?*

For further thought and study 1. Several times in the Gospels we read of Jesus healing people on the sabbath. It regularly led to criticism and showed the difference between the attitude of the Jewish leaders and the attitude of Jesus. See also 1:21–27, Luke 13:10–17, 14:1–6, John 5:1–18 and 9:1–41, and study in these passages these different attitudes.

2. Linking with the thought of Study 11, consider whether there are ways in which we (or the Church) make rules for ourselves and for other Christians which may hinder the healing and liberating work of Christ in our lives or in the lives of others? What is the right place of law in the Christian life?

Notes 1. Matthew 12:9–14 and Luke 6:6–11 are the parallels to this passage. Mark and Luke are very alike. Notice what Matthew 12:11–12 adds to what we have in Mark.

2. While the Romans ruled over Palestine, for many years they allowed members of the Herod family to have some power as local rulers. The Herodians would have been people who supported the Herods. The Pharisees, as strict Jews, had no love for them. The bitterness of their hatred for Jesus is shown by their willingness to plot with even the Herodians 'how to destroy him'.

PREACHING, EXORCISM AND PEOPLE'S RESPONSE

Mark 3:7—4:34

We have seen in the previous section (2:1—3:6) that five reasons are given for the Jewish religious leaders opposing Jesus. In the section after this (4:35—5:43) we will be shown four miracles that Jesus did when no other human help was of any use. In between we have this part of the Gospel which shows especially Jesus' work in teaching and preaching, and in His victory over the powers of evil.

We also see, in His parables and in the incidents that are told, the different responses of people to Him. The scribes said that He was an agent of the prince of demons. His relatives feared that He had gone mad. Twelve men accepted the call to share his work, 'to be with Him' and to be sent out 'to preach and have authority to cast out demons' as He did.

3:7–12	Jesus with the crowds, healing and casting out demons
3:13–19	Call of the twelve, to be with Him and share His work
3:20–30	Wrong explanation of what He was doing
3:31–35	His brothers and sisters, those who do God's will

Study 13: THE CROWDS AND THE CHOSEN TWELVE DISCIPLES

[7]Jesus withdrew with his disciples to the sea, and a great multitude from Galilee followed; also from Judea [8]and Jerusalem and Idumea and from beyond the Jordan and from about Tyre and Sidon a great multitude, hearing all that he did, came to him. [9]And he told his disciples to have a boat ready for him because of the crowd, lest they should crush him; [10]for he had healed many, so that all who had diseases pressed upon him to touch him. [11]And whenever the unclean spirits beheld him, they fell down before him and cried out, 'You are the Son of God.' [12]And he strictly ordered them not to make him known.

[13]And he went up on the mountain, and called to him those whom he desired; and they came to him. [14]And he appointed twelve, to be with him, and to be sent out to preach [15]and have authority to cast out demons: [16]Simon whom he surnamed Peter; [17]James the son of Zebedee and John the brother of James, whom he surnamed Boanerges, that is, sons of thunder; [18]Andrew, and Philip, and Bartholomew, and Matthew, and Thomas, and James the son of Alphaeus, and Thaddaeus, and Simon the Cananaean, [19]and Judas Iscariot, who betrayed him   (3:7–19a).

As so often in this Gospel, especially in the first half of it, we see Jesus with the crowds and we see Him with the disciples. So we have two different pictures of His work.

The two also picture for us different sides of the work of the Christian church today.

a. Crowds

Jesus sometimes taught people in homes, but on many occasions there was not room in a home for all who wanted to come to Him (2:1–2). Often He taught in the synagogues (1:21 and 3:1), but even in them there was not enough room (see 1:45). This time He was by the lake, and He used a boat 'to save him from being crushed by the crowd' (verse 9, New English Bible). In 1:45 it says 'people came to him from every quarter'. Here it speaks of people coming not only from Galilee and Judea and Jerusalem, but also from Idumea (or Edom) in the far south, from the east beyond the River Jordan and from Tyre and Sidon in the north-west (see map on page 25). The Jewish religious leaders opposed Jesus and even wanted to kill Him (verse 6), but the crowds of ordinary people came to Him because they had heard what He was doing (verse 8). Many were in need of healing of their sicknesses and diseases. They wanted 'to touch him' and be well.

We read again about the demon-possessed. As we have seen in 1:23–25 and 34, the demons recognized Jesus as the Son of God who had power to drive them out; but we see again that Jesus did not allow them to shout this out. People had to believe that for themselves and then honour and serve Him. Crowds! crowds! crowds! They came to Jesus for what they could receive of the blessings of God's kingdom. But not many would make Him Lord and Master of their lives. Jesus worked to help the crowds with all their needs, but He wanted, and needed, those who would be disciples and share His work.

b. Disciples

The crowds came from near and far. They came; they went away. But there were those who stayed with Him, willing, at least in some way, to share in His work. He had called four fishermen (in 1:16–20) and Levi, the tax-collector (in 2:13–14). They had answered His call. The word 'disciple' is used more than any other word in the Gospels for those who followed Jesus (more than 40 times in Mark). The word means 'learner' and the disciples had to learn from Jesus, but the Gospels also make clear that discipleship means obeying and serving Him.

Verses 14 and 15 tell us important facts about discipleship. 'He appointed twelve, to be with him, and to be sent out'. First, 'to be with Him'. They had to learn from Him, know His good news, see His lifestyle, understand His work. In Acts 1:21 it says that for one to be an apostle he needed to have been with Jesus from the beginning of His ministry through to His death and resurrection. Second, they were 'to be sent out'. They were to go, as and where He sent them, to share His work. This meant preaching – they had good news to tell. It also meant having authority and power from Jesus to conquer and drive out the powers of evil.

c. Those chosen

We see the great care with which Jesus chose these special disciples. In verse 13 it says, 'he went up on the mountain and called to him those he desired'. Luke 6:12 says that He spent the whole night in prayer before He did this.

Notice these things about His choice:

1. He chose twelve. Twelve was a special number, the number of the tribes of Israel in Old Testament days. His twelve were to be the beginning of a new community, a new people of God, a newly-formed Israel. This link between His twelve and the twelve tribes of Israel is made clear in Matthew 19:28 and Luke 22:30 and in the Book of Revelation (21:12–14).

2. They were very different people. Four were fishermen. One was a tax-collector, hated by loyal Jews. The second Simon was a 'Cananaean' and that means, not a man of

Canaan, but a very devoted Jew, determined to set his people free from Roman rule. (In Luke 6:15 he is called a 'zealot', a freedom fighter.) With Jesus as their Master and Teacher they had to learn to live together and work together as a team.

3. Some became famous and we know a good deal about them. Of others we know only their names. All are equally important to their Lord. He knows by name all who follow Him and He leads them (John 10:3–4).

4. One became a traitor. This shows that He does not compel anyone to follow Him and to keep faithful to Him. He chooses us to be His disciples. We have to accept His call and to receive His help to keep following Him to the end.

Meditation *'Come, I will send you' (Exodus 3:10). The call of God is always first 'come'. Then those who come to Him, He wants to 'send' to do His work in the world.*

For further thought and study 1. What do you think lies behind Jesus giving Simon the name Peter (= 'rock' or 'stone')? See Matthew 16:13–18 and John 1:40–42.

2. Why do you think Jesus called James and John 'sons of thunder'? Do Luke 9:51–56 and Mark 10:35–45 help to explain?

Notes 1. Luke 6:12–19 is parallel to this passage. Matthew 12:15–21 is parallel to verses 7–12 in Mark. Matthew 10:1–4 gives the list of the 'twelve' when they are first sent out by Jesus. We have the list of their names also in Acts 1:13.

2. There are small differences in the list of the 'twelve' in Mark and those given in Matthew, Luke and Acts. Matthew and Mark give the name of Thaddeus (in some early manuscripts Lebbaeus); Luke 6:16 and Acts 1:13 have instead the name 'Judas, the son of James'. Various explanations have been suggested for the differences but we do not really know the reason.

Study 14: MAD, DEMON-POSSESSED, OR
DOING THE WORK OF GOD?

Then he went home; ²⁰and the crowd came together again, so that they could not even eat. ²¹And when his family heard it, they went out to seize him, for people were saying, 'He is beside himself.' ²²And the scribes who came down from Jerusalem said, 'He is possessed by Be-elzebul, and by the prince of demons he casts out the demons.' ²³And he called them to him, and said to them in parables, 'How can Satan cast out Satan? ²⁴If a kingdom is divided against itself, that kingdom cannot stand. ²⁵And if a house is divided against itself, that house will not be able to stand. ³⁶And if Satan has risen up against himself and is divided, he cannot stand, but is coming to an end. ²⁷But no one can enter a strong man's house and plunder his goods, unless he first binds the strong man; then indeed he may plunder his house.

²⁸'Truly, I say to you, all sins will be forgiven the sons of men, and whatever blasphemies they utter; ²⁹but whoever blasphemes against the Holy Spirit never has forgiveness, but is guilty of an eternal sin' – ³⁰for they had said, 'He has an unclean spirit.'

³¹And his mother and his brothers came; and standing outside they sent to him and called him. ³²And a crowd was sitting about him; and they said to him, 'Your mother and your brothers are outside, asking for you.' ³³And he replied, 'Who are my mother and my brothers?' ³⁴And looking around on those who sat about him, he said, 'Here are my mother and my brothers!' ³⁵Whoever does the will of God is my brother, and sister and mother' (3:19b–35).

One of the things that Mark's Gospel shows us clearly is the response of different groups of people to Jesus, to what He was saying and doing. Ordinary people with open minds and needy hearts could see the truth of what He was teaching and recognized the power and love of God. So they came, and they kept coming, in crowds. We read this in verses 7–10 in this chapter and now it says again (in verse

20) that the crowds pressed on Him so much that there was no opportunity for Him to rest or even to eat. But we see also the reaction of His 'family' and of 'the scribes who came down from Jerusalem.'

a. His family

Jesus' family who had grown up with Him were worried about what He was doing. We can imagine their thoughts. Teaching, preaching all day long, healing people, sur-rounded by the crowds – it will be too much for Him. They could see He was stirring up the opposition of the religious leaders by what He was saying and claiming for Himself. He was calling people to follow Him and starting a new movement. What would He do next? 'People were saying, "He's gone mad!"' (verse 21, Good News Bible). It is sad that when people give themselves completely to the work of God they are often misunderstood. The apostle Paul was thought to be mad (Acts 26:24), and many Christians have had to face this accusation, sometimes from their closest relatives.

It was sad that Jesus' family did not understand. Later they did – after His resurrection (see Acts 1:13–14). But now when people said to Jesus, 'Your mother and your brothers are outside asking for you' (verse 32), His reply was, 'Whoever does the will of God is my brother, and sister, and mother' (verse 35). This was not because He did not care for His family. His care for His mother was such that even when He was experiencing the terrible pain and anguish of the cross, He thought of her and provided for her (John 19:25–27). But the closest of all family bonds are between people who put 'the will of God' first in their lives.

b. Scribes

Mark tells us much about the scribes. We have seen how people saw the great difference between the teaching of Jesus and that of the scribes (1:22). The scribes were offended at the thought of Jesus telling people that their sins were forgiven (2:6–7). They were angered that He should call a wicked tax-collector like Levi to be a disciple and then go to a feast in his home (2:13–16). They were jealous of the way the crowds went to Jesus and listened to His teaching. So they said that He was demon-possessed and 'by the prince of demons he casts out the demons' (verse 22).

Jesus had a straightforward answer for them. How would Satan want to cast out Satan? It would mean his kingdom was divided and a divided kingdom would not stand but would fall. The right explanation Jesus gave in a parable. You cannot enter a strong man's house and take his possessions unless you are stronger and able to 'bind the strong man'. Satan is strong, but the One who is stronger has come. This was the only true and sensible explanation of what Jesus was doing.

c. Unforgivable sin

The words of the scribes in verse 22 and Jesus' answer to them lead in verses 28–30 to His serious warning about the kind of sin that cannot be forgiven. People are sometimes troubled by these words. If a person says, 'I have committed the unforgivable sin,' we can help them to see that the Bible says again and again that if anyone *turns* from their sins and asks God's forgiveness, He *always* forgives. The danger is when a person refuses to repent and refuses God's offer of forgiveness, and when a person calls evil good and good evil. The scribes were in this danger. Here was Jesus driving out demons, conquering the powers of evil and they said, 'He has an unclean spirit' (verse 30). The Holy Spirit was showing them the Conqueror of evil, to whom they should turn for salvation, but they were resisting Him.

Prayer *Lord God, may the greatest desire of my life be to do Your will from day to day. Help me to accept as brothers and sisters all who seek to obey You through Jesus Christ our Saviour.* AMEN.

For further thought and study 1. Do the words of Hebrews 6:4–8 and 10:26–31 and 1 John 5:16 help us to understand what verses 28–29 say about the sin that cannot be forgiven?

2. How should a Christian continue to show love and concern for his or her own family when the members of that family do not understand what it means to live as a disciple of Christ, putting the will of God first? Should such a person's relationships in the family of Christian believers be more important than relationships in the human family?

Notes 1. We have parallels to these verses in Matthew 12:24–32 and 46–50 and in Luke 11:15–23, 12:10 and 8:19–21. Note the two things added in Jesus' answer to the scribes in Matthew 12:27–28 and Luke 11:19–20.

2. The RSV translates verse 19 as, 'he went home'. It may be simply He 'entered a house'; or it may be that the home of Simon and Andrew at Capernaum was His home base at this time. See also 2:1.

3. The name Be-elzebul for a demon prince or 'the prince of demons' is not known from earlier Jewish writings. The name may mean 'lord of the house'. Some early manuscripts have Be-elzebub, the name given to a Philistine deity in 2 Kings 1:2 which the Jews took as meaning 'lord of flies'.

4. Verse 27 may have a hint of the fulfilment of the words of the Old Testament in Isaiah 49:24–25 and 53:12.

Study 15: TEACHING IN PARABLES

[1]Again he began to teach beside the sea. And a very large crowd gathered about him, so that he got into a boat and sat in it on the sea; and the whole crowd was beside the sea on the land. [2]And he taught them many things in parables, and in his teaching he said to them: [3]"Listen! A sower went out to sow. [4]And as he sowed, some seed fell along the path, and the

birds came and devoured it. [5]Other seed fell on rocky ground, where it had not much soil, and immediately it sprang up, since it had no depth of soil; [6]and when the sun rose it was scorched, and since it had no root it withered away. [7]Other seed fell among thorns and the thorns grew up and choked it and it yielded no grain. [8]And other seeds fell into good soil and brought forth grain, growing up and increasing and yielding thirtyfold and sixtyfold and a hundredfold.' [9]And he said, 'He who has ears to hear, let him hear.'

[10]And when he was alone, those who were about him with the twelve asked him concerning the parables. [11]And he said to them, 'To you has been given the secret of the kingdom of God, but for those outside everything is in parables; [12]so that they may indeed see but not perceive, and may indeed hear but not understand; lest they should turn again, and be forgiven.' [13]And he said to them, 'Do you not understand this parable? How then will you understand all the parables?'   (4:1–13).

Jesus often spoke in parables. Sometimes the parable was a few words or a phrase as when He said that His disciples were to be as 'the salt of the earth' or 'the light of the world' (Matthew 5:13–14). Sometimes His parables were short sentences as when (in 2:20–22) He spoke about the patched garment and the wineskins. At other times they were stories, like the Good Samaritan (Luke 10:29–37). Why did Jesus teach in parables? We need to think clearly and look hard at the difficult verses 11–12 to answer the question.

a. Parables made Jesus' teaching clear for all kinds of people

He took His parables from everyday life so that the farmers and fishermen of Galilee as well as the scribes and scholars of Jerusalem could understand what He said. When he taught using illustrations from weddings and funerals, lost coins, lost sheep, lamps, hidden treasure and farm labourers, everyone could understand. Verse 33 of this chapter says, 'With many such parables he spoke the word to them, as they were able to hear it.' This was His way with the crowds (verse 2). No wonder it says that those crowds of ordinary people 'heard him gladly' (see 12:37).

b. Parables made Jesus' teaching challenging

In the Old Testament we see parables used to challenge people to think what they were doing. This was so with Jotham's story of the trees choosing a king over them (Judges 9:7–15) and more famously Nathan's parable of the poor man's lamb, addressed to David after he took Uriah's wife (2 Samuel 12:1–10). In Mark's Gospel the parable of the tenants of the vineyard was one that deeply challenged the Jewish religious leaders, because they saw 'that he had told the parable against them' (12:12). A good teacher makes his or her pupils think. So Jesus by His parables made people think and helped them to see the spiritual truths that applied to them.

c. People's attitude to parables shows their attitude to the truth

It is not a contradiction of our first reason for parables when it says in verse 11, 'To you has been given the secret of the kingdom of God, but for those outside everything is in parables.' God's truth is 'secret', or a 'mystery' as the word in this verse means literally, not because God wants to hide it from some people or make it mysterious. He wants people to understand and follow it, but only those who themselves *want* to understand and who want to obey it *will* understand. Others will hear the parables, enjoy the stories, but will not have the desire to know and apply them. The difference between true disciples and others was that the true disciples really wanted to understand and so they 'asked him concerning the parables' (verse 10). So the teaching of Jesus in general, and the teaching in the parables in particular, judged people's attitude to God's word. People either wanted the light of God to shine into their lives and make their lives different, or they just listened to the stories and did not want deeply to understand, to obey and have their lives changed. They saw, as verse 12 puts it, but did not 'perceive'; they heard but did not 'understand'. It was their decision and so God's judgment on them was that they should not 'turn again, and be forgiven.'

All these three reasons for parables are well shown in this parable of the sower. To understand this parable is to understand a great deal about Jesus' teaching in parables (verse 13). First, it made Jesus' meaning clear. Perhaps even as Jesus was teaching by the lake a sower could have been seen scattering his seed and letting it fall on different kinds of ground. Second, Jesus was certainly challenging people to 'listen' as He spoke (verse 3); and at the end He said, 'He who has ears to hear, let him hear' (verse 9). Thirdly, by this parable those who first heard it, and we who hear it today, are judged. What kind of soil am I for the seed of God's word? Do I hear and then think no more what God's word means for my life? Do I take notice for a little while and then do so no more, but let all the other voices crowd God's word out from my life? Or do I hear and want to understand, want to obey and to do what God's word calls me to do?

Prayer *All praise to You, our living God, that You speak to Your people simply and clearly, challenging us to listen and to follow in the way of life. When You speak, give us grace to obey and to do Your will.* AMEN.

For further thought and study 1. In verse 12 Isaiah 6:9–10 is quoted. Think what this means in its setting in the life of the prophet Isaiah, and why it is used in the New Testament, not only here and in Matthew 13:14–15 (parallel to this) but also in John 12:37–43 and Acts 28:23–28.

2. What can we learn from Jesus' use of parables for the ways we try to bring God's word to others, through preaching, teaching and personal witness?

Notes 1. The Good News Bible translation of the end of verse 12 is helpful: 'for if they did' (that is, if they did see and understand), 'they might turn to God and he would forgive them.'

2. It is an interesting and important link between chapter 3 and chapter 4 that 3:32 and 34 speaks of the disciples as those who were 'about him' and 3:31 and 32 speaks of those 'outside' (even His own human family), and 4:10–11 again speaks in the same terms of 'those who were about him' and 'those outside'.

———————————

Study 16: PARABLE OF THE SOILS

[14]**The sower sows the word.** [15]**And these are the ones along the path, where the word is sown; when they hear, Satan immediately comes and takes away the word which is sown in them.** [16]**And these in like manner are the ones sown upon rocky ground, who, when they hear the word, immediately receive it with joy;** [17]**and they have no root in themselves, but endure for a while; then, when tribulation or persecution arises on account of the word, immediately they fall away.** [18]**And others are the ones sown among thorns; they are those who hear the word,** [19]**but the cares of the world, and the delight in riches, and the desire for other things, enter in and choke the word, and it proves unfruitful.** [20]**But those that were sown upon the good soil are the ones who hear the word and accept it and bear fruit, thirtyfold and sixtyfold and a hundredfold** (4:14–20).

Some people understand these verses as Mark's explanation of the parable of verses 3–8 rather than Jesus' own explanation. They think that Jesus would not have explained His parables, but let people work them out for themselves. Some people think He would not have intended it to be interpreted point by point like an allegory, and even suggest that it would be more likely to be the way Christians would look back on the effects of the preaching of the Gospel after some years passed by. It is true that it does not actually say in verse 14 that Jesus was speaking, but that is the most natural way to see the link between verse 13 and what follows in verses 14–20. In fact it fits in well with what we have read before this in the Gospel, especially in this main section (3:7–4:34). These were the ways people were responding then as the kingdom of God came among them in the words and actions of Jesus. People were responding in a similar way to the preaching of the gospel at the time Mark wrote. They are the ways in which people respond – in which we respond – today. Jesus was the Sower, sowing the good seed of God's word (verse 14). All who are messengers of God's word join in the work of sowing. But the parable is principally about the different kinds of *soil*.

a. Seed sown along the path

Some seed fell on the well-trodden path across the field where the sower was sowing. There was no opportunity for the seed to go into the soil, put down roots and grow. The birds ate all that seed. So it is when God's word is preached, or when we read the Scriptures, and we do not allow that word to enter into our minds. It is the work of Satan to take away God's word from our minds so that it can have no effect on our lives. Jesus came to conquer Satan and to prevent his work going on (1 John 3:8). If we want to stop Satan's work and let God do His work in and through us, then when God's word comes to us we must stop, listen, think deeply, and apply His word to the practical things of our lives.

b. Seed sown on rocky ground

There was also seed that fell on ground where there was rock just below the surface. The seed could germinate, but roots could not go down deeply. In the heat of the sun the little plants soon withered and died. So there are those who receive God's word with joy and yet when things become hard and the way of obedience difficult, they no longer give the word of God place in their life. With great keenness one man said to Jesus, 'I will follow you wherever you go.' Jesus challenged him to realize how hard it would be to do as he said (Luke 9:57–58). Peter said, and all the other disciples with him, 'If I must die with you, I will not deny you' (Mark 14:31). Not many hours later 'they all forsook him and fled' (Mark 14:50). The parable challenges us – are we those who give up when trouble or persecution comes?

c. Seed sown among thorns

Some of the good seed fell into ground where there were also the seeds of thorns and weeds. The good plants grew but so did the thorns, and the thorns choked the good plants. How easily this can be applied! There are other forces in our lives as well as God's word. Verse 19 mentions three: 'The cares of the world' – our anxieties and worries; 'delight in riches' – putting possessions before God; the 'desire for other things' – not necessarily bad things but things that make the things of God, the will of God, the work of God, take second place. Then God's word 'proves unfruitful'.

d. Seed sown in good soil

Lastly, there was good soil where the seed could send down roots into the deep, rich earth. The plants could grow unchoked by thorns, and in due time bear fruit. So we have the picture of God's word heard, accepted and allowed to bear fruit (verse 20). Then the purpose of the work of Jesus is fulfilled in the lives of men and women.

Meditation *Ponder what James 1:22–25 says about being 'doers of the word, and not hearers only.'*

For further study and meditation 1. What teaching

does Jesus give to help us deal with 'the cares of the world' and the temptation to 'delight in riches'? See, for example, Matthew 6:25–34 and Luke 12:13–21.

2. What does this parable mean when it speaks of the word of God bearing fruit in people's lives? See John 4:34–38, 15:1–17, Galatians 5:22–23, Colossians 1:6 and 2 Peter 1:5–8.

Notes 1. Both Matthew (in 13:1–23) and Luke (in 8:4–15) give us the parable of the soils and its interpretation. Matthew has more details about the purpose of parables.

2. In verse 19, the word translated 'delight' in riches could also be translated (as in the New International Version) the 'deceitfulness' of riches. Certainly riches are deceitful, promising joy and blessings that they cannot give.

Study 17: WHAT TO DO WITH THE MESSAGE OF TRUTH

²¹And he said to them, 'Is a lamp brought in to be put under a bushel, or under a bed, and not on a stand? ²²For there is nothing hid, except to be made manifest; nor is anything secret, except to come to light. ²³If any man has ears to hear, let him hear.' ²⁴And he said to them, 'Take heed what you hear; the measure you give will be the measure you get, and still more will be given you. ²⁵For to him who has will more be given; and from him who has not, even what he has will be taken away (4:21–25).

As we have considered Jesus' teaching in parables, we have noted that sometimes His parables were stories, and sometimes comparisons that He made in a few words. In these verses we have six short sayings of Jesus, so full of meaning that they could be understood and applied in different ways. Jesus Himself may have used and applied them in different ways at different times (see 'For further thought and study'). Here they all apply to His work of teaching which is the special subject of this part of Mark's Gospel.

a. Purpose of the light of truth is to shine into the world

It is no use lighting a lamp and then putting it under a bowl or a barrel or under the bed. A sensible person puts the lamp on a lampstand. Then everyone can see it and can see into every corner of the room. Jesus came into the world to be 'the Light of the world' (John 8:12). He wanted people to hear and to understand and to follow the truth that He brought. It was sometimes necessary for certain things to be hidden for a time so that people could not misunderstand who Jesus was or the work that He had come to do. So He silenced the demons when they cried out about Him (1:34, 3:11–12), and tried to prevent people shouting about Him as a miracle-worker (1:43–44). But Jesus could certainly say, 'there is nothing hid, except to be made manifest; nor is anything secret, except to come to light' (verse 22).

b. We are given ears to hear God's word

God has given us a mouth to speak and, as Moses was reminded (Exodus 4:10–12), He who created our mouths is able to give us strength to use them to bring His message and His blessing to others. He has also given us ears to hear. Someone has said that God has given us *two* ears and only *one* mouth, but most of us are more ready to speak than to listen. James (1:19) says, 'Let every man be quick to hear, slow to speak'. Jesus often said to people what we have in verse 23, 'If any man has ears to hear, let him hear.' In other words, use your ears to listen. Then He said, 'Take heed what you hear'. Be sure, in other words, that you note the difference between what are human words, human ideas, human suggestions and what is God's word to us. The world shouts to us with ten thousand human voices – by radio and television, in books and newspapers, and in advertising. But through His messengers, in the Bible, and above all in Jesus Christ, God speaks His word to us. 'He who has ears to hear, let him hear' (verse 9).

c. God's truth is given to us to use

'The measure you give will be the measure you get' (verse 24). This applies to life in many ways. We will get out of work or study or friendship according to the measure that we put into it. But this is especially true in relation to God's word. If we earnestly seek to know the truth and live by it, we will understand it more and more and find the joy and blessing of it in our lives. Verse 25 means that if we use the truth that we have, we will gain more. On the other hand, what we do not use, we will lose (just as people can easily lose an art or a skill if they do not use it).

Meditation   *Use Matthew 7:24–27 as further meditation on this passage.*

For further thought and study   Compare the use of these sayings of Jesus in different parts of the Gospels, and notice the different ways in which they are applied. With verse 21 see Matthew 5:15 and Luke 8:16 and 11:33; with verse 22 see Matthew 10:26 and Luke 8:17 and 12:2; with verse 23 see Matthew 11:15 and 13:9 and 43; with verse 24 see Matthew 7:2 and Luke 6:38; with verse 25 see Matthew 13:12 and 25:29 and Luke 8:18 and 19:26.

Notes.   1. Verse 21 says literally 'Does a lamp come in order to be put under a bowl or under a bed?' This may suggest Jesus' 'coming' into the world to be the light of the world. See what is said about what He 'came' to do in 1:24, 38, 2:17 and 10:45.

2. The word which the Revised Standard Version translates as 'bushel' in verse 21 means a measure of about 9 litres or 2 gallons and so should be understood as a bowl or barrel that could contain this amount.

Study 18: PLANTS THAT GROW
AND GOD'S KINGDOM

[26]And he said, 'The kingdom of God is as if a man should scatter seed upon the ground, [27]and should sleep and rise night and day, and the seed should sprout and grow, he knows not how. [28]The earth produces of itself, first the blade, then the ear, then the full grain in the ear. [29]But when the grain is ripe, at once he puts in the sickle, because the harvest has come.'

[30]And he said, 'With what can we compare the kingdom of God, or what parable shall we use for it? [31]It is like a grain of mustard seed, which, when sown upon the ground, is the smallest of all the seeds on earth; [32]yet when it is sown it grows up and becomes the greatest of all shrubs, and puts forth large branches, so that the birds of the air can make nests in its shade.'

[33]With many such parables he spoke the word to them, as they were able to hear it; [34]he did not speak to them without a parable, but privately to his own disciples he explained everything   (4:26–34).

When we read the parables of Jesus and try to understand them, we must not think that a simple sentence will tell us everything about a parable's meaning. We may come back and back to a parable, as we can to a proverb, and see new ways in which it has meaning and application to our lives.

Here we have two parables about 'the kingdom of God' (verses 26 and 30) which both speak of the growth of plants. We have considered a little (in Study 4) what is meant by 'the kingdom of God'. It is God's rule in the lives of men and women. We pray in the Lord's Prayer, 'Your kingdom come'. How does God's kingdom, God's rule, come in the world and in people's lives? These two parables give an answer to that question.

a. How does a plant grow?

A child may plant a seed and expect it suddenly to become a plant. This is not God's way – neither in nature nor in people's lives. 'The kingdom of God is as if a man should scatter seed upon the ground.' The farmer does his work in sowing the seed. He looks forward to harvest time. There is little that he can do in between. While he goes about his work by day and while he sleeps at night, it grows, 'he knows not how'. For a plant there is a sowing time, a growing time, and then a harvest time. Jesus' parable of the sower (verses 3–8) said a lot about sowing time. His parable of the tares (Matthew 13:24–30 and 36–43) said something about the harvest time. This parable says more about the growing time. Growth is the work of God. In the work of God's kingdom it is what He does that is most important. Sometimes people have thought, as Jewish people sometimes did in New Testament times, that *they* could bring in God's kingdom – by political means, by military means, or by making people keep God's law.

We have our part to do, in obeying God and in sowing the seed of His word, but then we must leave God to do His work in people's lives. The apostle Paul had to remind the Christians in Corinth about this. Paul said, 'What then is Apollos? What is Paul? Servants through whom you believed, as the Lord assigned to each. I planted, Apollos watered, but God gave the growth. So neither he who plants nor he who waters is anything but only God who gives the growth' (1 Corinthians 3:5–7).

b. Small beginnings, great results

The second parable is about the growth of the mustard seed. Jewish people used to say, 'Small as a mustard seed'. It is a tiny seed, but when it grows it becomes a great shrub, two to three metres high. The work of the kingdom of God begins in a small way in a person's life, but it can have tremendous results. What began in a small way in the soil of

Palestine more than 1900 years ago when Jesus spoke these words has had tremendous results in the world. When Jesus spoke of the shrub growth from that tiny seed, putting forth 'large branches, so that the birds of the air can make nests in its shade,' some people would have thought of the Old Testament. The prophet Ezekiel (31:5–6) spoke of the great kingdom of Egypt in his time. He likened it to a tree that 'towered high above all the trees of the forest; its boughs grew large and its branches long.... All the birds of the air made their nests in its boughs.'. Then, to explain this Ezekiel said, 'under its shadow dwelt all nations.' (Similar things are said also in Ezekiel 17:22–24 and Daniel 4:10–14 and 20–22.) The Christian church has had the work of taking the good news of God's kingdom in Jesus to people of all nations and men and women of many nations have responded to that good news.

Verses 33–34 tell us again why Jesus used parables in His teaching. It was as people 'were able to hear' and understand His word. Then, as we have seen earlier in the chapter, those who wanted to understand more deeply and to follow the teaching of Jesus and become His disciples, asked to know more.

Prayer   *Lord God, we thank You for the work that You are doing by Your Spirit in the lives of men and women all over the world. Help us to rejoice in Your work, to trust in You, and to let You work in us to the glory of Your name.* AMEN.

For further thought and study   1. How should we see the work of the kingdom of God in the world in terms of sowing, growth, harvest? What is *our* work now, and what is God's work?

2. Consider those passages in the Bible which speak of the harvest as the fruit of sowing the seed of God's word in human lives (as in verse 20), and those that speak of the putting in of the sickle as God's judgment. See Joel 3:13–15, Matthew 13:30 and 39–42, and Revelation 14:14–16.

Note The parable of verses 26–29 is found only in Mark. The parable of the mustard seed is found also in Matthew 13:31–32 and Luke 13:18–19. We have a parallel to verses 33–34 in Matthew 13:34–35 where Matthew adds, as he often does, a quotation from the Old Testament (Psalm 78:2).

FOUR MIGHTY ACTS OF JESUS

Mark 4:35—5:43

In this next section we have four great miracles that Jesus did. In each case it is shown clearly that He did what no other person could do, and people were filled with fear and wonder. In the storm on Lake Galilee the disciples were in danger of death by drowning, but Jesus stilled the wind and waves and 'they were filled with awe, and said to one another, "Who then is this that even wind and sea obey him?"' (4:41). Then there was the man held by the power of demons, in danger of destroying himself. 'No one could bind him . . . no one had the strength to subdue him' (5:3-4), but Jesus drove out the demons. People 'were afraid' when they realized the power of Jesus, 'and all men marvelled', (5:15, 20). A woman in the grip of incurable sickness 'had suffered much under many physicians, and had spent all that she had, and was no better, but rather grew worse' (5:26). She touched Jesus and was healed and 'came in fear and trembling and fell down before him' (5:33). Lastly there was Jairus' daughter. Jesus showed His power over death itself and raised her to life, so that people 'were overcome with amazement' (5:42). All four were desperate situations which no other human help could change, but Jesus acted in His great power. In each case, He rebuked unbelief or encouraged faith in His disciples and in those who came to him (4:40, 5:19, 34, 36).

4:35–41	His power over wind and sea
5:1–20	His power over demons
5:21–23	People in need
5:24–34	His power over incurable sickness
5:35–43	His power over death

Study 19: THE STORM STILLED ON THE LAKE

[35]On that day, when evening had come, he said to them, 'Let us go across to the other side.' [36]And leaving the crowd, they took him with them in the boat, just as he was. And other boats were with him. [37]And a great storm of wind arose, and the waves beat into the boat, so that the boat was already filling. [38]But he was in the stern, asleep on the cushion; and they woke him and said to him, 'Teacher, do you not care if we perish?' [39]And he awoke and rebuked the wind, and said to the sea, 'Peace! Be still!' And the wind ceased, and there was a great calm. [40]He said to them, 'Why are you afraid? Have you no faith?' [41]And they were filled with awe, and said to one another, 'Who then is this, that even wind and sea obey him?' (4:35–41).

From this incident we can learn a great deal as we see the problem, the people concerned, and the power of Jesus. We can see what this incident must have meant to the first disciples of Jesus and then for those for whom Mark wrote who were facing the storms of persecution. It has deep meaning for us whatever storms of life we face.

a. Problem

It all began so naturally. It was Jesus' request to go to the other side of the lake (verse 35). He had been teaching the people from the boat (verse 1), and without going ashore 'they took him with them in the boat, just as he was'. Jesus, weary with the work of the day, went peacefully to sleep in the stern of the boat. Darkness fell and one of the sudden storms that so often arise on Lake Galilee came on them. The wind was fierce. The little boat was tossed about. Waves beat into it, and the water came in more quickly than they could bail it out. The situation was out of control; at least it was beyond the control of Jesus' disciples – as many of our human situations in times of trouble and danger and difficulty seem to be beyond us.

b. People

The disciples were in a panic, filled with fear, angry that Jesus was sleeping (and it was He who had suggested that they come across the lake). They stirred Him awake. 'Do you not care if we perish?' they said to Him. They were wrong in questioning His care for them. They were wrong in not trusting His power to help them. When everything was settled, He challenged them: 'Why were you afraid? Have you no faith?' (verse 40). He had been teaching them to trust Him, and He had been showing His love and care for those who came to Him. Could they not trust Him to deal with this problem?

c. Power of Jesus

'He awoke and rebuked the wind, and said to the sea, "Peace! Be still!"' The Lord can speak to the forces of nature to control them. God spoke to bring these forces of nature into being in the beginning (Genesis 1). The Old Testament speaks of God ruling the raging of the sea and stilling its waves (Psalm 89:9). Jesus was able to act with that power. When He said 'Be still', He used the same word He used to the demons (see 1:25), 'be muzzled'. He is able to control every power that threatens to harm and destroy human life.

Jesus did not keep them out of the storm, but He kept

them in the storm. At first they had a wrong kind of fear –
afraid of the storm, even though Jesus was with them. They
learnt a truer kind of fear. When they realized the power of
the Lord, 'they were filled with awe' (literally, 'they feared
a great fear'). 'Who then is this, that even wind and sea
obey him?'

Meditation   *'In the presence of Jesus we can have peace in
the wildest storms of life'* (W. Barclay).

For further thought and study   1. What passages of the
Bible speak of God's gift of sleep, when people are set free
from anxiety and worry? See, for example, Leviticus 26:6,
Job 11:18–19, Psalms 3:5 and 4:8. What things prevent
people having restful sleep in these days?

2. In what kind of 'storms' that Christians face today can
they find encouragement in the passage?

Notes   1. The parallels to this passage are Matthew 8:18, 23–27,
and Luke 8:22–25. It may be significant that Matthew 8:19–22
(just before this incident) has a passage about the cost of discipleship.

2. To some people today belief in miracles is difficult, especially
what are sometimes called 'nature miracles' (like this one of Jesus'
power over the storm, His feeding the crowds with a few loaves
and fish, or His raising the dead). We should ask *why* belief in such
miracles is found difficult. Is it because people think that the whole
of life must be explained by what we can see and hear and touch?
But if we believe (a) in the spiritual forces as well as the physical
ones in the universe, (b) in a God who has all power and wisdom,
and (c) in Jesus being the Son of God come into human life, we
should not think of 'miracles' as being impossible.

Study 20: STORM STILLED IN A HUMAN LIFE

[1]They came to the other side of the sea, to the country of the Gerasenes. [2]And when he had come out of the boat, there met him out of the tombs a man with an unclean spirit, [3]who lived among the tombs; and no one could bind him any more, even with a chain; [4]for he had often been bound with fetters and chains, but the chains he wrenched apart, and the fetters he broke in pieces; and no one had the strength to subdue him. [5]Night and day among the tombs and on the mountains he was always crying out, and bruising himself with stones. [6]And when he saw Jesus from afar he ran and worshipped him; [7]and crying out with a loud voice, he said, 'What have you to do with me, Jesus, Son of the Most High God? I adjure you by God, do not torment me.' [8]For he had said to him, 'Come out of the man, you unclean spirit!' [9]And Jesus asked him, 'What is your name?' He replied, 'My name is Legion; for we are many.' [10]And he begged him eagerly not to send them out of the country. [11]Now a great herd of swine was feeding there on the hillside; [12]and they begged him, 'Send us to the swine, let us enter them.' [13]So he gave them leave. And the unclean spirits came out, and entered the swine; and the herd, numbering about two thousand, rushed down the steep bank and were drowned in the sea.

[14]The herdsmen fled, and told it in the city and in the country. And people came to see what it was that had happened. [15]And they came to Jesus, and saw the demoniac sitting there, clothed and in his right mind, the man who had had the legion; and they were afraid. [16]And those who had seen it told what had happened to the demoniac and to the swine. [17]And they began to beg Jesus to depart from their neighbourhood. [18]And as he was getting into the boat, the man who had been possessed with demons begged him that he might be with him. [19]But he refused, and said to him, 'Go home to your friends, and tell them how much the Lord has done for you, and how he has had mercy on you.' [20]And he

**went away and began to proclaim in the Decapolis how
much Jesus had done for him; and all men marvelled**
(5:1–20).

In the last section we read what the Lord was able to do in
a situation that was completely out of control of the disciples
– the storm on Lake Galilee. Here is the situation of a man
who was out of control, a man with a mighty storm in his life
– and that storm, too, was stilled by Jesus.

a. A man out of control

Much of the work of Jesus was done on the western and
northern sides of Lake Galilee – in places like Bethsaida
and Capernaum, where many people lived. Sometimes, as
at this time, he went across to the eastern side 'to the
country of the Gerasenes' (see Note). In that whole area of
the Decapolis (verse 20) people were more Gentile than
Jewish, as is shown by the keeping of pigs which to Jews
were unclean (Leviticus 11:7–8). We have a vivid description of what happened when they reached the shore and
Jesus came out of the boat. He was met by 'a man with an
unclean spirit'. This demon-possessed man lived in a grave-
yard. He did things that no one could control. People had
tried to bind him with fetters and chains, as people in some
places still do with demon-possessed or mentally sick folk.
He broke off whatever bound him and 'no one had the
strength to subdue him' (verse 4). He often used his great
strength to hurt himself, bruising and cutting himself with
stones. He could not be controlled, by himself or by others.

b. Brought under control

The man, or the demons in him, feared no ordinary
human person. But in the presence of Jesus it was different.
As we have seen happen similarly before, in the case of
demon-possessed people (see 1:24 and 34 and 3:11), 'when
he saw Jesus from afar', he realized that he was in the
presence of the Conqueror of evil, the 'Son of the Most

High God'. He had reason to tremble before the One who had authority to give the command that every demon must obey. 'Come out of the man, you unclean spirit!' (verse 8). The pigs feeding on the hillside were the creatures who suffered from the demons, and 'rushed down the steep bank' into the lake; but the man was set free. The people saw the one who had been demon-possessed 'sitting there, clothed and in his right mind' (verse 15). Luke (8:35) says he was 'sitting at the feet of Jesus'. Before he had rushed about madly and restlessly. He was 'clothed', with respect for himself, and no longer like a wild animal. He was 'in his right mind', restored to sanity.

c. Response to the work of Jesus

As always happens when the word of God is preached and the work of Jesus Christ is seen in changing the lives of men and women, there were two kinds of response. There was the response of those who would rather Jesus did His work in other places and left them as they were. 'They began to beg Jesus to depart from their neighbourhood' (verse 17). Then there was the response of the man who knew that Jesus had given him new life and freedom. He wanted, above all things, to 'be with him' as a disciple (with verse 18 compare 3:14). However, Jesus had a different purpose. If he wanted to serve Jesus this was the way for him: 'go home to your friends, and tell them how much the Lord has done for you, and how he has had mercy on you' (verse 19). This was different from Jesus' command at other times when He had done miracles. In some places there was danger that Jesus might be known as Miracle-worker; then he told people to keep quiet about what He had done (see 1:44 and 3:11–12). Here, where Jesus could not Himself stay, this man must be the evangelist and tell and show 'how much Jesus had done for him' – and that he did gladly (verse 20).

Ever since Mark wrote his Gospel, people have seen in this incident a picture of what Jesus still does in the lives of men and women. They may not be demon-possessed. They may even be well-educated or rich but they are under the power of evil. They are not really in control of their lives, but are restless, destructive, useless. Only by the power of Jesus can they be set free from the power of evil and given peace and health, of body, mind and spirit. Then they are able to witness to the One who has become their Saviour and has changed their lives.

Meditation *'Everyone who commits sin is a slave to sin'* but *'if the Son makes you free, you will be free indeed'* (John 8:34, 36).

For further thought and study 1. Why do you think that these Gerasene people asked Jesus to leave their area? Are there similar reasons why people have tried to stop the preaching of the gospel, in the early days of the Church, or in our time? See Acts 4:15–18, 16:16–24 and 19:23–27 as examples.

2. In what other ways can we see that Jesus never forced Himself on people who did not want Him among them? What does this teach us for the preaching of the Gospel today? See Revelation 3:20.

Notes 1. Matthew (8:28–34) and Luke (8:26–39) record this incident but without as much detail as we have in Mark.

2. Verse 1 speaks of 'the country of the Gerasenes'. Some early copies of the Gospel had other place names. There was a Gerasa about 30 miles from the lake, but the place may have been that which today is known as Khersa (perhaps at that time also Gerasa). 'Decapolis' (in verse 20) means 'ten towns' since in that area there were these ten non-Jewish towns which came under the authority of the Roman governor of Syria.

3. In Study 5, Note 2, we considered the matter of demon-possession. There is much that we do not understand about the demonic. What is suggested by this passage is not only that demons recognize Jesus as Son of God, but that they also fear His power to drive them out and 'torment' them (verse 7). They appear to like

to remain in a place where they can possess humans (verse 10) –
and if not humans, then animals (verse 12). They do not like to be
left alone or to be in an uninhabited area. People sometimes
criticise the action of Jesus because of what happened to the pigs.
Yet we do not criticise the killing of numberless animals to provide
us with food! Jesus taught God's care for the sparrow and for all
His creatures (Matthew 10:29), but He also taught the special
value of a human life (Matthew 10:31). Even at great cost, the
Lord wants to set every human life free from possession by evil.

Study 21: FAITH, HEALING
AND PERSONAL BLESSING

[21]And when Jesus had crossed again in the boat to the other
side, a great crowd gathered about him; and he was beside
the sea. [22]Then came one of the rulers of the synagogue,
Jairus by name; and, seeing him, he fell at his feet, [23]and
besought him, saying, 'My little daughter is at the point of
death. Come and lay your hands on her, so that she may be
made well, and live.' [24]And he went with him.

And a great crowd followed him and thronged about him.
[25]And there was a woman who had had a flow of blood for
twelve years, [26]and who had suffered under many physicians, and had spent all that she had, and was no better but
rather grew worse, [27]She had heard the reports about Jesus,
and came up behind him in the crowd and touched his
garment. [28]For she said, 'If I touch even his garments, I shall
be made well.' [29]And immediately the haemorrhage ceased;
and she felt in her body that she was healed of her disease.
[30]And Jesus, perceiving in himself that power had gone forth
from him, immediately turned about in the crowd, and said,
'Who touched my garments?' [31]And his disciples said to
him, 'You see the crowd pressing around you and yet you
say, "Who touched me?"' [32]And he looked around to see
who had done it. [33]But the woman, knowing what had been

done to her, came in fear and trembling and fell down before him, and told him the whole truth. [34]And he said to her, 'Daughter, your faith has made you well; go in peace, and be healed of your disease' (5:21–34).

We have seen that the great purpose of this part of Mark's Gospel (4:35–5:43) is to show the power of Jesus to do what no other person could do – with the storm, with a demon-possessed man and now with an incurable illness. It is also part of the purpose of the Gospel to show the right way for people to come to Jesus with all their needs – humbly and in faith – and so find salvation and life.

a. Faith in Jesus

The two people of whom we read here came to Jesus in great need. Jairus came for his sick daughter who was, as we would say, 'at death's door' (verse 23). He was a man of importance, as 'ruler of the synagogue', responsible for the services and other life and work of the synagogue; but, without worrying about what people would think of him, he came humbly to Jesus and 'fell at his feet'. Because of what he knew that Jesus had done for others, he 'begged him earnestly.... Please come and place your hands on her, so that she will get well and live' (verse 23, Good News Bible).

Then there was the woman whose trouble had lasted for all the twelve years of the life-time of Jairus' daughter (verses 25 and 42). She had found no healing, but 'had heard the reports about Jesus'. Because He had healed others, she believed that He would heal her. There may have been a little superstition in the way that she thought of touching 'the fringe of his garment' (as Matthew and Luke put it), but she had faith. She said to herself, 'If I only touch his garment, I shall be made well.'

b. The touch of Jesus

No other person had been able to help that woman, and she had tried many doctors. Doctors had little of the knowledge and skills that they have today, and probably literally she 'had suffered much under many' of them. She had spent all her money 'and was no better but rather grew worse'. Then she came to Jesus. In faith, she touched His garment. 'And immediately... she felt in her body that she was healed of her disease.' Power, the healing power of God, went out from Jesus, and she was well again.

c. The word of Jesus

According to Jewish law, the woman's sickness made her ceremonially unclean (Leviticus 15:25–27). She could not go to the temple or the synagogue. Anyone whom she touched became unclean as well. She certainly would not want the crowd to know this. So she came up behind Jesus in the crowd, touched His garment, and was healed. But Jesus wanted her – like all the sick folk who came to Him – to receive more than healing for the body. He wanted added blessing to come to her, the blessing of His word and of her knowing Him personally. Therefore He asked that question, 'Who touched my garments?' To the disciples it was a foolish question – so many people were pressing in on Him.

To the one person whom it concerned it was not a foolish question. In fear and trembling she came, confessed what she had done and 'what had been done to her'. The words of Jesus must have changed her fear to joy. He showed that He cared for her by calling her 'daughter'. Then He encouraged her, 'Your faith has made you well' (literally 'has saved you', the same word is used both here in verse 34 and in verse 23). Then, 'go in peace' – peace with God, peace in her life, fullest health and well-being, the word means. You can be sure that you are 'healed of your disease'. Another needy life was changed by the presence, the power and the word of Jesus.

Meditation   *'When other helpers fail and comforts flee, Help of the helpless, abide with me'* (H. F. Lyte).

For further thought and study 1. When it says that for such a miracle to be done 'power had gone forth from him', what do you think this meant for Jesus Himself and for other people? See also Matthew 8:17, Luke 5:17, 6:19 and Acts 10:38.

2. 'Your faith has made you well' or 'your faith has saved you'. These words Jesus spoke not only to this woman but to others as well – see Luke 7:50, 17:19 and 18:42. What do you think that they meant to these people to whom they were spoken, and how can we apply them to ourselves? See John 3:16 and Acts 16:31.

Note The two incidents of which we read in verses 21–43 are also linked together in Matthew (9:18–26) and Luke (8:40–56) but there is not the detail which we have in Mark.

Study 22: DEATH CONQUERED

[35]While he was still speaking, there came from the ruler's house some who said, 'Your daughter is dead. Why trouble the Teacher any further?' [36]But, ignoring what they said, Jesus said to the ruler of the synagogue, 'Do not fear, only believe.' [37]And he allowed no one to follow him except Peter and James and John the brother of James. [38]When they came to the house of the ruler of the synagogue, he saw a tumult, and people weeping and wailing loudly. [39]And when he had entered, he said to them, 'Why do you make a tumult and weep? The child is not dead but sleeping.' [40]And they laughed at him. But he put them all outside, and took the child's father and mother and those who were with him, and went in where the child was. [41]Taking her by the hand he said to her, 'Talitha cumi'; which means, 'Little girl, I say to you, arise.' [42]And immediately the girl got up and walked (she was twelve years of age), and they were immediately

overcome with amazement. ⁴³And he strictly charged them that no one should know this, and told them to give her something to eat (5:35–43).

Jairus had come to Jesus to ask Him to come to heal his daughter. She was 'at the point of death' (verse 23), but he could well feel, 'While there's life, there's hope.' The delay while Jesus healed and spoke to the woman who came and 'touched his garment' meant that the girl died while Jesus was on the way.

a. Natural human attitude to death

All that the messengers from the home of the ruler at the synagogue could say was, 'Your daughter is dead. Why trouble the Teacher any further?' There was no longer any hope. Jesus might be able to heal, but He could do no more, they thought. So at the house where the girl had died people began 'weeping and wailing loudly'. It was the custom in Palestine not only for the families to weep and mourn, but they paid people to play flutes and wail loudly. The Jewish writer, Josephus, says that even poor people would pay at least two flute-players and one woman to mourn. People cried out loudly, tore their clothes and their hair and beat their breasts. This was the 'tumult' that Jesus found when He came to the house (verse 38).

b. Attitude of Jesus to death

In every way the attitude of Jesus to death was different from the natural human attitude. When the message that his daughter had died came to Jairus, Jesus encouraged him to keep on believing; even though she had died. 'Do not fear', He said to him. When He came to the house, He put out all the weeping and wailing mourners. He said, 'Why do you make a tumult and weep? The child is not dead but sleeping'. They knew that, on any human reckoning, she was dead, and so 'they laughed at him' (verse 40). No one had any doubt that she had died. To Jesus she was asleep, because her death was not final – she was soon to be restored to life again. It was as when on onother occasion He went to restore the dead Lazarus to life, and He said, 'Our friend Lazarus has fallen asleep, but I go to awake him out of sleep' (see John 11:11–15).

c. Action of Jesus

The message had come that Jairus' daughter had died, but Jesus still went to Jairus' home. When He arrived, He said He wanted with Him only the parents and the three disciples, Peter, James and John (verse 37). All of the others He sent out. As with His other miracles (see 1:43–44 and 3:12), He wanted no broadcasting of the fact that He was a great miracle-worker (see also verse 43). Then with these few He 'went in where the child was'. He spoke with tenderness but with authority. His words in Aramaic, the language of that home, would always be remembered by those who heard them: 'Talitha cumi', meaning 'Little girl, I say to you, arise.' She got up, began to walk about, and Jesus reminded them of her need of food.

This is the last and greatest of the miracles that Mark records in this part of his Gospel (4:35—5:43) – a twelve-year-old girl raised from death to life. People 'were immediately overcome with amazement' (verse 42). These were the signs of the kingdom, of the rule of God, God's power at work in Jesus. The storm was stilled, demons were cast out, the sick were healed, the dead raised to life (see Luke 7:22). In Jesus Christ we have a gospel which is good news of victory over all evil and victory over death. In the face of death, Jesus' words to us are still, 'Do not fear'. 'Do not mourn as others without hope' (see 1 Thessalonians 4:13). Those who believe have eternal life (John 3:16). Death for them is the gateway to the fulness of life with God.

Meditation   '*Even though I walk through the valley of the shadow of death, I fear no evil; for thou art with me;...*

Surely goodness and mercy shall follow me all the days of my life; and I shall dwell in the house of the Lord for ever' (Psalm 23:4, 6).

For further thought and study 1. Why do you think that Jesus chose the three disciples, Peter, James and John to be with Him when He raised Jairus' daughter? They were with Him also on two other special occasions. See Mark 9:2–3 and 14:32–42. Do you think that the principle of Deuteronomy 19:15, quoted in 2 Corinthians 13:1 and other places, helps to answer the question?

2. Why is death often spoken of in the New Testament as 'sleep'? See 1 Corinthians 15:6, 16–18 and 1 Thessalonians 4:13–15.

WIDER MINISTRY, FAITH AND UNBELIEF, THE TRAINING OF DISCIPLES

Mark 6:1—8:30

These three themes link together what we have in this next main part of the Gospel. The scope of the ministry of Jesus was widened as He sent out the twelve disciples to continue His work (6:7–13). People kept on coming to Him from near and far (6:55–56). He went into parts of the country that were more Gentile than Jewish and helped people there (7:24–37). The teaching that Jesus gave about the Jewish law of clean and unclean meats pointed to the way that the great barrier between Jews and Gentiles would be broken down (7:1–23). The disciples had to learn what it meant to share life and work with Jesus, not only when the crowds came to Him, but when, as in His own home town of Nazareth, people would not believe in Him (6:1–6). The fact that John the Baptist was put to death because of his faithfulness to his ministry (6:17–29) pointed to what would happen to Jesus.

The disciples at this time had to grow in faith and understanding. The miracles in this part of the Gospel are linked with the work of Jesus in training them and leading them to fuller faith in Him. When Jesus had the hungry crowds around Him, He challenged the disciples to have compassion for them (6:30–44 and 8:1–10). He expected them to learn from His power to provide for their needs. It says that they had fear instead of faith, 'for they did not understand about the loaves' (6:52). Later, when they were weak in faith He reminded them of what He had done and how that should encourage them to trust Him (8:19–21). Two of the miracles told have a special point. He took a deaf man aside from the crowds and made him able to hear (7:31–37) and He took a blind man aside and made him able to see (8:22–26). Then Jesus challenged His disciples: 'Having eyes do you not see, and having ears do you not hear?' (8:18). He took them aside and Peter was led to make the great confession of faith. 'You are the Christ' (8:27–30). It is a high point of the Gospel. All that has gone before has led up to this. What follows from this point concerns the way that Jesus went to the cross and how He prepared His disciples.

We may divide this part of the Gospel into the following sections:

Study 23: RESULTS OF UNBELIEF AND OF FAITH

¹He went away from there and came to his own country; and
his disciples followed him. ²And on the sabbath he began to
teach in the synagogue; and many who heard him were
astonished, saying, 'Where did this man get all this? What is
the wisdom given to him? What mighty works are wrought
by his hands! ³Is not this the carpenter, the son of Mary and
brother of James and Joseph and Judas and Simon, and are
not his sisters here with us?' And they took offence at him.
⁴And Jesus said to them, 'A prophet is not without honour,
except in his own country, and among his own kin, and in his
own house.' ⁵And he could do no mighty work there, except
that he laid his hands upon a few sick people and healed
them. ⁶And he marvelled because of their unbelief.

⁷And he called to him the twelve, and he went about among
the villages teaching, and began to send them out two by
two, and gave them authority over the unclean spirits. ⁸He
charged them to take nothing for their journey except a
staff; no bread, no bag, no money in their belts; ⁹but to wear
sandals and not put on two tunics. ¹⁰And he said to them,
'Where you enter a house, stay there until you leave the
place. ¹¹And if any place will not receive you and they refuse
to hear you, when you leave, shake off the dust that is on
your feet for a testimony against them.' ¹²So they went out
and preached that men should repent. ¹³And they cast out
many demons, and anointed with oil many that were sick
and healed them   (6:1–13).

In these verses we see two different pictures. In Nazareth
the people had opportunity of seeing the 'wisdom' of Jesus'
teaching and the power of His 'mighty works', but they
were not willing to believe and let Him do His work among
them. Then we see the disciples, still with much to learn
and still to grow in true faith in the Lord Jesus, and yet
willing to be sent out to work for Him. In His power they go
preaching, casting out 'many demons' and healing 'many
that were sick' (verses 12–13).

a. Jesus in Nazareth

Nazareth was Jesus' home town where He had been brought up (see Matthew 2:23 and Luke 2:39, 51), and often He was called 'Jesus of Nazareth'. In the midst of His ministry in other parts of Galilee He went there. As in other places, people 'who heard him were astonished' (verse 2). They asked the right questions: 'Where did this man get all this? What is the wisdom given to him? What mighty works are wrought by his hands!' They could see the wisdom of His teaching and they had heard of His 'mighty works' in other places. They asked the right questions, but they were not willing to receive the right answers. They thought of Him as one of them. They knew Him as their carpenter. He could not be more than that, they thought. They were not willing to see that God could trust His message and give His power to a carpenter – indeed that the Son of God could have lived the life of a carpenter in Nazareth. They were not willing to believe. They were not willing to let His power work among them. Just 'a few sick people' found healing. As once He 'marvelled' at the faith of a Roman soldier who had not had all the opportunities that the Jews had (Matthew 8:10), so here 'he marvelled because of their unbelief.' They missed their great opportunity. Jesus went on to other villages and taught there (verse 6; compare 1:38).

b. Disciples on a mission

In 3:14 we have read how Jesus called and appointed the twelve disciples 'to be with him and to be sent out...'. They still had many things to learn by being with Him and in these chapters we will see how they also had to overcome unbelief and truly trust Him; but they were willing to learn and to serve. So Jesus sent them out, and they found that His power was given to them. They were able to cast out demons and heal the sick like their Master. Like Him they 'preached that men should repent' (verse 12), for in turning from their sin back to God people could come to know the blessings of the kingdom of God.

Jesus sent the disciples out 'two by two'. The agreement of two witnesses was always important to the Jews because, as we have seen, this was a principle laid down in the law (see Deuteronomy 19:15). More important, 'two are better than one', because one can support and encourage the other (see Ecclesiastes 4:9–10). This is always a good principle in the work of Christ. They had to go out simply, taking no food or money with them. In a practical way they had to trust His promise that if they put first the work of His kingdom, then their needs would be provided (Matthew 6:25–33).

So the disciples learnt to enter into and share the work and ministry of their Master. As we have noticed, they also learnt with Him what it meant for His message to be rejected. The disciples, verse 1 tells us, were with Jesus in Nazareth when people there were not willing to believe in Him. They were also told what to do when people refused to listen to them (verse 11). Jewish people returning from Gentile areas shook the dust from their feet. So the disciples were to show people what they were doing when they acted as unbelievers, when they had the opportunity to hear God's word and rejected it. (See also Acts 13:51 and 18:6.)

Meditation *'There is laid on us the tremendous responsibility that we can either help or hinder the work of Jesus Christ. We can open the door wide to Him – or we can slam it in His face'* (W. Barclay).

For further thought and study   1. Verse 3 here tells us all that we know of the life of Jesus from the age of 12 (Luke 2:42) to the age of 30 (Luke 3:23): that he was a 'carpenter'. What does that tell us about Jesus Himself and about how we should think of the ordinary work that people do?

2. When the disciples were sent out they went with the power and authority of Jesus (verse 7). How do other passages in the Bible show that when the Lord gives to men

and women His call and His authority to do His work He also gives them His power? See Matthew 28:18–20 and Acts 1:8 and remember the call of people like Moses, Joshua, Elisha and Jeremiah in the Old Testament.

Notes 1. Matthew 13:53–58 tells us of the same event as verses 1–6 here. Luke 4:16–30 tells also what happened to Jesus in the synagogue at Nazareth, but it is not clear whether it refers to the same time as the things recorded here. With verses 7–13 we should compare Matthew's account (10:1, 5–15) and Luke's account (9:1–6) of the sending out of the twelve. There are differences of detail but the same things are emphasised.

2. Luke 10:7–9 help us to understand verse 10. The disciples were to accept what was offered to them and not try to find a better place or a richer home.

3. Verse 10 says that they anointed many sick people with oil. Oil was used in those days as medicine (see Luke 10:34 and Isaiah 1:6); but here it was probably used (in the way James 5:14 speaks of this) to help people's faith, as an outward sign of the healing work that God was able to do through His servants.

Study 24: DEATH OF THE FAITHFUL FORE-RUNNER

[14]**King Herod heard of it; for Jesus' name had become known. Some said, 'John the Baptizer has been raised from the dead; that is why these powers are at work in him'** [15]**But others said, 'It is Elijah.' And others said, 'It is a prophet, like one of the prophets of old.'** [16]**But when Herod heard of it he said, 'John, whom I beheaded, has been raised.'** [17]**For Herod had sent and seized John, and bound him in prison for the sake of Herodias, his brother Philip's wife; because he had married her.** [18]**For John said to Herod, 'It is not lawful for you to have your brother's wife.'** [19]**And Herodias had a grudge against him, and wanted to kill him. But she**

could not, [20]for Herod feared John, knowing that he was a righteous and holy man, and kept him safe. When he heard him, he was much perplexed; and yet he heard him gladly. [21]But an opportunity came when Herod on his birthday gave a banquet for his courtiers and officers and the leading men of Galilee. [22]For when Herodias' daughter came in and danced, she pleased Herod and his guests; and the king said to the girl, 'Ask me for whatever you wish, and I will grant it.' [23]And he vowed to her, 'Whatever you ask me, I will give you, even half of my kingdom.' [24]And she went out, and said to her mother, 'What shall I ask?' And she said, 'The head of John the baptizer.' [25]And she came in immediately with haste to the king, and asked, saying, 'I want you to give me at once the head of John the Baptist on a platter.' [26]And the king was exceedingly sorry; but because of his oaths and his guests he did not want to break his word to her. [27]And immediately the king sent a soldier of the guard and gave orders to bring his head. He went and beheaded him in the prison, [28]and brought his head on a platter, and gave it to the girl; and the girl gave it to her mother. [29]When his disciples heard of it, they came and took his body, and laid it in a tomb   (6:14–29).

The work of Jesus had become more and more widely known as He had gone to many towns and villages (verse 6) and had sent out the twelve disciples. Herod Antipas, who, under the Roman authority, was ruler (and sometimes called 'king') over Galilee and the area east of the River Jordan called Perea, heard about Jesus. Some people were saying that Jesus was Elijah come back as was foretold in the Old Testament (Malachi 3:1 and 4:5). Others said He was a prophet because He preached God's word with such authority (Matthew 21:11, Luke 7:16 and 24:19). Herod said that it must be John the Baptist risen from the dead. He said this because he was afraid and still felt guilty for putting John to death.

a. John, faithful to death

We have read of John's faithful preaching and humble life at the beginning of the Gospel (1:4–8). To him the favour of God meant more than the favour of kings. So he was not afraid to rebuke Herod and to tell him, 'It is not lawful for you to have your brother's wife.' Herod knew that John was not only faithful in preaching; he was a 'righteous and holy man' in the way he lived (verse 20). Herod knew that he should listen to the word of God that such a man preached – a man who was willing to be put in prison and to die rather than be silent.

b. Herodias, determined to kill

Herod did not like John's word of rebuke when he took his brother's wife, Herodias. Herodias hated it. She wanted to silence the voice that spoke against her. She was not satisfied even to have John put in prison (as the Jewish writer Josephus tells us, in the awful fortress of Machaerus by the Dead Sea). She 'wanted to kill him' (verse 19). At first she 'could not' because of Herod's respect for John. She waited her time and made her plan. Herod had been enticed by the beauty of her daughter. So at the birthday feast when Herod ate and drank with 'his courtiers and officers and the leading men of Galilee', Herodias' daughter danced before him. He, perhaps partly drunk, made her the promise, 'Whatever you ask of me, I will give you.' This was the chance for Herodias to silence for ever the accusing voice of John. The girl did what her mother wished and asked for 'the head of John the Baptiser'.

Herod was pulled both ways. He knew the truth of John's preaching but he did not want to displease Herodias. Nor did he want to go back on his word spoken before all his guests (verse 26). So he had John the Baptist put to death. But he continued to feel guilty for what he had done and so the reports about Jesus made him fear that John had come to life again, and 'these powers are at work in him' (verse 14).

Mark told this story in full for us to learn from the

courage of John, to see in Herodias the hatred of God's word and in Herod the lack of courage to do what he knew was right and to refuse what he knew was wrong. Yet Mark knew also that as John suffered (as the prophet Elijah had done), so Jesus Himself was going to suffer because He spoke and lived out the truth (see 9:12–13). As Herodias set out to put John to death, so the Jewish leaders plotted to kill Jesus (see 3:6). As Herod let himself do what Herodias wanted, so Pilate would let himself do what the Jewish leaders demanded. The disciples had to learn the way that they, too, were called to follow.

Meditation *'Be faithful unto death, and I will give you the crown of life'* (Revelation 2:10).

For further thought and study 1. What other examples come to your mind, from the Bible or from the history of the Christian Church, of people who like John the Baptist suffered for their courage in speaking the truth?

2. What does the Bible teach about vows and promises that people may make? See Psalm 141:3, Ecclesiastes 5:1–6 and Matthew 5:33–37. Is it better to break or to keep a promise when to keep it would clearly be to do wrong?

Notes 1. Matthew 14:1–12 is parallel to these verses in Mark and Luke 9:7–9 to verses 14–16. Luke does not tell of the death of John.

2. The Jewish writer, Josephus, tells us that Herodias was not married to Philip the Tetrarch who is named in Luke 3:1 as Herod's brother. He says that Herodias was the wife of another Herod – but possibly this one also had the name Philip.

Study 25: FEEDING OF THE FIVE THOUSAND

[30]The apostles returned to Jesus and told him all that they

had done and taught. [31]And he said to them, 'Come away by yourselves to a lonely place, and rest a while.' For many were coming and going, and they had no leisure even to eat. [32]And they went away in the boat to a lonely place by themselves. [33]Now many saw them going, and knew them, and they ran there on foot from all the towns, and got there ahead of them. [34]As he went ashore he saw a great throng, and he had compassion on them, because they were like sheep without a shepherd; and he began to teach them many things. [35]And when it grew late, his disciples came to him and said, 'This is a lonely place, and the hour is now late; [36]send them away, to go into the country and villages round about and buy themselves something to eat.' [37]But he answered them, 'You give them something to eat.' And they said to him, 'Shall we go and buy two hundred denarii worth of bread, and give it to them to eat?' [38]And he said to them, 'How many loaves have you? Go and see.' And when they had found out, they said, 'Five, and two fish.' [39]Then he commanded them all to sit down by companies upon the green grass. [40]So they sat down in groups, by hundreds and by fifties. [41]And taking the five loaves and the two fish he looked up to heaven, and blessed, and broke the loaves, and gave them to the disciples to set before the people; and he divided the two fish among them all. [42]And they all ate and were satisfied. [43]And they took up twelve baskets full of broken pieces and of the fish. [44]And those who ate the loaves were five thousand men   (6:30–44).

Verses 7–13 of this chapter told of the sending out of the twelve disciples. Verses 14–29 broke into the story to tell us what Herod thought when he heard of the work of Jesus and of His representatives, and to tell us how Herod put John the Baptist to death. Now we are told of the return of the disciples. How much they would want to tell Jesus of their experiences, of all that they had done and taught. Weary with their work and with so much to tell, they were glad of Jesus' invitation to them, 'Come away by yourselves to a lonely place, and rest a while'. They, like Christians still today, had to learn their need of rest and of time apart with their Master. They had also to learn, however, that rest would often be interrupted by people coming with their needs.

a. Compassion of Jesus

The disciples thought of the crowds that came when they wanted to be quiet and alone as an interruption and a great nuisance. Yet Jesus 'had compassion on them because they were like sheep without a shepherd' (verse 34). Those who (as shepherds) should have protected them and led them in the right way had failed to do so (compare Ezekiel 34:1–6). So Jesus would be their Shepherd and 'he began to teach them many things.' It was surely time, the disciples thought, for the crowds to go. So they said to Jesus, 'the hour is now late; send them away, to go into the country and villages round about and buy themselves something to eat.' But Jesus wanted His disciples to enter into His compassion; '*You* give them something to eat,' he said.

b. Power of Jesus

The disciples had no great desire to help the hungry crowd. Nor did they see any way that they could. Could they buy 'two hundred denarii worth of bread'? That was the money a man might earn in eight or nine months (see Matthew 20:2). Probably they had nothing like this amount of money. If they had, where would they buy? If they did buy, they still could not feed such a crowd. Jesus asked them: 'How many loaves have you?' He would use the little that they could offer and make it enough for the crowd to eat and to be 'satisfied'. He who could heal the sick, raise the dead, still the storm, could increase the five loaves and two fish to feed five thousand. They still had to learn of His power and to trust Him. The question of Psalm 78:19–20 was answered, 'Can God spread a table in the wilderness? Can he also give bread... for his people?'

c. Methods of Jesus

The disciples had much to learn from the way Jesus acted. Those who deal with needy crowds have to insist on order. Jesus sat them down on the green grass 'in groups, by hundreds and by fifties'. Then as Jesus took the bread and the fish 'he looked up to heaven', and, like the Jewish father of the family, blessed God for His good gift. He broke the loaves, divided the fish and the meal was shared with all. Finally, Jesus allowed no waste. 'They took up twelve baskets full of broken pieces and of the fish.'

The disciples had to learn of the compassion, the power and the methods of Jesus. Mark will come back to these lessons again (6:52, 8:1–10, 17–21). Later, the broken bread will speak of the body of Jesus broken that He might be for the world the Bread of life (14:22). This miracle leads us to the heart of the good news of Jesus.

Meditation *Jesus said, 'I am the bread of life; he who comes to me shall not hunger, and he who believes in me shall never thirst'* (John 6:35).

For further thought and study 1. What should we learn from the fact that so many of the words used in verse 41 are used also in 8:6, 14:22, Luke 24:30 and 1 Corinthians 11:23–24?

2. What further lessons does John chapter 6 teach about this miracle as a 'sign' showing who Jesus is and the purpose of His coming?

Notes 1. All four Gospels have the record of this miracle. See Matthew 14:13–21, Luke 9:10–17, John 6:1–14. In modern times there have been many attempts to explain this story without making it a miracle of increasing the loaves and fish by an act of God's creative power. Some have seen it as a fellowship meal or a sacramental meal, satisfying people by its meaning rather than meeting their bodily hunger. In all the Gospels, however, it is clearly presented as a miracle.

2. In verse 30 the disciples are called 'apostles' because 'apostle' means 'one sent' and they had been *sent* by Jesus.

Study 26: DIFFERENT RESPONSES TO THE MIGHTY WORKS OF JESUS

[45]Immediately he made his disciples get into the boat and go before him to the other side, to Bethsaida, while he dismissed the crowd. [46]And after he had taken leave of them, he went up on the mountain to pray. [47]And when evening came, the boat was out on the sea, and he was alone on the land. [48]And he saw that they were making headway painfully, for the wind was against them. And about the fourth watch of the night he came to them, walking on the sea. He meant to pass by them, [49]but when they saw him walking on the sea they thought it was a ghost, and cried out; [50]for they all saw him, and were terrified. But immediately he spoke to them and said, 'Take heart, it is I; have no fear.' [51]And he got into the boat with them and the wind ceased. And they were utterly astounded [52]for they did not understand about the loaves, but their hearts were hardened.

[53]And when they had crossed over, they came to land at Gennesaret, and moored to the shore. [54]And when they got out of the boat, immediately the people recognized him, [55]and ran about the whole neighbourhood and began to bring sick people on their pallets to any place where they heard he was. [56]And wherever he came, in villages, cities, or country, they laid the sick in the market places, and besought him that they might touch even the fringe of his garment; and as many as touched it were made well   (6:45–56).

These verses show us different ways in which people responded to the things that Jesus was doing and show how the love and power of God were working wonderfully through Him.

a. Dangerous response

When we read verse 45 carefully we realize that something strange and unusual was happening. Jesus 'made his disciples get into the boat and go before him to the other side' of the lake. It could even be translated, He 'compelled them to go'. Then He 'dismissed the crowd'. Why did He do this? John 6:15 helps us to understand. After He had fed the hungry crowd, the people 'were about to come and take him by force to make him king'. But He had not come to be that kind of leader. He had not come only to provide food for the body, or to be a political ruler and to free the people from the rule of Rome. He had come to lead people back to the ways of God and to know the kingdom and rule of God. So the response of the crowd was dangerous to the people themselves, as it would lead them in a wrong direction, and for the disciples, if they were caught up in a movement to make Jesus a king of that kind. Perhaps it was even dangerous for Jesus Himself and brought back the temptation that He had faced at the beginning (see 1:13 and Matthew 4:3–10). So for His own sake, for the sake of the disciples and for the sake of the crowd, He needed to be alone 'on the mountain to pray' (verse 46).

b. Surprised response

From the Lord alone on the mountain in prayer, our thoughts are turned to the disciples in the boat on the lake. They were rowing hard, but, as happens when tide or current or wind is against a rower, 'they were making headway painfully, for the wind was against them' (verse 48). They must have rowed for a long time, and become more and more distressed. Jesus saw them and 'about the fourth watch of the night' (that watch began about 3 o'clock in the morning) 'He came to them, walking on the sea'. They were 'terrified' when they saw Him, and at first they thought that they saw a ghost. His word brought them comfort, 'Take heart, it is I; have no fear.' In His presence there was peace. 'The wind ceased.' 'And they were utterly

astounded.' Mark shows us again the lesson of faith that
they should have learnt. He who could provide food for the
crowd would not fail them in any storm, in any dangerous
situation when (serving and obeying Him) they seemed
only to be 'making headway painfully'.

c. Response to people in need

Verses 53–56 tell what happened after they arrived at the
shore. They were in the area of Gennesaret, between
Capernaum and Tiberias, a fertile area where many people
lived (see map). 'The people recognized him and ran about
the whole neighbourhood' and brought all their sick and
needy friends to Jesus. Not only in Gennesaret but wherever He came, 'in villages, cities or country, they laid their
sick in the market places'. They knew His power to heal.
Like the woman of whom we read in 5:25–34, they believed
that if they could only touch 'the fringe of his garment' they
would be healed; 'and as many as touched it were made
well' (verse 56).

Here was faith, an attitude so different from the unbelief
that Jesus found in Nazareth (verses 1–6). Yet it is one
thing – then or now – to come to Jesus with our needs, our
prayers, our requests. It is another thing to come to Him as
disciples, to learn from Him, to obey Him and to serve
Him.

Prayer   *Lord God, You show Your power and love to all
who turn to You through Jesus Christ. Help us to trust You,
and increase our faith in You; then may we not only bring to
You our needs, but also bring our lives to serve You in
thankfulness and praise, now and always.* AMEN.

For further thought and study   1. We find the words 'take
heart' or 'be of good cheer' which we have in verse 50 are
used also in Matthew 9:2, 22; Mark 10:49, and John 16:33.
What were these other situations in which these words
brought comfort and hope?

2. What does it mean when it says in verse 52 that 'their hearts were hardened'? How may our hearts be hard to God's word and to faith in Him? See also 8:17–18, 10:5 and Hebrews 3:7–15.

Notes 1. This passage has parallels in Matthew 14:22–36 and also in John 6:15–21.

2. It is hard to understand what is meant when verse 48 says, 'He meant to pass by them'. Perhaps, as in Luke 24:28–29, the disciples had to show their desire to welcome Jesus.

3. The words 'it is I' in verse 50 could mean, 'I, Jesus, am here with you'; but the words 'I AM' are important in John's Gospel, as in the Old Testament (in Exodus 3:14, Isaiah 41:4 and 43:10), and express the name of God.

4. The disciples thought that they saw 'a ghost'. People have different views about ghosts and about spirits of the departed. There are many things that we do not know about life after death and about spiritual beings. Two things can be said clearly on the basis of the Bible's teaching: (a) Those who trust in the power of the living Lord Jesus need never fear what any ghost or spirit can do to them. By His death and resurrection Jesus has conquered all spiritual powers against Him; and, as Colossians 2:15 puts it, all these powers are under His rule. (b) There is no basis in the Bible for the idea of reincarnation, that is, of a spirit of a person who has died coming into another person. Hebrews 9:27 says, 'it is appointed for men to die once, and after that comes judgment.'

Study 27: THE CLEAN AND THE UNCLEAN

¹Now when the Pharisees gathered together to him, with some of the scribes, who had come from Jerusalem, ²they saw that some of his disciples ate with hands defiled, that is, unwashed. ³(For the Pharisees, and all the Jews, do not eat unless they wash their hands, observing the traditions of the elders; ⁴and when they come from the market place, they do not eat unless they purify themselves; and there are many

other traditions which they observe, the washing of cups and pots and vessels of bronze.) ⁵And the Pharisees and the scribes asked him, 'Why do your disciples not live according to the tradition of the elders, but eat with hands defiled?' ⁶And he said to them, 'Well did Isaiah prophesy of you hypocrites, as it is written,

> "This people honours me with their lips,
> but their heart is far from me;
> ⁷in vain do they worship me,
> teaching as doctrines the precepts of men."

⁸You leave the commandment of God, and hold fast the tradition of men.'

⁹And he said to them, 'You have a fine way of rejecting the commandment of God, in order to keep your tradition! ¹⁰For Moses said, "Honour your father and your mother"; and, "He who speaks evil of father or mother, let him surely die"; ¹¹but you say, "If a man tells his father or his mother, What you would have gained from me is Corban" (that is, given to God) – ¹²then you no longer permit him to do anything for his father or mother, ¹³thus making void the word of God through your tradition which you hand on. And many such things you do.'

¹⁴And he called the people to him again, and said to them, 'Hear me, all of you, and understand: ¹⁵there is nothing outside a man, which by going into him can defile him; but the things which come out of a man are what defile him.' ¹⁷And when he had entered the house, and left the people, his disciples asked him about the parable. ¹⁸And he said to them, 'Then are you also without understanding? Do you not see that whatever goes into a man from outside cannot defile him, ¹⁹since it enters, not his heart but his stomach, and so passes on?' (Thus he declared all foods clean.) ²⁰And he said, 'What comes out of a man is what defiles a man. ²¹For from within, out of the heart of man, come evil thoughts, fornication, theft, murder, adultery, ²²coveting,

wickedness, deceit, licentiousness, envy, slander, pride, foolishness. [23]**All these evil things come from within and they defile a man** (7:1–23).

We have seen in the earlier parts of the Gospel (2:1—3:6) the reasons why the Jewish religious leaders were against Jesus. We read in 3:22 what 'scribes who came down from Jerusalem' said about Him. Here now (verse 1) there were Pharisees and scribes who came down from Jerusalem and criticized Jesus.

a. Tradition of the elders about cleanness

If we want to keep healthy, we will wash our bodies well, and especially wash our hands before we eat. But the reason why the Pharisees emphasized washing was not for health. They said to Jesus, 'Why do your disciples not live according to the tradition of the elders, but eat with hands defiled?' (verse 5). Because most of Mark's readers were not Jews, he explained in verses 3 and 4 these traditions of the Jewish elders. People were thought to be religiously unclean unless they washed in exactly the way that the elders said they should wash. Contact with non-Jewish people in the market would make them 'unclean'. Therefore they must be careful to wash. The Pharisees were not thinking of the health of the disciples when they criticized them; they were saying that they were not good, religious Jews.

Jesus was troubled by their criticisms for two reasons. They were making their rules and traditions more important than the love of God; and they thought outward cleanness more important than purity of heart.

b. Human rules and traditions or the law of God

When Jesus answered the scribes and Pharisees He quoted from the Old Testament, from Isaiah 29:13. That verse spoke of the people saying with their lips that they served God, when their hearts were far from Him. It also spoke of the people teaching human traditions rather than God's word.

The scribes had made so many rules in addition to the Law that sometimes they lost the great purpose and principles of the Law itself. Jesus gave one example. The fifth commandment said, 'Honour your father and your mother' (Exodus 20:12 and Deuteronomy 5:16). It even said that a person who failed to do so deserved to die (Exodus 21:17). But by the Jewish tradition a person might avoid giving what he should to his parents. He might say, 'This money of mine is "Corban", that is, it is an offering given to God.' Perhaps he would only actually give a small part of it to God, but by what he had said, as a vow or promise, he was freed from his duty to his parents. So Jesus said, in this and in 'many such things', 'you leave the commandment of God' and reject it 'in order to keep your tradition' (verses 8–9).

c. Unclean food or unclean hearts

The Pharisees emphasized washing for the sake of religious cleanness. The Old Testament law said also that certain kinds of meat should be treated as unclean and not eaten (Leviticus 11 and Deuteronomy 14). Jesus showed that in the deepest way 'there is nothing outside a man, which by going into him can defile him' (verse 15). It cannot affect his 'heart', that is, what he truly is before God (verse 19). What comes out from a person's life is what makes him or her unclean – 'evil thoughts' and then all the wrong words and actions to which such evil thoughts lead (verses 21–22). 'All these evil things come from within,' Jesus said, 'and they defile a man.'

When we read a section of the Gospel it is good to think of it in three ways:

1. what it meant in the work of Jesus' own ministry;
2. how it applied to the people for whom the Gospel was written;
3. the part that it played in the Gospel that Mark wrote.

We have seen that Jesus in answering the scribes and Pharisees showed clearly that the word of God must be obeyed before the traditions and teachings of men, and that cleanness of heart matters more than what happens to the body. The teaching that 'unclean' meats could not make a person unclean in heart meant that in principle 'he declared all foods clean' (verse 19). This was the lesson that Peter had to learn with great difficulty when God sent him to the home of the Gentile Cornelius to preach the gospel (Acts 10). This was the principle that broke down the barrier between Jews and Gentiles so that they could be one in Christ and have fellowship together and eat together. We can understand why it is that after Mark has given us this teaching of Jesus, he goes on at once to tell us what Jesus did for a Gentile, the Greek Syro-Phoenician woman who came to ask for help for her daughter (verses 24–30).

Prayer *'Create in me a clean heart, O God, and put a new and right spirit within me'* (Psalm 51:10). Read also Psalm 24:3–6.

For further thought and study 1. In what ways is it possible for us to put human traditions, from our own culture, or even Christian customs and rules, above the clear principles of the word of God?

2. In what ways can we be guilty of the wrong things mentioned in verses 21–22, especially when we remember the teaching of Jesus in Matthew 5:21–48 about sins in our thoughts and desires?

Notes 1. Matthew (15:1–20) is the only gospel that has a parallel to this section; but note the similar teaching in Luke 11:37–41.

2. Mark often tells us how Jesus gave His teaching to all who came to hear Him, and then in a 'house' alone with His disciples He explained things more (with verse 17 see 9:28, 33 and 10:10).

Study 28: OUTREACH OF CHRIST'S COMPASSION

[24]And from there he arose and went away to the region of Tyre and Sidon. And he entered a house, and would not have any one know it; yet he could not be hid. [25]But immediately a woman, whose little daughter was possessed by an unclean spirit, heard of him, and came and fell down at his feet. [26]Now the woman was a Greek, a Syrophoenician by birth. And she begged him to cast the demon out of her daughter. [27]And he said to her, 'Let the children first be fed, for it is not right to take the children's bread and throw it to the dogs.' [28]But she answered him, 'Yes, Lord; yet even the dogs under the table eat the children's crumbs.' [29]And he said to her, 'For this saying you may go your way; the demon has left your daughter.' [30]And she went home, and found the child lying in bed, and the demon gone.

[31]Then he returned from the region of Tyre, and went through Sidon to the Sea of Galilee, through the region of the Decapolis. [32]And they brought to him a man who was deaf and had an impediment in his speech; and they besought him to lay his hand upon him. [33]And taking him aside from the multitude privately, he put his fingers into his ears, and he spat and touched his tongue; [34]and looking up to heaven, he sighed, and said to him 'Ephphata,' that is, 'Be opened.' [35]And his ears were opened, his tongue was released, and he spoke plainly. [36]And he charged them to tell no one; but the more he charged them, the more zealously they proclaimed it. [37]And they were astonished beyond measure, saying, 'He has done all things well; he even makes the deaf to hear and the dumb speak   (7:24–37).

We have here two incidents in which we see the compassion of Christ reaching out to those in need, first to a Gentile (non-Jewish) woman, and then to a deaf man.

a. Gentile woman's prayer

We have seen that the teaching of Jesus about the clean and the unclean broke down in principle the barrier be-

tween Jews and Gentiles. Because of the laws about unclean
meat, Jews and Gentiles could not eat together, and for a
long time even Jews who became Christians were not willing
to eat with Gentiles. Immediately after that teaching of
Jesus which 'declared all foods clean' (verse 19), Mark tells
us of Jesus travelling to the Gentile area of Tyre and Sidon
(verse 24). He did not go there for public ministry to the
crowds. Perhaps He went there because He wanted to be
alone with His disciples. 'He entered a house, and would
not have any one know it'; but reports of what He had done
had reached this area (see Luke 6:17) and so 'he could not
be hid'. In particular a woman from those parts (Greek by
her culture, and from this Syrian Phoenician area) came to
Him in great need and 'begged him to cast the demon out of
her daughter' (verse 26). Although Jesus loved and cared
for all people, Matthew (15:24) says He told this woman, 'I
was sent only to the lost sheep of the house of Israel'. He
said, 'Let the children first be fed, for it is not right to take
the children's bread and throw it to the dogs.' Hard words?
They seem so. Probably Jesus meant that His ministry was
first to the Jews (as the children of the house) but Gentiles
also would have a place. Jews often spoke of Gentiles as
'dogs'. Jesus (perhaps as a joke) used the word that meant
'puppies'. The woman seems to have been encouraged,
rather than discouraged, by the way that Jesus spoke. So
she could answer, 'Yes, Lord; yet even the dogs under the
table eat the children's crumbs.' Jesus praised the faith that
she showed and gladly answered her prayer. He sent her
home to find that the demon had gone from her daughter.

b. Deaf man's need

Verse 31 tells of more travelling in Gentile territory –
north to Sidon, south-east to Galilee, further east to the
area of Decapolis. There 'they brought to him a man who
was deaf and had an impediment in his speech, and they
besought him to lay his hand upon him' (verse 32). Notice
the kindness and thoughtfulness with which Jesus acted. It

is hard to deal with a deaf person in a crowd. So Jesus took him aside privately. Then, since he could not hear Jesus' words, He showed by His actions what He wished to do. 'He put his fingers into his ears.' 'He spat', because spittle was sometimes used in ancient healings. He touched the man's tongue. He looked up to heaven and, by sighing, showed His concern and His prayer. Then He spoke – one word of authority, remembered by people in the language in which it was spoken – 'Ephphatha', that is, 'Be opened'. Then 'his ears were opened, his tongue was released, and he spoke plainly' (verse 35).

As at other times (see 1:44–45 and 5:43) Jesus told people not to talk about the miracle, but they could not keep quiet. They said, 'He has done all things well.' They echoed the Old Testament words from Genesis 1:31. There those words spoke of what God did in creation at the beginning. Now Jesus is making human lives new. 'He even makes the deaf hear and the dumb speak.' The great prophecies of the Old Testament were also coming true, 'Then the eyes of the blind shall be opened, and the ears of the deaf unstopped: . . . and the tongue of the dumb sing for joy' (Isaiah 35:5–6).

Prayer *Lord Jesus, continue Your work in us, we pray; drive out all evil from our lives, and may our ears hear Your words and our tongues praise You, today and always.* AMEN.

For further thought and study 1. How do the Gospel and the life of the early Church show the truth of what Paul says in Romans 1:16 about the good news coming 'to the Jew first and also to the Greek'?

2. What do verses 32–35 teach us about the ways in which we should help those who have special needs and handicaps in life?

Note Matthew 15:21–28 is parallel to verses 24–30; the other Gospels do not have the miracle recorded in verses 31–37 (but see Matthew 15:29–31).

Study 29: CROWD, DISCIPLES AND PHARISEES

[1]In those days, when again a great crowd had gathered, and they had nothing to eat, he called his disciples to him and said to them, [2]'I have compassion on the crowd, because they have been with me now three days, and have nothing to eat; [3]and if I send them away hungry to their homes, they will faint on the way; and some of them have come a long way.' [4]And his disciples answered him, 'How can one feed these men with bread here in the desert?' [5]And he asked them, 'How many loaves have you?' They said, 'Seven'. [6]And he commanded the crowd to sit down on the ground; and he took the seven loaves, and having given thanks he broke them and gave them to his disciples to set before the people; and they set them before the crowd. [7]And they had a few small fish; and having blessed them, he commanded that these also should be set before them. [8]And they ate, and were satisfied; and they took up the broken pieces left over, seven baskets full. [9]And there were about four thousand people. [10]And he sent them away; and immediately he got into the boat with his disciples, and went to the district of Dalmanutha.

[11]The Pharisees came and began to argue with him, seeking from him a sign from heaven, to test him. [12]And he sighed deeply in his spirit, and said, 'Why does this generation seek a sign? Truly, I say to you, no sign shall be given to this generation.' [13]And he left them, and getting into the boat again he departed to the other side   (8:1–13).

In this Gospel, we have often read of three groups of people – the crowds, the disciples, the scribes and Pharisees – and how they each related to Jesus. In these verses we see all three and we will study the ways they responded to Jesus and to what He was doing.

a. Hungry crowd

Nearly forty times in this Gospel we are told of the 'crowds' that came to Jesus – great numbers of people coming to Him constantly with all their needs. Often they came for healing or brought their friends to be healed. They came to know of His love and His power, and so they came for what He could do for them. They were also attracted by His teaching, so different from that of the scribes. Jesus saw them as 'sheep without a shepherd' (Matthew 9:36), needing to be guided in the ways of God and needing to be fed with food for their souls. But He also cared for their bodily needs. On this occasion the crowds had stayed with Him for three days (verse 2), because they so greatly wanted to learn from Him. He had compassion on them, and, as He had done before, He took the loaves that were brought to Him, 'and having given thanks he broke them and gave them to his disciples to set before the people' and so also the fish. 'And they ate and were satisfied', and the broken pieces were taken up so that there was no waste.

b. Disciples, and lessons they had to learn

The disciples always appear in the Gospels as a group different from the crowds. They had not come for what they could get from Jesus. They had, in some way at least, accepted His call to stay with Him and to share His work. They had to learn again (see 6:34–37) to share the Lord's love and compassion. Verse 1 says He 'called his disciples to him, and said to them, "I have compassion on the crowd".' They replied, 'Where in this desert can anyone find enough food to feed all these people?' (verse 4, Good News Bible). They had to learn again the lesson of trust in their mighty Lord. 'How many loaves have you?' He asked them. Again, He wanted to take what they could provide and use it to meet the needs of the crowd.

c. Pharisees, unwilling to believe

From chapter 2 of the Gospel, we have read how the Pharisees came to Jesus to criticize Him for what He said and did. Their minds were closed to the truth that He spoke. Their hearts were closed to His love. They would not think of His miracles as signs of God's power and of God's kingdom. This time they came 'to argue with him' and asked for 'a sign from heaven'. A later book of the teaching of the rabbis said that when the Messiah came, he would stand on the temple, and those who doubted would see a light from heaven shining brightly on him. At the beginning of His ministry Jesus was tempted by Satan to give people this kind of sign (see Matthew 4:5–7). In fact, however, He was giving them all the time the true signs of God's love and power working in Him. So He felt a great sadness at their unwillingness to believe. He 'sighed deeply in his spirit' and said that no such sign would be given.

Jesus 'left' the Pharisees because they were unwilling to learn from anything that He said and did. (See verse 13 and Luke 4:30 and Matthew 21:15–17 for other times when Jesus is said to have 'left' people who had been with them.) Verse 10 said about the crowd that 'he sent them away', and perhaps He needed to do this, as in 6:45 (see Study 26), lest they should follow Him for the wrong reasons as a leader who would always provide their bodily needs. He sent the crowds away. He left the Pharisees. Only the disciples remained with Him. We will see in the next two studies that the time ahead was to be a special time of their learning from Him and of growing in their trust in Him.

Prayer *Lord, give to us today, we pray, more of Your love and compassion, and show us ways to feed the hungry, care for those in need and share with those around us the good news of Your Kingdom.* AMEN.

For further thought and study 1. Compare other passages in the Gospels that speak of people asking Jesus for a 'sign' and notice the answers that He gives. See Matthew 12:38–42, 16:1–4, Luke 11:16, 29–32, 12:54–56, John 6:30 and refer also to the words of the apostle Paul in 1 Corinthians 1:22–24. In what ways do people today ask for that kind of sign to make them believe?

2. What do other New Testament passages teach about the Christian duty to feed the hungry? See Matthew 25:31–46, Acts 2:44–47, 6:1–6, 11:27–30, James 2:14–17 and 1 John 3:17–18. How should we link together our caring for people's bodily needs and our caring for their spiritual needs?

Notes 1. Matthew (15:32–39) is the only other Gospel that gives the account of the feeding of the 4,000 as well as the feeding of the 5,000. Some people have suggested that the two stories may be different accounts of the same incident. We do see similar details when we read the two accounts side by side, but there are definite differences in the numbers of the crowds, of the loaves, of the fish, of the baskets of broken pieces taken up, and in other ways. Verses 19–20 in this chapter show that Mark understood the two as different incidents. Other people have suggested that in the first case Jesus provided for the needs of a Jewish crowd, and in this case for a Gentile crowd, but the Gospel does not say this.

2. It is not known where Dalmanutha is (verse 10), or whether this was the name originally given. Some of the very old copies of the Gospel have Magadan or Magdala, which were on the western side of Lake Galilee.

Study 30: DO YOU NOT UNDERSTAND?

[14]Now they had forgotten to bring bread; and they had only one loaf with them in the boat. [15]And he cautioned them, saying, 'Take heed, beware of the leaven of the Pharisees and the leaven of Herod.' [16]And they discussed it with one another, saying 'We have no bread.' [17]And being aware of it, Jesus said to them, 'Why do you discuss the fact that you have no bread? Do you not perceive or understand? Are your hearts hardened? [18]Having eyes do you not see, and having ears do you not hear? And do you not remember?

[19]When I broke the five loaves for the five thousand, how many baskets full of broken pieces did you take up?' They said to him, 'Twelve.' [20]And the seven for the four thousand, how many baskets full of broken pieces did you take up?' And they said to him, 'Seven.' [21]And he said to them, 'Do you not yet understand?'   (8:14–21).

Jesus, having met the needs of the crowds has 'sent them away' (verse 10). He has 'left' the Pharisees who have refused to believe unless they are given the kind of 'sign' that they want (verse 11). He is now alone with the disciples, wanting to help them to believe and to trust Him more fully.

a. Jesus' teaching

In His teaching at this time, He has one special warning for them. 'Beware of the leaven of the Pharisees and the leaven of Herod' (verse 15). In making bread a little leaven or yeast is mixed with a lot of flour, and before long its effect is seen on the whole lot. In one of Jesus' parables (in Matthew 13:33), He used this work of leaven to picture the spreading influence of the kingdom of God in human lives. Often leaven was used as a picture of the spread of the influence of evil (see 1 Corinthians 5:6–8 and Galatians 5:9). That is the case here. Luke 12:1 speaks of 'the leaven of the Pharisees' as 'hypocrisy'. They wanted to appear to others as much better than they were. In some ways the Pharisees, the religious leaders, and Herod, the political leader, were very different. But they were alike in the way that they wanted power for themselves and influence over the lives of men and women. 'They loved the praise of men more than the praise of God' (John 12:43). Jesus did not want this kind of attitude to have influence with His disciples.

b. The disciples' misunderstanding

When some special concern or worry fills our minds, we can hardly think of anything else, and we easily misunderstand what others are saying. It was like this with the disciples at this time. Jesus was talking about 'the leaven of the Pharisees and the leaven of Herod' meaning their evil influence. The disciples thought of leaven and so of bread, and of the fact that they had only one loaf of bread (verse 14), and perhaps they were arguing and blaming one another for not bringing the bread that they needed. So Jesus, instead of going on with what He was wanting to teach them, took up the worry that they had.

c. The disciples' slowness to believe

Their worry showed their lack of trust in Him and their lack of the kind of faith to which He was trying to lead them. Could they not see with their eyes and realise the Lord's love and power? They were like the blind man of whom we are to read in verses 22–26 who needed his eyes to be opened. Could they not hear with their ears and understand what the Lord had been teaching? They were like the deaf man of whom we have read in 7:31–37 who needed his ears to be opened. Could they not remember – what He did for the 5,000 and for the 4,000, and how He met their needs so abundantly that there were baskets of broken pieces left over? Were their hearts so hard that they could not let the realization of what Jesus had done lead them to trust Him (compare verse 17 with 6:52)? Jesus did not want the disciples to trust Him only to provide the food they needed, but He longed for them to trust Him as the One who had come to meet all the deepest needs of human lives and to be the Saviour and Lord of all.

Meditation   *The Bible often calls us to* remember *what God has done for us, to* see *His work, to* hear *His word, to* understand *– and so not to be hard of heart, but to* trust, love *and* serve *our mighty Lord.*

For further thought and study Verse 18 echoes words from the Old Testament, like those of Isaiah 6:9–10 (used already in Mark 4:12), Jeremiah 5:21, Ezekiel 12:2 and Deuteronomy 29:2–4. In what ways were the people of Israel blind to God's work and deaf to His word? How may this be the case with Christian people today? In what ways is the prayer for spiritual sight in Ephesians 1:15–23 an important one for us to pray?

Note Matthew 16:5–12 is parallel to this passage; Luke 12:1 has a similar warning to that of verse 15 here, but Luke does not record the whole incident.

Study 31: THE EYES OF THE BLIND OPENED

²²And they came to Beth-saida. And some people brought to him a blind man, and begged him to touch him. ²³And he took the blind man by the hand, and led him out of the village; and when he had spit on his eyes and laid his hands upon him, he asked him, 'Do you see anything?' ²⁴And he looked up and said, 'I see men; but they look like trees, walking.' ²⁵Then again he laid his hands upon his eyes; and he looked intently and was restored, and saw everything clearly. ²⁶And he sent him away to his home, saying, 'Do not even enter the village.'

²⁷And Jesus went on with his disciples, to the villages of Caesarea Philippi; and on the way he asked his disciples, 'Who do men say that I am?' ²⁸And they told him, 'John the Baptist; and others say, Elijah; and others one of the prophets.' ²⁹And he asked them, 'But who do you say that I am?' Peter answered him, 'You are the Christ.' ³⁰And he charged them to tell no one about him (8:22–30).

In these verses we read of two things that happened, the first one to a blind man, the second to Jesus' disciples. They seem very different, but in fact they are similar when we study them.

a. Sight for a blind man

First we read of this blind man whose friends brought him to Jesus and 'begged' Jesus 'to touch him'. Jesus treated him as He treated the deaf man of whom we read in 7:31–37. He took him by the hand and led him away from the crowd to a quiet place outside the village. Then Jesus did three things to help the man to understand what He wished to do and to help him to have faith. He put spittle on his eyes (since in those days people linked spittle with healing). He laid His hands on him. He spoke to him and asked, 'Do you see anything?' Then, as may happen today, when a doctor operates on a person's eyes blinded by cataracts, the man gained his sight in two stages. At first he looked up and saw men, but 'they looked like trees walking'. Jesus again laid His hands on the man's eyes and he was able to focus and to see everything clearly. How greatly the man would have rejoiced! But Jesus, as He has often done before, told him not to go and shout about the miracle in the village (see 1:44, 3:12, 5:43).

b. Peter sees and believes

Jesus took the deaf man away from the crowd (7:32–33), helped him to believe in Him and then opened his ears so that he could hear. Now He has taken the blind man away from the crowd (verse 25), helped him to believe in Him and opened his eyes so that he can see. The disciples, Jesus said, were like people who had eyes and yet could not see; they had ears and yet could not hear (verse 18). They needed Jesus to help them to see and hear and understand. So He took them away from the crowds 'to the villages of Caesarea Philippi', a quieter part north of Lake Galilee. As He talked with them, He began by asking them what other people were saying about Him. They gave answers like those which we have read in 6:14–15. Some thought He was

John the Baptist come to life again. Others thought He was Elijah for whose return the people hoped. Then when Jesus asked the disciples, 'But who do you say that I am?', Peter was able to answer, 'You are the Christ'.

c. A turning-point in the Gospel

As Mark wrote his Gospel and told the story of the work and ministry of Jesus, he clearly wanted to show how important was this statement by Peter. In the first verse of the Gospel Mark has said that he is telling the story of how the good news began – the good news of Jesus Christ, Son of God. Mark has told of Jesus' teaching and preaching of the kingdom of God, of His miracles as showing God's kingdom at work amongst men and women. He has called disciples to follow Him, to see His work and learn from His teaching. He has been disappointed at their slowness to understand and believe in Him. Now there is faith, surer and clearer than ever before. Peter still had many things to learn and to understand, but he could now say to Jesus from his heart, 'You are the Christ.'

d. Believing in Jesus as the Christ

Why was it so important that the disciples should believe in Jesus as the Christ? Certainly the whole New Testament sees it as important, as it uses the word 'Christ' more than 350 times, nearly always as a name or title of Jesus. We considered in our first Study what it meant to call Jesus 'Christ' and 'Son of God'. Christ, Messiah – both words meant 'anointed'. Priests, kings and prophets were anointed in Old Testament days, because they were people set apart for the special service of God. Jesus came and did the work of all three – prophet, priest and king. More important still, as we saw in Study 1, the Old Testament prophets gave to the Hebrew people the hope of one who, beyond all others, would be the Anointed One, sent by God to be their Saviour, who would rule in justice and in peace. Jesus was this Christ of whom the Old Testament prophets spoke.

We are left with one important question from these verses. If it was so important when Peter confessed Jesus as 'the Christ', why (in verse 30) did He tell His disciples 'to tell no one about him'? The reason was that most of the people were looking for a very different kind of Christ. Jesus goes on, as we will see in our next Study, to tell the disciples that He is the kind of Christ who must suffer and die.

Prayer *Lord God, we ask You to open the eyes of our understanding, that we may see You more clearly, believe in You more deeply, and serve You more truly, through Jesus Christ our Saviour.* AMEN.

For further thought and study 1. How many similar points can you find between Jesus' two miracles in 7:31–37 and 8:22–26? Are these points similar to those in 8:27–30 also?

2. What can you learn from the places in this Gospel where Jesus is spoken of as Christ (1:1, 8:29, 14:61 and 15:32), and also from the fact that He is not called Christ more often in the chapters of the Gospel?

Note There is no record of the miracle of verses 22–26 in the other Gospels, but with verses 27–30 we can compare Matthew 16:13–20, Luke 9:18–21 and perhaps also John 6:66–69.

As we move into this next part of the Gospel, the scene changes and the emphasis is different from before. Up to this time Jesus has been much with the crowds in Galilee – and there have been many miracles, and much teaching of the people in their synagogues, in their homes, and in the open air. There has been some teaching of the disciples by themselves, but now this becomes of great importance. There are fewer miracles. There is increasing opposition from the Jewish leaders. The faith of the disciples has been encouraged to the point where Peter has confessed Jesus as the Christ. Now He tells them how He must suffer, but He speaks also of future glory. The way for the disciples also is one of glory but only through suffering and humble service. Like a drum beat through this part of the Gospel are the predictions of His suffering and death (8:31, 9:31, 10:32–34) and the emphasis on what discipleship means.

This section may be divided as follows:

8:31–33	Necessity of Christ's sufferings (first passion prediction)
8:34–38	Cross of discipleship
9:1–8	Transfiguration
9:9–13	Elijah and the Son of man

Study 32: THE WAY OF THE CROSS

[31]And he began to teach them that the Son of man must suffer many things, and be rejected by the elders and the chief priests and the scribes, and be killed, and after three days rise again. [32]And he said this plainly. And Peter took him, and began to rebuke him. [33]But turning and seeing his disciples, he rebuked Peter, and said, 'Get behind me, Satan! For you are not on the side of God, but of men.'

[34]And he called to him the multitude with his disciples, and said to them, 'If any man would come after me, let him deny himself and take up his cross and follow me. [35]For

whoever would save his life will lose it; and whoever loses his life for my sake and the gospel's will save it. [36]For what does it profit a man, to gain the whole world and forfeit his life? [37]For what can a man give in return for his life? [38]For whoever is ashamed of me and of my words in this adulterous and sinful generation, of him will the Son of man also be ashamed, when he comes in the glory of his Father with the holy angels   (8:31–38).

Peter had confessed Jesus as 'the Christ' (verse 29). Straight after this we read that Jesus 'began to teach them' that 'the Son of man must suffer' (verse 31), and that the disciple must 'deny himself and take up his cross and follow' (verse 34). There is a cross for Jesus and a cross for the disciple.

a. The cross for Jesus

We have noticed in our last Study that although Peter had rightly confessed Jesus as 'the Christ', Jesus spoke of Himself as 'the Son of man'. (See also Note 2 on Study 8.) A suffering Christ, a suffering Messiah, was something most Jews found hard to understand. But His sufferings 'must be', because of the purpose of the Father and the work that Jesus had been sent into the world to do. He had come to be Saviour, to bring men and women God's forgiveness, to conquer sin and evil by His death, to conquer death itself and 'after three days rise again' (verse 31).

'He said this plainly', but it was hard for disciples to accept. Peter, who had just made his great confession of faith, took Jesus aside (as verse 32 literally says). He felt that he should 'rebuke' his Master for thinking and speaking like this. 'God forbid, Lord! This shall never happen to you,' were his words, as Matthew (16:22) puts them. Yet for Peter's sake, and knowing how the other disciples could easily be led astray in a similar way, Jesus 'rebuked Peter'. He was 'not on the side of God'. He was not thinking of God's way, God's will, God's purposes, but was thinking in the very human way that would always choose to avoid suffering. Peter was even as 'Satan' to Jesus, bringing back to Him the temptation to avoid the way of the cross that He had faced when His public ministry began (see Study 3).

b. The cross for the disciple

Jesus taught that there are three things involved in being His disciple, or follower.

1. We must deny self. Jesus does not tell us to deny ourselves things that we can do without, but to deny *self*. This means to say 'No' to selfish desires and to self-will, that we may say 'Yes' to God's will, and to work for His kingdom. This is what we pray every time we say the Lord's Prayer.

2. The disciple must take up the cross. This is the first time that the word 'cross' is used in the Gospel. For us the cross is so common a sign of the Christian faith that we find it hard to realize what it must have meant for the first disciples. At that time, death by crucifixion was the death of a criminal, a revolutionary, a runaway slave, the most painful and shameful death that people knew. The condemned person had to carry the cross to the place of execution. Now Jesus said the disciple must 'take up his cross'. This meant not only death to self-centred living, but being willing for Christ's sake to suffer shame and pain at the hands of the world.

3. The disciple is called to 'follow' Jesus. He calls us to go no other way but that which He first has gone Himself – but He does call us to go that way and not to try to avoid it.

In the words of Matthew 7:13–14 this way is a 'narrow' and a 'hard' way. There is a 'wide' and 'easy' way, the natural human way, which we follow when we try to gain 'the whole world' or as many of its joys and possessions as we can (verse 36). To choose that way will often make us ashamed of confessing Christ. We will want to realize our own ambitions, and use life for ourselves rather than give it to serve Christ and others. But the end of that way is to lose the life that is true life; and when we stand before our Lord on the Judgment Day to give account of ourselves, we will find that He is not able to own us as His own (verse 38).

These verses make it very clear that there is a cross for Jesus and a cross for the disciple. They also show that beyond the cross for Jesus was the resurrection, and the cross is the way of life and glory for the disciple.

Prayer — *Lord Jesus, for the joy that was set before You, You 'thought nothing of the disgrace of dying on the cross'. Help us to follow in the way that You lead us, and so share with You Your life, Your work, and Your kingdom, now and for ever.* AMEN.

For further thought and study 1. What does it mean in verse 35 and similarly in 10:29, to speak of disciples doing things not only for Jesus' sake but also for the sake of the gospel?

2. What does Jesus mean when He speaks of 'the world' in verse 36 and 'this adulterous and sinful generation' in verse 38? See John 12:31, 2 Corinthians 4:4, James 4:4 and 1 John 2:15–17.

3. Verses 34–38 set out conditions of discipleship; how would you put these in terms of life today and what it means in your own situation to be a faithful disciple of Christ?

Notes 1. We have parallels to these verses in Matthew 16:21–27 and Luke 9:22–26.

2. In verse 31 and in several passages later in the Gospel it speaks of 'chief priests'. The Jews only accepted one high priest, who held the position till the end of his life. The Roman authorities on a number of times took the office away from one high priest and put in another. In this way there was more than one chief priest among the people.

Study 33: JESUS IN HIS TRUE GLORY

[1]And he said to them, 'Truly, I say to you, there are some standing here who will not taste death before they see that the kingdom of God has come with power.'

[2]And after six days Jesus took with him Peter and James and John, and led them up a high mountain apart by themselves; and he was transfigured before them, [3]and his garments became glistening, intensely white, as no fuller on earth could bleach them. [4]And there appeared to them Elijah with Moses; and they were talking to Jesus. [5]And Peter said to Jesus, 'Master, it is well that we are here; let us make three booths, one for you and one for Moses and one for Elijah.' [6]For he did not know what to say, for they were exceedingly afraid. [7]And a cloud overshadowed them, and a voice came out of the cloud, 'This is my beloved Son, listen to him.' [8]And suddenly looking around they no longer saw any one with them but Jesus only   (9:1–8).

At the end of chapter 8 we have read how Jesus taught the disciples that He must suffer and die, and that if they followed Him, they must 'take up the cross'. Yet He also made clear that the end for Him and for faithful disciples was not death but life, victory and glory. So now in the first verse of this chapter, following on from this teaching and leading to the great event that we call the 'transfiguration', we have Jesus' promise that some of those standing with Him would 'not taste death before they saw the kingdom of God come with power. When does the kingdom of God come with power? In one way, when Jesus rose from the dead on the first Easter Day. In another way, on the day of Pentecost when the Holy Spirit came in power to the disciples. In the greatest way, the kingdom of God will come in power when Jesus comes again in His glory. Yet in what they were now going to see, three of the disciples were to have a glimpse of this glory before time. So Mark goes on from the words of verse 1 to tell what happened 'after six days'.

a. What Peter, James and John saw

The first verse of this Gospel spoke of Jesus as 'Son of God'. Yet He became one of us, truly human, and in His life on earth, it was as if His glory was veiled – otherwise we would have been dazzled and blinded by His splendour. Above all, that glory would be veiled or hidden as He allowed Himself to die, rejected and put to death by those He came to save. Before that happened, the inner group of three disciples were allowed to see, for a few moments, His real glory. 'He was transfigured' – that is, His normal human form was changed. His glory was shown as intense brightness; it shone, as it were, through his clothes which became far whiter than any washing could make them. (Some translations use the old word 'fuller' for one who washes clothes.) All that the disciples could say in later years about this was, 'With our own eyes we saw his greatness! We were there when he was given honour and glory by God the Father.' (See 2 Peter 1:16–18.)

b. What the transfiguration meant

What we see or hear we can only understand in the light of what we have known and experienced before. The Old Testament helped the disciples to understand what the transfiguration meant. In the vision which they saw on the mountain, Moses and Elijah were 'talking to Jesus'. Moses, the Lawgiver of Israel, had seen God's glory on Mount Sinai, and something of the brightness of that glory was reflected on him (see Exodus 24:12–18, 33:17–23 and 34:29–35). Elijah knew what it was to stand in the presence of the living God (1 Kings 17:1). He knew God's greatness, heard His word and faithfully preached it to others. Moses' and Elijah's desires for their people were being realized in what Jesus was doing and what He would do by His death and resurrection.

A cloud 'overshadowed them, and a voice came out of the cloud.' In Old Testament days God had shown His presence in a 'pillar of cloud', and spoken out of the cloud (see Exodus 13:21–22, 33:9–11, 34:5–7, 40:34–35 and 1 Kings 8:10–11). In the vision of Daniel 7:13–14 'with the clouds of heaven there came one like a Son of man, and he came to the Ancient of days…and to him was given dominion and glory and kingdom'. These Old Testament passages would have helped the three disciples to understand what they saw. Peter and James and John had a tremendous sense of wonder and 'were exceedingly afraid', realizing more than ever before the presence of God in the person of Jesus their Master.

c. Jesus only

We are not surprised that as Jesus 'was transfigured before them', those disciples did not know what to say or do. Peter, being the person that he was, had to say something. He said first, 'it is well that we are here', and without doubt they would have loved to stay there for ever. That was not to be. They would soon have to go down the mountain to a needy world (as verses 14–29 show). Then Peter said, 'Let us make three booths' ('tents' in the Good News Bible) 'one for you and one for Moses and one for Elijah'. The Festival of Booths (or Tabernacles) was a great annual festival in Israel and the prophecy of Zechariah 14:16–21 gave the people the hope that in the final coming of God's kingdom there would be a glorious celebration of that festival. Perhaps Peter thought and hoped that the day had come.

Then they saw Moses and Elijah no longer – only Jesus with them; but they heard a voice from heaven, as at His baptism (1:11). The One whom they had followed, though He would soon be rejected by the Jewish leaders and put to death, was truly God's Son. The greatest thing that they could do was to 'listen to him' – listen to His teaching, try to understand, keep following, and keep on obeying and serving Him.

Prayer   *Lord Jesus, You showed Yourself to Your disciples*

*in the humility of Your life, in the glory of Your transfigura-
tion, in the sacrifice of Your death and in the victory of Your
resurrection; help us to listen to Your word to us and give us
strength to obey.* AMEN.

For further thought and study   1. What is said about the
transfiguration of Jesus in 2 Peter 1:16–18? What is said in
the verses that follow in 2 Peter concerning those of us who
have never had such a vision of His glory?

2. The word that is used for the transfiguration of Jesus
is used also in the New Testament for what should happen
to the Christian in Romans 12:2 and 2 Corinthians 3:18.
What do these verses teach us?

Notes   1. We have similar accounts of the transfiguration of Jesus
in Matthew 17:1–8 and Luke 9:28–36. The small differences from
Mark should be noticed. John does not tell of the transfiguration
but he says a great deal of the 'glory' of Christ.

2. There may be an intended link between the 'six days' of verse
2 and the 'six days' of Moses' preparation for seeing the glory of
God of which we read in Exodus 24:15–17; also between the words
'listen to him' in verse 7 and what we read about the prophet like
Moses in Deuteronomy 18:15–19.

Study 34: THE PROMISED ELIJAH

⁹**And as they were coming down the mountain, he charged
them to tell no one what they had seen until the Son of man
should have risen from the dead. ¹⁰So they kept the matter to
themselves, questioning what the rising from the dead
meant. ¹¹And they asked him, 'Why do the scribes say that
first Elijah must come?' ¹²And he said to them, 'Elijah does
come first to restore all things; and how is it written of the
Son of man, that he should suffer many things and be
treated with contempt? ¹³But I tell you that Elijah has come,**

and they did to him whatever they pleased as it is written of him (9:9–13).

The three disciples, Peter, James and John had had the wonderful experience of seeing Jesus in His true glory, 'transfigured' before their eyes on the mountain. There were still things, however, which they found hard to understand. Notice their three questions here.

a. 'What does this rising from death mean?'

This is the way that the Good News Bible translates the question of verse 10. Jesus had told the three who had been with Him on the mountain not to tell others for the present what they had seen. For those who did not believe it would be meaningless and only lead to misunderstanding and criticism. Jesus said they should not tell others 'until the Son of man should have risen from the dead.' Jesus had told them before that He would be rejected by the Jewish leaders, suffer and die, but be raised from death (8:31). They could not understand. We wonder why they were slow to learn. But we live after Jesus' resurrection; and we have to remember that although many Jews believed that there would be a resurrection of the dead, they thought that would be 'at the last day' (see John 11:24). That Jesus should die and then as soon as the third day rise again was something that they could not take into their thinking. Soon they would understand and then they would go out witnessing to their risen Lord (Acts 1:8, 21–22).

b. Must Elijah come first?

We have seen (in Study 24) that there was an Old Testament prophecy that said that Elijah would be sent by God 'before the great and terrible day of the Lord comes' (Malachi 4:5). So the scribes taught that the prophet would come back. Jesus said that the scribes were right. But Elijah's coming was in a different way from what they expected. Several New Testament passages help us to understand. Luke 1:17 says of John the Baptist that he would go before the Lord preparing the way for Him 'in the spirit and power of Elijah'. It is true that when John the Baptist was asked the question 'Are you Elijah?', in his humility not wanting to make any claims for himself, he replied 'I am not' (John 1:21). In Matthew 11:13–14 Jesus made it plain, 'all the prophets and the law prophesied until John; and if you are willing to accept it, he is Elijah who is to come.' In the parallel to this passage in Matthew 17:9–13 it says that 'the disciples understood that he was speaking to them of John the Baptist.'

c. Why, after Elijah's coming, must the Son of man suffer?

We have seen that the disciples found it hard to accept what Jesus said about His being rejected and put to death (8:31–33). Here was an added problem for them. The old prophecy about Elijah in Malachi 4:5–6 said that the prophet would come to prepare the way of the Lord (see also Malachi 3:1); he would 'turn the hearts of fathers to their children and the hearts of children to their fathers'. People would repent of the evil of their lives. Surely 'the Son of man' who followed him would be welcomed and accepted? But, 'as is written' in 1 Kings 17–19, Elijah had to suffer because he preached God's message. So John the Baptist, as we have seen in 6:17–29, had to suffer because he preached God's message. 'They did to him whatever they pleased' – and so they would do to Jesus.

We may have questions like those of the disciples. We live on the other side of the cross and resurrection of Jesus. We know the victory that He won for us over sin and death. But we still live by faith and not by sight, in hope of the final showing forth of the glory of Christ. Until that final day of victory, we, like Elijah, like John the Baptist, like Jesus Himself, have to struggle and suffer; but the risen Lord is with us and the power of His spirit is given to us.

Meditation *Consider 1 Peter 5:10–11 in the light of the words of these verses.*

For further thought and study 1. What similarities are there in the ways that Elijah had to suffer and the way John the Baptist suffered? See the passages referred to above, 1 Kings 17–19 and Mark 6:17–29.

2. Is there any special application to us now of the words of verse 9? Are there things that we understand about Jesus that we should keep to ourselves or should we be witnesses to all that we know of Him? Consider Matthew 7:6 and Acts 1:8.

Study 35: THE VALLEY OF HUMAN NEED

[14]And when they came to the disciples, they saw a great crowd about them, and scribes arguing with them. [15]And immediately all the crowd, when they saw him, were greatly amazed, and ran up to him and greeted him. [16]And he asked them, 'What are you discussing with them?' [17]And one of the crowd answered him, 'Teacher, I brought my son to you, for he has a dumb spirit; [18]and wherever it seizes him, it dashes him down; and he foams and grinds his teeth and becomes rigid; and I asked your disciples to cast it out, and they were not able.' [19]And he answered them, 'O faithless generation, how long am I to be with you? How long am I to bear with you? Bring him to me.' [20]And they brought the boy to him; and when the spirit saw him, immediately it convulsed the boy, and he fell on the ground and rolled about, foaming at the mouth. [21]And Jesus asked his father, 'How long has he had this?' And he said, 'From childhood. [22]And it has often cast him into the fire and into the water, to destroy him; but if you can do anything, have pity on us and help us.' [23]And Jesus said to him, 'If you can! All things are possible to him who believes.' [24]Immediately the father of the child cried out and said, 'I believe; help my unbelief!'

²⁵And when Jesus saw that a crowd came running together, he rebuked the unclean spirit, saying to it, 'You dumb and deaf spirit, I command you, come out of him, and never enter him again.' ²⁶And after crying out and convulsing him terribly, it came out, and the boy was like a corpse; so that most of them said, 'He is dead.' ²⁷But Jesus took him by the hand and lifted him up, and he arose. ²⁸And when he had entered the house, his disciples asked him privately, 'Why could we not cast it out?' ²⁹And he said to them, 'This kind cannot be driven out by anything but prayer (9:14–29).

In the beginning of this chapter we have read how the glory of Jesus was seen in His transfiguration. Now for Him the road leads on to Jerusalem and to the cross, and in the rest of the Gospel we see what the cross meant to Him. We also have much of His teaching given to the disciples, showing them what it meant to follow Him. There are few miracles told now, but we can see special reasons why this miracle is told in some detail – especially for what the disciples had to learn from what happened.

a. Down from the mountain – to human suffering

Peter and James and John would have loved to have stayed for ever on the mountain where they saw Jesus in His glory and heard Moses and Elijah talking with Him (verses 4–5). They had to learn that they must go down the mountain, back to the world, and again be alongside people with great needs – the sick, the demon-possessed, the troubled, the anxious. Here was a father who had brought his son who took epileptic fits, but whose fits (as verse 20 makes clear) were caused by demon possession. The disciples had to learn to share the compassion and concern of Jesus for deep human needs caused by the attack of the demonic on precious human lives. Jesus, as long as He was on earth, would continue to minister to the suffering and to those battered and beaten by the forces of evil. His disciples are still called to share in His work.

b. Failure – through lack of faith

Added to the sickness and demon-possession of the boy, there was a further problem for the father and for all those involved. Although Jesus' disciples had been sent out with power to heal and to cast out demons (see 3:14–15 and 6:7–13), they had been unable to help in this case. When Jesus came down from the mountain He found them discouraged at their failure, the 'scribes arguing with them' (verse 14), and the father more troubled than ever. 'If you can do anything, have pity on us and help us,' he said to Jesus (verse 22). He need not have said to Jesus, 'If you can'. He should have believed in the power of Jesus to do for his son what He had done for others. The father and the disciples themselves were so slow to believe. The scribes who professed to be religious teachers and leaders were no better. No wonder Jesus had to say of them all, 'O faithless generation, how long am I to be with you? How long am I to bear with you?' (verse 19). He had done so much to help people to see the love and mighty power of God. Could they not believe?

c. Compassion for need and power to help

In the valley of human need Jesus showed His love and compassion. Immediately the father was invited to bring his son to Him. At the approach of the One who had all power over the forces of evil, the demon made a final attack on the boy's life. 'It convulsed the boy, and he fell to the ground and rolled about, foaming at the mouth.' Jesus spoke with authority; 'You dumb and deaf spirit, I command you, come out of him, and never enter him again.' The demon had to go, but the boy was left – so it seemed to people around – lifeless. 'But Jesus took him by the hand and lifted him up, and he arose.' Such is always the work of Jesus. He not only frees our lives from the power of evil, He also gives new life.

This passage ends with a question that the disciples asked Jesus and with the answer He gave. 'Why could we not cast it out?' they asked when they were alone with Him (verse 28). His answer was, 'This kind cannot be driven out by anything but prayer' (verse 29). Perhaps the disciples thought that in the past when Jesus had sent them out, they had been given the power that they needed. What they did then, they could do again. They had to learn – and it is a lesson for Christians still – they could not depend on a past experience of the power of God. For each day and for each hour, for each challenge of the power of evil, they must rely on the power of God. Prayer is the link – to be kept renewed all the time – between the power of God and the need and weakness of men and women, of us all. It is like the link wire between the source of electric power and the light bulb. It is like the link pipe between the abundant source of water in the reservoir, lake or river and the tap in home, hospital or factory where the water is needed. There must be the link between the source of power and the place where it is needed – and that link is our dependence on God by the prayer of faith.

Prayer   *Forgive, Lord, our lack of faith. Help us to know in our own lives more of Your love and power and to be channels of Your grace to our needy world, to the blessing of others and to the glory of Your name.* AMEN.

For further thought and study   1. Consider other ways in which Jesus spoke of the need of His disciples to have a growing faith in Him. See Mark 11:22–24, Matthew 17:20, 21:21–22.

   2. Someone has said, 'The scene in the valley is a picture of the world today: youth in the grip of evil, parents in anguish, the Church not using its full powers, and hostile critics.' Is that a fair comment?

Notes   1. The passages parallel to this in other Gospels are Matthew 17:14–21 and Luke 9:37–43. Again the slightly different details in these passages should be noted.

2. Some of the old manuscripts in verse 29 have 'prayer and fasting'. We have considered (in Study 10) the attitude of Jesus to fasting. By fasting we may be able better to give all our attention to our prayer and dependence on God. It is important, however, to be sure that our motive in fasting is not to try to win the favour of God or to impress other people (see Matthew 6:1–8 and 16–18).

Study 36: HIGHEST OR LOWEST

[30]**They went on from there and passed through Galilee. And he would not have anyone know it;** [31]**for he was teaching his disciples, saying to them, 'The Son of man will be delivered into the hands of men, and they will kill him; and when he is killed, after three days he will rise.'** [32]**But they did not understand the saying, and they were afraid to ask him.**

[33]**And they came to Capernaum; and when he was in the house he asked them, 'What were you discussing on the way?'** [34]**But they were silent; for on the way they had discussed with one another who was the greatest.** [35]**And he sat down and called the twelve; and he said to them, 'If any one would be first, he must be last of all and servant of all.'** [36]**And he took a child, and put him in the midst of them; and taking him in his arms, he said to them,** [37]**'Whoever receives one such child in my name receives me; and whoever receives me, receives not me but him who sent me.'**

[38]**John said to him, 'Teacher, we saw a man casting out demons in your name, and we forbade him, because he was not following us.'** [39]**But Jesus said, 'Do not forbid him; for no one who does a mighty work in my name will be able soon after to speak evil of me.** [40]**For he that is not against us is for us.** [41]**For truly, I say to you, whoever gives you a cup of water to drink because you bear the name of Christ, will by no means lose his reward** (9:30–42).

We have seen that from the time when Peter confessed

Jesus to be the Christ (or Messiah), Jesus began to teach the disciples that He must be a suffering Messiah and what it would mean for them to follow Him (8:27–37). Now we read that He wanted to avoid the crowds coming to Him, so that He might teach the disciples the things that were so important for them to learn – how He must die (verses 30–32) and how they must follow Him (verses 33–50).

a. Handed over to die

In a similar way to what we have read in 8:31, Jesus speaks here of the death He must die. He also tells the way He will rise from death. The Gospel gives us His words: 'The Son of man will be delivered into the hands of men.' The Good News Bible puts it, 'handed over to men'. Jesus could have avoided this happening, but He did not. The same words are used in the Gospel to tell how He allowed Judas to 'hand Him over' to the Jewish leaders (14:10–11, 43–45), the Jewish leaders to 'hand Him over' to Pilate (15:1), and Pilate to 'hand Him over' to the soldiers for Him to be crucified (15:15). It is the same word each time in the Greek language in which Mark wrote. The disciples could not understand the words of Jesus at the time (verse 32). They understood later. It was the Father's purpose that Jesus should be 'handed over' to die (see Acts 2:23 and Romans 8:32) – and to rise again. Each of us who is a disciple can now say like the apostle Paul, 'The Son of God loved me and handed Himself over for me (Galatians 2:20, which uses the same word).

b. First or last

When Jesus allowed Himself to be 'handed over' to His enemies and when He died on the cross, He was willing to be treated as the least and lowest of all people. He was teaching the disciples how this must be the way for Him, but they were arguing about which of them was the greatest and should be the first. They were ashamed to reply when Jesus said, 'What were you discussing on the way?' They, like us who are His disciples today, had a hard lesson to learn. In hundreds of ways we have to decide either to put ourselves forward or to help others along the road to life. Do we want to be seen among important people? Or are we willing to love and to serve those who can do nothing for us in return? As He often did, Jesus taught by action as well as word. He took a little child into His arms and said that to receive a little child in His name was like receiving God Himself (verse 37)!

c. Receiving or rejecting

Verses 36–37 are about 'receiving' others. The disciples, like us very often, were busy 'rejecting' others. We like to put ourselves first and think our own concerns are the most important. It is natural to put first those who belong to our group – our congregation or fellowship, our tribe or people. But if we do, then we can easily do what the disciples did here. Here was one who acted in the name of Jesus and he must have had the power of Jesus, because the evil spirits were driven out. John said, 'We told him to stop, because he doesn't belong to our group' (verse 38, Good News Bible). The disciples had to learn to receive rather than reject such a person. God Himself accepts as valuable in His sight the smallest action done in His name when it is done to those who belong to Him (verse 41). The true servant of God treats as brother or sister all who truly serve God and who are fighting with God against the forces of evil.

Meditation   *'Live in harmony with one another; do not be haughty, but associate with the lowly; never be conceited'* (Romans 12:16).

For further thought and study   1. Compare the words of verse 40 with those of Matthew 12:30 and Luke 11:23. How do the settings of the words help us to see that both can be true and help us to understand both?

2. Why do you think that Jesus placed such emphasis on the attitude that a person shows to children?

Notes 1. We find parallels to verses 30–32 in Matthew 17:22–23 and Luke 9:43–45; to verses 33–37 in Matthew 18:1–5 and Luke 9:46–48 (see also Luke 22:24–27); to verses 38–40 in Luke 9:49–50.

2. Verse 33 is one of several places in this Gospel where we read of private conversations between Jesus and His disciples (see also 4:10, 34, 7:17, 9:28 and 10:10).

3. Verse 37 brings out the emphasis on Jesus as 'sent' by the Father, as we find it often in the Gospels. See Matthew 15:24, Luke 4:18, John 3:17, 7:28–33 and 20:21.

Study 37: CAUSES OF STUMBLING

[42]'**Whoever causes one of these little ones who believe in me to sin, it would be better for him if a great millstone were hung round his neck and he were thrown into the sea.** [43]**And if your hand causes you to sin, cut it off; it is better for you to enter life maimed than with two hands to go to hell, to the unquenchable fire.** [45]**And if your foot causes you to sin, cut it off; it is better for you to enter life lame than with two feet to be thrown into hell.** [47]**And if your eye causes you to sin, pluck it out; it is better for you to enter the kingdom of God with one eye than with two eyes to be thrown into hell,** [48]**where their worm does not die, and the fire is not quenched.** [49]**For every one will be salted with fire.** [50]**Salt is good; but if the salt has lost its saltness, how will you season it? Have salt in yourselves, and be at peace with one another** (9:42–50).

The order in which we find things in Mark's Gospel is not always that of time. Sometimes similar sayings or actions of Jesus are brought together, like His parables in 4:1–34, and in 4:35–5:43 His miracles to show who He is. Here we have teaching which Jesus may have given on different occasions, but which Mark may have brought together because they deal with the same subject. Verse 41 has spoken about giving even a cup of water to a person in the name of Christ. In contrast verse 42 gives a warning about causing 'little ones' who are believers to stumble in the way of life. Then verses 43–48 give serious warnings of ways in which we ourselves may be caused to stumble. Finally in this section, verses 49–50 bring together three sayings of Jesus about salt.

a. Causing others to stumble

In verses 36–37 Jesus has shown how those who are least important in the eyes of the world are precious to Him. The worst thing that any of us can do is to cause another person, however small or unimportant, to stumble and turn aside from the ways of God. This happens in the world in many ways. Weak people are led to ruin their lives with drugs or alcohol, or led to a career of crime or dishonesty and corruption. Perhaps we may not be guilty of leading people to such sins, but we can cause others to stumble by laughing at the simple faith of a believer, or by our own failure to live out the faith we profess, or by encouraging others to put money or power or popularity before God. The words of Jesus are a serious warning, 'Whoever causes one of these little ones who believe in me to sin, it would be better for him if a great millstone were hung round his neck and he were thrown into the sea.'

b. Causing ourselves to stumble

Jesus has used strong language in warning us of the danger of causing others to stumble. He also uses strong language in speaking of ways in which we may stumble and sin ourselves. Our 'hand' may cause us to sin, by doing what is contrary to God's ways, against other people, against our own well-being. Our 'foot' may lead us to sin, by our going to places where we will fall into temptation. Our 'eye' may cause us to sin, as we see and covet and desire what we know God would not wish us to have (compare Genesis 3:6 and 1 John 2:16). Jesus says 'cut off' your hand or foot, 'pluck out' your eye. We are not to take this literally, but as sometimes a surgeon has to cut off a limb to save the whole body, sometimes we have to take strong action to stop ourselves falling into sin.

So also it is picture language when Jesus speaks of 'hell, where their worm does not die, and the fire is not quenched' (verse 48). Heaven and hell can only be spoken of in picture language, in terms of what we know in this life. This is not saying that they do not exist, but that the reality is far more wonderful and terrible than anything we can express in words. By His goodness and love we can choose the way of life. It is a great mistake if we ever think we can go on rejecting God and His ways in this life, and then expect to be accepted by Him in the life to come.

c. Salt sayings

In verses 49–50 there are three sayings about salt. The first links with what has been said about 'fire' in verse 48. Fire burns rubbish and the Bible often speaks of the cleansing work of fire and used it as a picture of the purifying of human lives. Salt also preserves food from corruption. To be 'salted with fire' possibly means to be purified by trial and suffering (as this is spoken of in 1 Peter 1:6–7).

Second, salt gives flavour to our food, and in Matthew 5:13 Jesus says to His disciples, 'You are the salt of the earth'. There He continued as He says here, 'if the salt has lost its saltness, how will you season it?' We must never lose the flavour and goodness that Christians should bring to the world, that is, love, truth, purity, justice, kindness, shown in word and action.

Thirdly, Jesus says, 'Have salt in yourselves, and be at peace with one another.' Living at peace with others – the New Testament often calls Christians to this – is part of what it is to be 'salt' in the earth. People in those days spoke of fellowship as 'eating salt together' (the word is used in the Greek of Acts 1:4). Christians in their life together are to show the world love and peace more than anything else (see John 13:35 and Romans 12:18 and 14:19).

Meditation *St Augustine prayed that he might have 'towards God a heart of flame, towards others a heart of love, and towards himself a heart of steel.'*

For further thought and study 1. What can we learn by linking the words of verses 43–48 with similar words in Matthew 5:27–30?

2. Compare the teaching of these verses about leading others to sin with what is said in such New Testament passages as Matthew 18:7, 23:13, Romans 14:13–23 and 1 Corinthians 8. The Old Testament shows the responsibility of those in leadership positions who may either lead others in the ways of God or who, like King Jeroboam I 'made Israel to sin' (e.g. see 1 Kings 14:16).

Notes 1. We have parallels in the other Gospels; with verse 42, Matthew 18:6–7 and Luke 17:1–2; with verses 43–48, Matthew 18:8–9; with verse 50, Matthew 5:13 and Luke 14:34–35.

2. In most Bibles there is no verse 44 or 46, because these words, originally written as our verse 48, came to be repeated in the other two places.

3. The word used for 'hell' in these verses is Gehenna, a name that comes from the Valley of Hinnom outside Jerusalem, a rubbish dump where worms continually fed on refuse and fires burned continually – hence the words of verse 48.

4. 'To enter life' here (in verses 43 and 45) is the same thing as 'to enter the kingdom of God' (verse 47).

Study 38: FAMILY MATTERS

¹And he left there and went to the region of Judea and

beyond the Jordan, and crowds gathered to him again; and again, as his custom was, he taught them.

²And Pharisees came up and in order to test him asked, 'Is it lawful for a man to divorce his wife?' ³He answered them, 'What did Moses command you?' ⁴They said, 'Moses allowed a man to write a certificate of divorce, and to put her away.' ⁵But Jesus said to them, 'For your hardness of heart he wrote you this commandment. ⁶But from the beginning of creation, "God made them male and female." ⁷"For this reason a man shall leave his father and mother and be joined to his wife, ⁸and the two shall become one flesh." So they are no longer two but one flesh. ⁹What God has joined together, let not man put asunder.'

¹⁰And in the house the disciples asked him again about this matter. ¹¹And he said to them, 'Whoever divorces his wife and marries another, commits adultery against her; ¹²and if she divorces her husband and marries another, she commits adultery.'

¹³And they were bringing children to him, that he might touch them; and the disciples rebuked them. ¹⁴But when Jesus saw it he was indignant, and said to them, 'Let the children come to me, do not hinder them; for to such belongs the kingdom of God. ¹⁵Truly, I say to you, whoever does not receive the kingdom of God like a child shall not enter it.' ¹⁶And he took them in his arms and blessed them, laying his hands upon them   (10:1–16).

As Mark in his Gospel continues to show from the teaching of Jesus what it means to be disciples of Christ, we can see how wisely he sets side by side with the answer Jesus gives to a question about divorce (verses 2–9), further teaching about marriage (verses 10–12), and an incident that shows His love and concern for children (verses 13–16).

a. Marriage

The Pharisees came to Jesus with a question about divorce that the Jewish teachers often discussed. What is sufficient reason for a man to divorce his wife? Some of the rabbis said there could only be divorce if the wife was unfaithful to her husband. Others made divorce possible for little things like spoiling her husband's food by her bad cooking. They wanted to 'test him' and to see whose side He would take. He answered with a question to them. 'What did Moses command you?' They replied by saying what the Mosaic Law *allowed* about *divorce* (Deuteronomy 24:1–4). He turned them to what the beginning of the Law *taught* about *marriage*. God's purpose 'from the beginning of creation' is given in the words, 'God made them male and female'. Man and woman are both made in 'the image of God' (Genesis 1:26–27). Marriage is part of God's good plan and in it 'a man shall leave his father and mother and be joined to his wife.' There is a *leaving* – leaving behind the closest relationship of the past (child to parent) for what becomes now the closest relationship, in the *joining* of husband and wife. God's purpose is that that should be a lasting relationship, the secure foundation for home and family life. 'What therefore God has joined together, let not man put asunder.' Genesis 2:24 quoted here says that in marriage 'the two shall become one'. In the Old Testament, as in many societies in the world now, polygamy is often practised, but it is against God's highest purpose of which Genesis speaks – the partnerships of equals, one man, one woman, in lasting marriage.

In most cases a marriage is blessed with children, but, in the Bible teaching, childlessness in marriage is not a reason for divorce or for a couple to separate.

b. Divorce

The Pharisees quoted Deuteronomy 24:1 to Jesus, 'Moses allowed a man to write a certificate of divorce' and put his wife away. Yes, the Mosaic Law, like laws in our countries today, provides for divorce. But Jesus said, it is 'for your hardness of heart' that there are such laws. It is always human weakness and failure when marriage breaks down and divorce takes place. There is no doubt that the Bible shows that God's plan and purpose is that a man and woman joined in marriage should remain as husband and wife until they are parted by death. The teaching of Jesus 'in the house' with His disciples later (verse 10), made clear that it was adultery for a man to divorce his wife or a woman to divorce her husband and marry another.

God's plan and purpose is clear, but in the life of the Church today we have to deal with the breakdown of marriage as with every other failure and sin. We should act in love and concern for those whose marriages have broken down, just as we should act wisely and with understanding with those whose customs have allowed polygamy for centuries. But of the purpose of God for the lasting partnership of one man and one woman in marriage we should have no doubt, and we should work and pray for the strengthening of Christian marriage and home life.

c. Children

Few things on earth are more beautiful than a home where there is a secure marriage, and children are brought up in love and trust and true discipline. Where marriage breaks down, the children often suffer most. Here in the setting of Jesus' teaching about marriage and divorce, we see His love and concern for children. When children were brought 'that he might touch them', the disciples took the attitude that Jesus would not have time for them. They thought children could not understand what He was saying and doing. But they were wrong, and 'when Jesus saw it he was indignant'. His words were, 'Let the children come to me, do not hinder them'; and 'he took them in his arms and blessed them, laying his hands upon them'. He had even more to say and to teach about children, 'for to such belongs the kingdom of God.' Then with His powerful emphasis, 'Truly, I say to you', He added, 'whoever does not receive the kingdom of God like a child shall not enter it.' In what way are we to be like children to 'receive' and to 'belong to' the kingdom of God'? A child is trustful, but we, as we get older, are often suspicious. A child is open to spiritual things, but we, as we grow older, are influenced more and more by material things. It is easier for a child than for an older person to make God King and to accept the blessings and the tasks of His Kingdom.

Prayer *Lord, in our community and nation, strengthen, we pray, the love and loyalty of husbands and wives, and may our children grow up to know and serve You in the joy of Your Kingdom.* Amen.

For further thought and study 1. What do you consider to be the main principles of Christian marriage? How do you think the church should help in preparing those who are planning to be married.?

2. Along with verses 13–16 consider what is said about children in 9:36–37 and Matthew 18:1–6. What do these passages suggest about what should be the Church's attitude to children and to work among children?

Notes 1. We have parallel passages in the other Gospels – to verses 2–12, Matthew 19:3–9 (and see 5:31–32); to verses 13–16, Matthew 19:13–15 and Luke 18:15–17.

2. Verse 1 shows that Jesus had come south from Galilee and that He spent time east of the Jordan and in Judea. The rest of the Gospel tells of His journey to Jerusalem (verse 32) and what happened there.

3. The 'certificate of divorce' (verse 4) to which the law in Deuteronomy 24 refers was to protect the wife. In Jewish law a man could divorce his wife, but a woman could not divorce her husband. In Roman law, however, a woman could divorce her husband. This Roman law would have been well-known in Palestine, and so verse 12 would be meaningful.

Study 39: RICHES AND DISCIPLINE

[17]And as he was setting out on his journey, a man ran up and knelt before him and asked him, 'Good Teacher, what must I do to inherit eternal life?' [18]And Jesus said to him, 'Why do you call me good? No one is good but God alone. [19]You know the commandments: "Do not kill, Do not commit adultery, Do not steal, Do not bear false witness, Do not defraud, Honour your father and mother."' [20]And he said to him, 'Teacher, all these I have observed from my youth.' [21]And Jesus looking upon him loved him, and said to him, 'You lack one thing; go, sell what you have, and give to the poor, and you will have treasure in heaven; and come, follow me.' [22]At that saying his countenance fell, and he went away sorrowful; for he had great possessions.

[23]And Jesus looked around and said to his disciples, 'How hard it will be for those who have riches to enter the kingdom of God!' [24]And the disciples were amazed at his words. But Jesus said to them again, 'Children, how hard it is to enter the kingdom of God! [25]It is easier for a camel to go through the eye of a needle than for a rich man to enter the kingdom of God.' [26]And they were exceedingly astonished, and said to him, 'Then who can be saved?' [27]Jesus looked at them and said, 'With men it is impossible, but not with God; for all things are possible with God.' [28]Peter began to say to him, 'Lo, we have left everything and followed you.' [29]Jesus said, 'Truly, I say to you, there is no one who has left house or brothers or sisters or mother or father or children or lands, for my sake and for the gospel, [30]who will not receive a hundredfold now in this time, houses and brothers and sisters and mothers and children and lands, with persecutions, and in the age to come eternal life. [31]But many that are first will be last, and the last first' (10:17–31).

As the teaching of the Gospel continues about what it means to be a disciple, we read Jesus's teaching about the disciple's attitude to riches. It is given in three ways – first, in answer to a rich man's question, then in teaching given by the Lord about those who hold on to riches, and thirdly about those who for His sake give up what they have.

a. Rich man's question

The Pharisees of whom we read in verse 2 came to Jesus with a question 'to test him'. This man with his question seems to have been sincere, enthusiastic and humble; he 'ran up and knelt before him'. 'Jesus looking upon him loved him' (verse 21). His question was an important one, about 'eternal life', but the way he asked and the way the conversation continued showed things that were wrong in his attitude. He addressed Jesus as 'Good Teacher'. That was right, but did he realize what he was saying when he used the word 'good'? He thought that he also was good. He had kept all the commandments from childhood, he thought. Yet was there something more that he should 'do' 'to inherit eternal life'? We can see his mistake. We realize when we think of the commandments, that we have all failed to keep them, so that we no longer have any hope of acceptance with God by our 'doing' – only by His forgiving us. But Jesus knew He must test this young man. Did he really love his neighbour as himself (as the commandments require – see Romans 13:9)? Then would he go and sell his possessions and give the money to the poor? Did he love God with all his heart and soul and mind and strength (see 12:28–30)? Then would he 'come, follow' Jesus? When Jesus spoke like this, 'he went away sorrowful; for he had great possessions.'

b. Those who hold on to riches

The man with the question about eternal life 'went away sorrowful' because, when it came to the test, his riches meant more to him than other things – more than loving his neighbour, more than loving God, more than the hope of eternal life. That is the danger of earthly possessions. That is why it is hard, as Jesus said, 'for those who have riches to enter the kingdom of God.' A person who is comfortable and satisfied in this life can easily forget God and not care about His Kingdom. Humorous, but challenging, was Jesus' picture of a camel trying to get through the eye of a needle! It is as hard as that for a rich person to get into God's kingdom! We are not surprised that the disciples said, 'Then who can be saved?' They had been taught that riches were a sign of God's favour and blessing, and there are some churches which teach this today. It is true that all a rich person has, all that any of us have, is by God's gift; but we can so easily think more of the gifts than the Giver. Humanly speaking it is hard to bring self-satisfied people to the kingdom of God. Yet God's love and grace can work in any person's life and what with us seems impossible is 'possible with God.'

c. Those who give up riches

As the disciples heard what Jesus said, perhaps they were proud because they could honestly say, 'we have left everything and followed you'. Notice the way that Jesus answered. Yes, God richly blesses those who have left home and family for His sake to tell His gospel to others. They will find in the fellowship of His followers those who will be to them 'brothers and sisters and mothers and children' (verse 30). They will have eternal life. But as He warned them before, in following Him they will face 'persecutions'. The way of discipleship is a way of blessing, but it is hard and painful. Finally, as a warning to their pride, Jesus said, 'many that are first will be last, and the last will be first'. There will be some surprises when finally we see things as God has seen them all along. Some who have been thought great, and have thought themselves great in God's service, will be seen as less important, while others who have hardly been noticed will be honoured most in God's presence.

Meditation *The rich man was challenged about those parts of his life where he had not put God first and had not loved*

*and cared for others. What are the parts of our life where the
Lord would challenge us to obey Him and serve others?*

For further thought and study 1. Consider other passages
in the Bible which speak of the dangers of riches – for
example Psalm 62:10, Matthew 6:19–24, Luke 12:13–21
and 1 Timothy 6:6–19. What special dangers would you
list?

2. Consider the place that is given in the Bible to the
emphasis that those who serve God should care for the
poor. For example see Deuteronony 24:19–22, Matthew
25:34–40, John 13:29, Acts 2:44–45, 4:32–37 and 6:1–6.
How should we apply this to ourselves?

Notes 1. The parallel passages to these verses in other Gospels
are Matthew 19:16–30 and Luke 18:18–30.

2. The commandment 'Do not defraud' (in verse 19) may be a
way of putting the 10th commandment against coveting, or it may
be a way of putting such laws as Deuteronomy 24:14–15.

3. Some early copies of the Gospel in verse 24 had 'how hard it
is for those who trust in riches', but probably what our translation
has is what was originally written.

4. Three times in these verses (21, 23 and 27) we read of the way
Jesus looked on people. It was clearly something that those who
were present never forgot (compare Mark 3:5, 34, 5:32 and Luke
22:61).

Study 40: TO SERVE AND TO GIVE HIS LIFE

³²**And they were on the road, going up to Jerusalem, and
Jesus was walking ahead of them; and they were amazed,
and those who followed were afraid. And taking the twelve
again, he began to tell them what was to happen to him,
³³saying, 'Behold, we are going up to Jerusalem; and the Son
of man will be delivered to the chief priests and the scribes,**

and they will condemn him to death, and deliver him to the
Gentiles; ³⁴and they will mock him, and spit upon him, and
scourge him, and kill him; and after three days he will rise.'

³⁵And James and John, the sons of Zebedee, came forward
to him, and said to him, 'Teacher, we want you to do for us
whatever we ask of you.' ³⁶And he said to them, 'What do
you want me to do for you?' ³⁷And they said to him, 'Grant
us to sit, one at your right hand and one at your left, in your
glory.' ³⁸But Jesus said to them, 'You do not know what you
are asking. Are you able to drink the cup that I drink, or to
be baptized with the baptism with which I am baptized?'
³⁹And they said to him, 'We are able.' And Jesus said to
them, 'The cup that I drink you will drink; and with the
baptism with which I am baptized, you will be baptized;
⁴⁰but to sit at my right hand or at my left is not mine to grant,
but it is for those for whom it has been prepared.' ⁴¹And
when the ten heard it, they began to be indignant at James
and John. ⁴²And Jesus called them to him and said to them,
'You know that those who are supposed to rule over the
Gentiles lord it over them, and their great men exercise
authority over them. ⁴³But it shall not be so among you; but
whoever would be great among you must be your servant,
⁴⁴and whoever would be first among you must be slave of all.
⁴⁵For the Son of man also came not to be served but to serve,
and to give his life as a ransom for many'   (10:32–45).

'And they were on the road, going up to Jerusalem...'.
The disciples had still much to learn about what it meant to
the Lord that He was going up to Jerusalem, and what it
meant for them to follow Him.

a. The future for Jesus
For the third time now Jesus talks to the disciples about
what lies ahead of Him in Jerusalem. His words are similar
to what we have read in 8:31 and 9:31. It is added here that
the chief priests and scribes would hand Him over to the
Gentiles. They did not recognize that in Him all the greatest

hopes and prophecies of the Old Testament were coming true. They did not want to give Him any place in their lives or in their nation; and because the Romans ruled over them and they had no power to put anyone to death (John 18:31), they had to hand Him over to the Gentiles to fulfil their desire to kill Him. Added here are the insults and abuse He would bear: 'they will mock him, and spit upon him, and scourge him.'

We are told also how those who were with Him felt as 'Jesus was walking ahead of them'. Those who saw Him 'were amazed'. He knew that in Jerusalem there would be rejection, suffering, death; but He would not turn back. He was willing to suffer. He had come, as the last verse of this passage puts it, 'to give his life as a ransom for many.' They 'were amazed', and 'those who followed were afraid' – afraid for Him and afraid for themselves (compare John 11:7–10).

b. Disciples' hopes

It is clear from the request that James and John made that the disciples had not understood the words of their Master. Perhaps they were thinking of His promises about prayer (like Matthew 7:7–11, 18:19 and 21:22) when they said, 'Teacher, we want you to do for us whatever we ask of you.' What was their request? A selfish one, that thought nothing of what their Master was suffering, nothing of their fellow disciples: 'Grant us to sit, one at your right hand and one at your left, in your glory.' Glory was what they wanted – the places next to Him. But Jesus' glory was first in His suffering on the cross. Who were on His right hand and on His left then? (See 15:27.) James and John had made their request and the other ten disciples 'began to be indignant' at them. It was all very human; and we who are disciples today still are tempted to look for the places of honour and importance!

c. Disciples' calling

Patiently Jesus taught His disciples again what it means to follow Him. Those who want to be near the Master in His glory must share His cup of suffering and His baptism of pain and death. In the end James did this as he met a martyr's death (Acts 12:2), and John as he lived a long life of service and suffering. The way of Christ is not the world's way. Gentile rulers 'lord it over' people. They love authority and power. 'It shall not be so among you', Jesus says to those who follow Him. The greatest among His followers must be 'servant' and 'slave of all'. This is easy to say, but hard to live out! We follow the One who lived that way to the end. He came 'to serve, and to give his life as a ransom for many'. Often the New Testament speaks of the suffering and death of Christ as an example for us to follow – but never just as an example. The New Testament teaching and preaching repeat again and again that on the cross He did *for* us what we needed most, and what He alone could do. It is described in many ways. Here it is 'ransom'; a price paid to set free a slave. We were slaves to sin. To receive forgiveness of sin, and the power to overcome evil, is to know freedom. The good news that we have is that Jesus died and rose from the dead to gain that freedom for us.

Meditation *'You know what was paid to set you free.... It was not something that can be destroyed, such as silver or gold; it was the costly sacrifice of Christ.'* (1 Peter 1:18–19, Good News Bible).

For further thought and study 1. What did Jesus mean by the 'cup' that He would drink? With verse 38 consider also 14:36, John 18:11 and in the Old Testatment, Psalm 23:5, 75:8 and Isaiah 51:17.

2. How do other New Testament passages help to explain what it meant for the death of Christ to be spoken of as 'ransom' or 'redemption'? For example, see Romans

3:23–26, 1 Corinthians 6:20, 1 Timothy 2:6, Titus 2:14 and 1 Peter 1:18–19.

3. In the light of verses 43–45 what kind of ambition do you think it is right for a Christian to have?

Notes 1. Matthew 20:17–19 and Luke 18:31–34 are parallel passages to verses 32–34; Matthew 20:20–28 parallels verses 35–45, but there the mother of James and John makes the request. Teaching like that of verses 42–45 is found in Luke 22:24–27.

2. Although the Old Testament speaks of the 'cup', it does not speak of baptism. It does speak of people being overwhelmed as waters pour over them (Psalm 42:7, 69:15 and 124:2–5). Notice also the words of Jesus in Luke 12:50. Part of the meaning of Christian baptism is that the person baptized is made one with Jesus in His death and resurrection (Romans 6:1–4).

3. Verse 40 may mean that this was one of the things that was in the Father's hands and not in the hands of Jesus as Son of God (compare 13:32). On the other hand, it may mean that these positions could not be given to any one whom He might choose; the kind of people for whom those places have been 'prepared' has already been decided.

4. Some people have thought that Jesus' prediction of His death, and in particular such details as we have in verses 33–34 may have been brought into its present form after His death and resurrection. However, as well as having the gift of prophecy, Jesus (a) knew of the Jewish opposition to Him and how any attempt to put Him to death must bring in the Roman rulers, and (b) He must often have thought deeply of Old Testament passages that spoke of the sufferings of faithful servants of God. Behind His words in verse 45 we can understand His thinking of Isaiah 53:11–12.

Study 41: WELCOME TO THE SON OF DAVID

⁴⁶**And they came to Jericho; and as he was leaving Jericho with his disciples and a great multitude, Bartimaeus, a blind**

beggar, the son of Timaeus, was sitting by the roadside.
⁴⁷And when he heard that it was Jesus of Nazareth, he began
to cry out and say, 'Jesus, Son of David, have mercy on me!'
⁴⁸And many rebuked him, telling him to be silent; but he
cried out all the more, 'Son of David, have mercy on me!'
⁴⁹And Jesus stopped and said, 'Call him.' And they called
the blind man, saying to him, 'Take heart; rise, he is calling
you.' ⁵⁰And throwing off his mantle he sprang up and came
to Jesus. ⁵¹And Jesus said to him, 'What do you want me to
do for you?' And the blind man said to him, 'Master, let me
receive my sight.' ⁵²And Jesus said to him, 'Go your way;
your faith has made you well.' And immediately he received
his sight and followed him on the way.

11: ¹And when they drew near to Jerusalem, to Bethphage
and Bethany, at the Mount of Olives, he sent two of his
disciples, ²and said to them, 'Go into the village opposite
you, and immediately as you enter it you will find a colt tied,
on which no one has ever sat; untie it and bring it. ³If anyone
says to you, "Why are you doing this?" say, "The Lord has
need of it and will send it back here immediately."' ⁴And they
went away, and found a colt tied at the door out in the open
street; and they untied it. ⁵And those who stood there said to
them, 'What are you doing, untying the colt?' ⁶And they
told them what Jesus had said; and they let them go. ⁷And
they brought the colt to Jesus, and threw their garments on
it; and he sat upon it. ⁸And many spread their garments on
the road, and others spread leafy branches which they had
cut from the fields. ⁹And those who went before and those
who followed cried out, 'Hosanna! Blessed is he who comes
in the name of the Lord! ¹⁰Blessed is the kingdom of our
father David that is coming! Hosanna in the highest!'

¹¹And he entered Jerusalem, and went into the temple;
and when he had looked round at everything, as it was
already late, he went out to Bethany with the twelve
(10:45—11:11).

Sometimes the singing of a choir in a great song of joy

begins with a single voice leading. In the customs of some people when a special visitor is welcomed there is first one voice and then many voices join in the welcome. It is good to read the end of chapter 10 and the beginning of chapter 11 together. As Jesus went on His way to Jerusalem a blind beggar called out to Him as Son of David. Later 'when they drew near to Jerusalem', the crowds welcomed Him with the words, 'Blessed is the kingdom of our father David that is coming!'

a. First voice

It was the last visit of Jesus to Jericho before He went to Jerusalem to be arrested and to die. A great crowd was around Him as He left Jericho. A blind beggar heard the sounds of the crowd, and when he asked the reason, people told him that Jesus of Nazareth was there. Two things he was confident about because of what he had heard of this Jesus of Nazareth. First, he knew that He was no ordinary person. He called out to Him as 'Son of David', the expected Messiah. Second, he believed that this One could do what no other could do, and restore his sight. When he called out, 'Jesus, Son of David, have mercy on me,' people tried to silence him. But he knew that this was his great opportunity and 'he cried out all the more.' Jesus did act in mercy. He 'stopped', and said 'Call him'. Without a moment's delay, 'he sprang up and came to Jesus'. When Jesus asked him, 'What do you want me to do for you?' he replied immediately and received his sight'.

Often the poor and the weak are the most ready to believe and to follow the Lord (see Matthew 11:25 and 1 Corinthians 1:26–29). This 'blind beggar' pointed the way for others.

b. Preparations for entering Jerusalem

Often in this Gospel we have read how crowds would come to Jesus just for miracles, and we have seen how He tried to avoid this (1:44, 5:43 and 7:36). When people (whether demon-possessed or believers) shouted to the world that He was 'Messiah' or 'Son of God', He stopped them (see 1:25, 3:12 and 8:30). Yet He did not silence Bartimaeus calling Him 'Son of David', and He even made careful plans for a public procession into Jerusalem. He arranged for a donkey that had never been ridden before to be brought to him. On this He was to ride, fulfilling, as Matthew 21:4–5 says, the prophecy of Zechariah 9:9: 'Rejoice greatly, O daughter of Zion! Shout aloud, O daughter of Jerusalem! Lo, your King comes to you; triumphant and victorious is he, humble and riding on an ass.' He came as King, but He came humbly. He came for all to see Him come – but not on a horse, the animal of war, but as Prince of peace, riding on a donkey. For once He let the crowds do what they wished.

c. Welcome

The crowds welcomed Him with great keenness. Some put their clothes on the donkey. Others spread theirs on the road, or put leafy branches down to make a carpet. In Palestine as in many African countries, this was the welcome for a king (compare 2 Kings 9:13). They shouted their welcome to Jesus as the one 'coming in the name of the Lord.' These words, from Psalm 118:26, could be the welcome to any pilgrim coming up to a festival at the Jerusalem temple – but they could mean more (see Matthew 23:39). The people spoke, too, of the kingdom of David. They were looking for the Messiah descended from David, the one of whom the prophets had spoken. Was this he? Using Psalm 118:25 they cried, 'Hosanna!'. This might be a shout of praise, like 'Glory in the highest!', but Hosanna' was really a prayer, 'Save us now' 'Save us from highest heaven'. What did the people in the crowd mean? Perhaps, as usual with a crowd, some meant one thing and some another. At least this was the welcome He deserved – so different from the reception the religious leaders were planning for Him.

The welcoming crowds, the hostile leaders – what would

Jesus do in Jerusalem itself? Just then, nothing, as verse 11 says. He 'looked round at everything'. He saw all that was happening. Next day would be His time to take action.

Prayer *Psalm 24:7 is a fitting prayer of welcome to the Lord to the 'temple' of our lives today: 'Lift up your heads, O gates!...that the King of glory may come in.'*

For further thought and study 1. We can understand the hope of 'the kingdom...of David' and of the Davidic Messiah as we read such Old Testament passages as 2 Samuel 7:11–16, Psalm 89:4, 132:11, Isaiah 9:6–7, Jeremiah 23:5–6 and Ezekiel 37:24–25.

2. The idea behind Jesus riding an animal which had never been ridden before (verse 2), is probably that something to be used in God's special purposes should never have been used before. For this see Deuteronomy 15:19, 21:3 and 1 Samuel 6:7.

Notes 1. Parallels to this passage are Matthew 20:29—21:11 and Luke 18:35–43 and 19:28–40.

2. Usually the names of those for whom Jesus does His miracles are not given. Perhaps the name of Bartimaeus is given because he was well-known in the life of the early Church.

3. What Jesus says in verse 2 could be based on God-given knowledge of these things. On the other hand it may be that He had made arrangements before with the owners of the donkey, and now the disciples had their part in carrying out the plan.

All that we read earlier in this Gospel about the relationship between Jesus and the Jewish religious leaders has led up to the climax of which we now read. Jerusalem was the centre of the religious life of Israel – the 'holy city'; the temple was the 'holy place'. There Jesus challenged the religious leaders and they challenged Him. He challenged their use of the temple (11:15–17); for being unfruitful in God's service (12:1–11); for what they had done to God's messengers, down to John the Baptist (11:29–32); and for what they were thinking about the Messiah (12:35–37). They challenged His authority (11:27–28), and tried to catch Him with their hard questions (12:13–34).

He showed up the pride and selfishness of the scribes and their desire for the praise of other people and to get gain for themselves even at the expense of poor widows (12:38–40). Then in contrast He showed them a poor widow who had no desire to get, but rather gave all that she had to God (12:41–44).

We may subdivide this part of the Gospel into the following sections:

11:12–14   Cursing of the fig tree
11:15–19   Cleansing of the temple

Study 42: WHEN THE LORD COMES TO HIS TEMPLE

[12]On the following day, when they came from Bethany, he was hungry. [13]And seeing in the distance a fig tree in leaf, he went to see if he could find anything on it. When he came to it, he found nothing but leaves, for it was not the season for figs. [14]And he said to it, 'May no one ever eat fruit from you again.' And his disciples heard it.

[15]And they came to Jerusalem. And he entered the temple and began to drive out those who sold and those who bought in the temple, and he overturned the tables of the money-changers and the seats of those who sold pigeons; [16]and he would not allow anyone to carry anything through the temple. [17]And he taught, and said to them, 'Is it not written, "My house shall be called a house of prayer for all the nations"? But you have made it a den of robbers.' [18]And the chief priests and the scribes heard and sought a way to destroy him; for they feared him, because all the multitude was astonished at his teaching. [19]And when evening came they went out of the city.

[20]As they passed by in the morning, they saw the fig tree withered away to its roots. [21]And Peter remembered and

said to him, 'Master, look! The fig tree which you cursed has withered.' [22]And Jesus answered them, 'Have faith in God. [23]Truly, I say to you, whoever says to this mountain, "Be taken up and cast into the sea," and does not doubt in his heart, but believes that what he says will come to pass, it will be done for him. [24]Therefore I tell you, whatever you ask in prayer, believe that you have received it, and it will be yours. [25]And whenever you stand praying, forgive, if you have anything against any one; so that your Father also who is in heaven may forgive you your trespasses' (11:12–25).

In this section of the Gospel we have the record of what the Lord did in the temple in Jerusalem between the two parts of the story of what happened to a fig tree which had no fruit. The meaning of what Jesus did in the temple and the meaning of what happened to the fig tree belong together.

a. Unfruitful fig tree

It is easy to criticize what is said in verses 12–14 if we do not understand it as it was intended. Was it because Jesus was hungry that He was disappointed and angry, when he found no fruit on the fig tree? Since 'it was not the season for figs', should He have condemned the tree, and have said that no one should ever find fruit on the tree? But what Jesus did was an acted parable. Often the Old Testament speaks of Israel as a fig tree planted by God in the land He gave to them (Jeremiah 8:13). He expected fruit – the fruit of godly living, justice and kindness towards others (see Micah 7:1–6). Often He found no such fruit. There is a parable about an unfruitful fig tree in Luke 13:6–9. Now as Jesus saw this fig tree without fruit, He wanted to show that He had come to His people expecting to find fruit. Instead, what kind of conduct did He find as He came to Jerusalem and to the temple?

b. Misused temple

If the people of Israel, and their religious leaders had been fruitful in God's service, the temple would have been a true place of worship. But what did people find as they came from near and far to worship in the temple? The noise of bargaining and the dishonest dealing of the money-changers and those who sold pigeons for sacrifices. The Old Testament prophets had looked forward to Gentiles coming to know the one true God and to worshipping Him in the Jerusalem temple (see Isaiah 2:2–4). But any Gentiles who came would find the one part of the temple that they could enter (the Court of the Gentiles) made into a market. So when the Lord suddenly came to His temple (Malachi 3:1), He drove out those who were trading there. Quoting Isaiah 56:7, He said what was God's purpose: 'My house shall be called a house of prayer for all nations'. He said, too, what Jeremiah (7:11) had told the people of his time, 'you have made it a den of robbers'.

In a life full of acts of kindness and healing, the action of Jesus against the fig tree stands out and makes us think, just as His act of protest and judgment in the temple stands out. It was intended to make the leaders of the people think and take the warning.

c. Power in prayer

Mark goes on to tell us how the next morning after Jesus had driven the traders from the temple, the disciples 'saw the fig tree withered away to its roots' and they were surprised. The great lesson for them was about the way that God's people have become unfruitful in their lives and useless in the service of God. For all time it has a lesson to teach about faith.

The disciples should not have been surprised at what had happened. The word of Jesus is a word of power. God is always powerful to bring about what His word says (see Isaiah 55:11). If we pray for what we know (by His word) is God's will to give and His purpose to do, we know that He will answer. It may be a matter of moving a mountain of difficulty (verse 23). It may be something else. We can pray in faith when we know God's purpose. We should ask Him to show us His plan and purpose, and then pray with such confidence that we believe that we have received already what we ask for (verse 24).

God's work in us is hindered and we cannot truly pray if we do not forgive others. God is a forgiving God, and if we want fellowship in prayer with Him, we must forgive. So He taught His disciples to pray, 'forgive us...as we have forgiven others', and in Matthew 6:14–15 Jesus says, 'If you do not forgive men their trespasses, neither will your Father forgive your trespasses'.

Meditation *1 Corinthians 6:19 speaks of our individual lives as temples of God and 2 Corinthians 6:16 speaks of the fellowship of Christians as His temple. What things does the Lord need to drive out of His temple today?*

For further thought and study 1. Think about the New Testament teaching (a) about faith in prayer – see other passages like Hebrews 11, Matthew 17:20, Luke 17:5–6, James 1:5–8; (b) about forgiving others – see Matthew 6:12–15, 18:21–35, Luke 6:36–37, Ephesians 4:32, Colossians 3:13.

2. Does the action of Jesus in the temple support the actions of Christians today making public protests about things that are wrong in society? If so, what kind of public protests are right? and for what causes?

Notes 1. Parallels to this passage are found in Matthew 21:12–22 and Luke 19:45–48. There is a record of the 'cleansing of the temple' near the beginning of John's Gospel (2:13–22). Perhaps Jesus cleansed the temple twice; it may be, however, that John is not giving things in order ot time, but showing the meaning for Israel and for the world of the different things that the Lord did in the time of His ministry.

2. People have tried to explain in different ways the difficulties of verses 12–14, considering the time of the year that this may have taken place, such as the idea of small figs being formed before the main crop. As suggested above, however, we are probably wise to understand what happened as an enacted parable, a little like such actions of which we read in the Old Testament (see Jeremiah 19:1–13 and Ezekiel chapters 4 and 5). It is interesting also to read the words that speak about judgment on 'the trees of the field' (in Jeremiah 7:20) that follow what is quoted in verse 17 from Jeremiah 7:11.

3. In Jerusalem most of the markets where birds and animals were sold for sacrifice in the temple were on the Mount of Olives outside the city, but not long before this time a market had been allowed in the temple courts. Jews had to pay the temple tax in the Jewish money or that of Tyre; so, if they came from other countries, they would need to change their money. Jeremiah 17:27, Zechariah 14:21 and Malachi 3:1 help us to think what the action of Jesus in the temple would have meant to those who knew their Scriptures well.

4. The most recent translations of the Bible leave out verse 26 as not found in most of the oldest copies of the Gospel.

Study 43: WHOSE AUTHORITY?

[27] And they came again to Jerusalem. And as he was walking in the temple, the chief priests and the scribes and the elders came to him, [28] and they said to him, 'By what authority are you doing these things, or who gave you this authority to do them?' [29] Jesus said to them, 'I will ask you a question; answer me, and I will tell you by what authority I do these things. [30] Was the baptism of John from heaven or from men? Answer me.' [31] And they argued with one another, 'If we say "From heaven", he will say, "Why then did you not believe him?" [32] But shall we say, "From men"?' – they were afraid of the people, for all held that John was a real prophet. [33] So they answered Jesus, 'We do not know.' And

Jesus said to them, 'Neither will I tell you by what authority I do these things' (11:27–33).

A great deal is said in this Gospel about authority. In 1:22 it says how people 'were astonished at his teaching', because 'he taught them as one who had authority, and not as the scribes.' He also acted 'with authority' that made them 'all amazed' – even the evil spirits obeyed Him (1:27). He gave that same authority to His disciples (3:15 and 6:7). He acted with authority in the temple (verses 15–18) where the chief priests thought that they were the authorities.

a. Jewish leaders' question

Jesus 'was walking in the temple', acting freely and teaching in the temple courts where the rabbis often walked and talked with people (see Luke 20:1). All the Jewish leaders were challenged by what He said and did. So 'the chief priests and the scribes and the elders came to him.' They had one most important question to ask Him, 'By what authority are you doing these things, or who gave you this authority to do them?'

There are three kinds of authority that a person may have. It may be given to a person by others. Those who rule a country may give certain people authority to act as police, as judges, as officers in different government departments, or in the army. A Roman centurion (army officer) came to Jesus and said how he was 'a man under authority', under the authority of Roman rulers, and so could command those under him (Matthew 8:9). Second, a person may take authority, as in a military 'coup', and act as a self-chosen leader or dictator. Thirdly, a person may have authority from God, to speak His word and do His work. So it was with people like Moses and Joshua in Old Testament days, and with the prophets and prophetesses.

The Jewish religious leaders wanted no-one to teach or act in religious matters without their authority. So the question they put to Jesus was really, 'Why are you doing these things without our authority?'

b. Jesus' question

As He often did, Jesus answered a question with another question. His question, if they answered it properly, would have given the answer to theirs. Did John the Baptist, when he preached and baptized people, have authority from heaven (that is, from God) or from men? 'Answer me', Jesus said twice, as He challenged them. It *was* a challenge to them. They knew that they could not say 'from men', as it was clear that neither they nor any other person gave John authority. He came from the wilderness and preached with great power and sincerity. He had courage to rebuke sin even though he was imprisoned and put to death for doing so. The ordinary people with open minds saw that 'John was a real prophet'. Yet these Jewish leaders were not prepared to answer 'from heaven' because they had not been willing to accept and respond to his preaching.

If they had listened to John, they would have been prepared to accept the God-given authority of Jesus, for John had prepared people for the coming of Jesus (as we saw in 1:2–8). Like John, only far more, Jesus had spoken in truth and sincerity, and had acted without fear of people's opposition or desire for their favour.

b. No answer

The Jewish leaders could only answer, 'We do not know'. They were not willing to admit that they had been wrong not to accept John. They wanted to keep in favour with the people, and they wanted to keep their own position of power and authority. But those who 'love the praise of men more than the praise of God' (John 12:43) can never know the truth. By their unwillingness to answer the question about John they showed that they had no right to be called religious authorities in the nation.

Jesus gave no answer, but for a different reason. He knew that they had no desire for the truth. They were not willing to listen to it. There is a warning for people of every age and nation here. God shows His truth to those who are willing to receive it and act on it. If we are not willing to hear and to act on what we see is right, we will never know the truth.

Meditation *'If anyone wants to do God's will, he will know whether my teaching is from God, or whether I merely speak on my own authority'* (John 7:17, Phillips' translation).

For further thought and study 1. What can we learn from this Gospel about the authority of Jesus and of His disciples (see 1:22, 27; 2:10; 3:15 and 6:7)? In what ways can Christians speak and act with authority in the name of Christ today?

2. How may we be tempted today to speak what we know people will like to hear rather than with the truth?

Note. In the other Gospels Matthew 21:23–27 and Luke 20:1–8 are parallel to this passage. It is usually thought that Jesus was asked this question about His authority after His action in the temple. The Jewish leaders, however, may have been asking about Jesus' authority in all that He was teaching and doing.

Study 44: PARABLE OF THE VINEYARD

[1]And he began to speak to them in parables. 'A man planted a vineyard, and set a hedge around it, and dug a pit for the wine press, and built a tower, and let it out to tenants, and went into another country. [2]When the time came, he sent a servant to the tenants to get from them some of the fruit of the vineyard. [3]And they took him and beat him, and sent him away empty-handed. [4]Again he sent to them another servant, and they wounded him in the head, and treated him shamefully. [5]And he sent another, and him they killed; and

so with many others, some they beat and some they killed.
⁶He had still one other, a beloved son; finally he sent him to
them, saying, "They will respect my son." ⁷But those
tenants said to one another, "This is the heir; come, let us
kill him, and the inheritance will be ours." ⁸And they took
him and killed him, and cast him out of the vineyard. ⁹What
will the owner of the vineyard do? He will come and destroy
the tenants, and give the vineyard to others. ¹⁰Have you not
read this scripture:

"The very stone which the builders rejected
has become the head of the corner
¹¹this was the Lord's doing,
and it is marvellous in our eyes"?'
¹²And they tried to arrest him, but feared the multitude,
for they perceived that he had told the parable against them;
so they left him and went away   (12:1–12).

The chief priests and the scribes and the elders had
challenged Jesus with their question, 'By what authority
are you doing these things?' (11:27–28). Jesus challenged
them, as their prophets had often done, by speaking 'in
parables'. Often a parable has one main point and the
details may be part of the story and without special meaning. In this story many of the details could be seen as
meaningful, telling what the leaders of Israel had done in
the past and what they were doing. They could see 'that he
had told the parable against them' (verse 12).

a. Tenants of the vineyard

In the Old Testament there is a parable like this one in
Isaiah 5:1–7. The owner planted a vineyard, put a hedge
around it to protect it, installed a wine press where the
grapes were to be pressed and dug a pit for the juice. He
looked forward to good grapes and rich wine from the
vineyard. Isaiah said, 'Israel is the vineyard of the Lord
Almighty; the people of Judah are the vines he planted'
(Good News Bible). Often the Old Testament spoke of

Israel as God's vineyard or vine, planted by the Lord, protected by Him, and expected to be fruitful in living for Him. (See Psalms 80:8–11, and compare also what we have seen in the description of Israel as a fig tree in Study 42.)

This parable, however, has differences from the one in Isaiah. As often happened with vineyards in the Jordan Valley and in Galilee in the time of Jesus, the owner left tenants in charge of his vineyard. Their work was to look after the vineyard. They could keep part of the fruit for themselves as payment for their work. The other part of the grapes and the wine they had to give each year to the owner when he sent his servants for it.

b. Servants and son

The first servant whom the owner sent the tenants beat and sent away without any of the fruit of the vineyard. A second 'they wounded... in the head, and treated him shamefully.' Others they beat or killed. The Jewish leaders who listened to Jesus and who knew all that the Old Testament said about Israel as God's vineyard understood well what Jesus was saying. Stephen, the martyr, later said (in Acts 7:52), 'Which of the prophets did not your fathers persecute?' Jesus said the same thing in His parable.

The owner of the vineyard tried once more to bring the tenants to act rightly. 'He had still one other' whom he could send, 'a beloved son'. Surely they would respect his son! But the tenants thought that if they killed him, they could do what they liked in the vineyard. The Jewish leaders could hardly fail to see what Jesus meant as they were planning to kill Him (see 11:18).

c. End of the story

What kind of treatment did the tenants of the vineyard deserve? Jesus asked, 'What will the owner of the vineyard do?' Anyone with a mind for justice could only say. 'He will come and destroy the tenants and give the vineyard to others.'

But what about the Son? The greatest interest in the story is what happened to the Son. The leaders of Israel rejected and killed Him, but the words of Psalm 118:22 are true: 'The very stone which the builders rejected has become the head of the corner.' It has been thought that when the temple was built, one great stone that seemed of no use was set aside by the builders. Later it was found useful as the cornerstone of the whole building. Psalm 118 speaks of a person, rejected like that, who becomes more important than all others. This was supremely true of Jesus, and the early Christians loved to use the words of Psalm 118 to speak of Him (see Acts 4:11 and 1 Peter 2:7). What happened to Him 'was the Lord's doing and it is marvellous in our eyes.'

Meditation   *Use Philippians 2:5–11 as you think over this parable.*

For further thought and study   1. For accounts of the way that God's servants were persecuted in Old Testament days see 1 Kings 18:13, 19:1–2, 22:26–27, 2 Chronicles 24:20–22, 36:15–16, Nehemiah 9:26, Jeremiah 25:3–7, 37:11–21, 38:1–13, Amos 7:10–13.

2. The parable speaks of the vineyard being given to others (verse 9). Consider how in Romans chapters 9 to 11 Paul applies this to the offer to Gentile (non-Jewish) people of the privileges of being God's people; at the same time it emphasises that whoever we are, of whatever race, our privileges are by God's grace and not because we deserve them.

Note   Both Matthew (21:33–46) and Luke (20:9–19) have this parable, closely similar to its words here in Mark.

Study 45: SHOULD WE PAY TAXES

¹³And they sent to him some of the Pharisees and some of the Herodians, to entrap him in his talk. ¹⁴And they came and said to him, 'Teacher, we know that you are true, and care for no man; for you do not regard the position of men but truly teach the way of God. Is it lawful to pay taxes to Caesar, or not? ¹⁵Should we pay them, or should we not?' But knowing their hypocrisy, he said to them, 'Why put me to the test? Bring me a coin, and let me look at it.' ¹⁶And they brought one. And he said to them, 'Whose likeness and inscription is this?' They said to him, 'Caesar's.' ¹⁷Jesus said to them, 'Render to Caesar the things that are Caesar's, and to God the things that are God's'. And they were amazed at him (12:13–17).

In this chapter of Mark we now have three questions put to Jesus (verses 13–34), and one that He asked as He taught in the temple (verses 35–37). The first was planned by those who wanted to 'entrap him in his talk'.

a. Question

Two groups of people were sent together to try to trap Jesus with their question, the Pharisees and the Herodians (see 3:6 and Note 2 on Study 12). The Pharisees, as we have seen, were very religious people, and had no pleasure in the rule of the Romans. The Herodians supported the rule of the Herods who held power only because the Romans allowed them to do so. Pharisees and Herodians together asked this question, 'Is it lawful to pay taxes to Caesar or not?' He could not please both by this reply. If He said 'Yes', the Pharisees could show that He was against the freedom and independence of the Jewish people. If He said 'No', the Herodians would be displeased, and His reply could be used against him before the Roman authorities. (Luke 23:2 shows that His reply was used against Him, but unjustly.) Jesus' enemies were determined to get a 'Yes' or 'No' answer from Him. They said, 'Teacher, we know you are an honest man. You don't worry about what people think, because you pay no attention to what a man seems to be, but you teach the truth about God's will for man' (verse 14, Good News Bible). They thought His answer to them must be 'Yes' or 'No'. 'Should we pay...or not?'

b. Answer

Jesus saw their trick and how they were trying to catch Him. He had an answer far wiser than they thought. He asked them to bring to Him the Roman coin that was called the 'denarius'. It had the value of a day's wages for a labourer (see Matthew 20:2). Every adult citizen had to pay at least one denarius as tax to Rome. On the coin was the picture of the Roman emperor and writing that spoke of him. So when Jesus asked 'Whose likeness and inscription' was on the coin, they said immediately 'Caesar's'. A country's coins often show who rules in the country. The coins with the head of Caesar, the Roman emperor, showed that Rome ruled Palestine. Jesus said, 'Well, then, pay to the Emperor what belongs to him, and pay to God what belongs to God' (verse 17, Good News Bible).

What did Jesus' answer mean and what does it say to us today?

1. There is a duty to pay taxes to those who rule our country and provide our roads and many other things for us.

2. The greatest of all our duties is to give to God what belongs to Him, the service of our lives.

3. Jesus showed by His answer that He was not trying to overthrow the power of Rome. He had a more important work to do in bringing people to accept the kingdom of God, God's rule over them.

4. At the same time, if Caesar or any political ruler asks of us that loyalty, worship and service that are due only to God, we are right to say 'No'. That was the case for some Christians for whom Mark wrote, and often in many countries since.

There was such wisdom in the reply Jesus gave – able to be applied to all our different political situations – we can understand that people 'were amazed at him'.

Meditation *The coin had the image of the Roman emperor on it – to him it belonged. We are made in the image of God (Genesis 1:26–27); to Him we belong, and we only have true life when we are under His loving rule.*

For further thought and study What do Romans 13:1–7, Titus 3:1 and 1 Peter 2:13–17 teach about the attitude of Christians to Government? The Book of Revelation shows a different attitude as it was written at a time when Rome (called Babylon in Revelation) persecuted Christians and called on them to worship the emperor (See especially Revelation 17.) What should Christians do when there is injustice or corruption in the political life of their community?

Notes 1. Matthew 22:15–22 and Luke 20:20–26 are parallels to these verses in Mark.
2. When they said that Jesus 'cares for no man' and 'does not regard the position of men', it means that He did not think rich or powerful people are more important than the poor and the weak. The Bible often shows that this is the attitude of God and it should always be the attitude of Christians. See Acts 10:34 and James 2:9.

Study 46: QUESTION ABOUT THE RESURRECTION

[18]And Sadducees came to him, who say that there is no resurrection; and they asked him a question, saying, [19]'Teacher, Moses wrote for us that if a man's brother dies and leaves a wife, but leaves no child, the man must take the wife, and raise up children for his brother. [20]There were seven brothers; the first took a wife, and when he died left no

children; [21]and the second took her, and died, leaving no children; and the third likewise; [22]and the seven left no children. Last of all the woman also died. [23]In the resurrection whose wife will she be? for the seven had her as wife.'

[24]Jesus said to them, 'Is not this why you are wrong, that you know neither the scriptures nor the power of God? [25]For when they rise from the dead, they neither marry nor are given in marriage, but are like angels in heaven. [26]And as for the dead being raised, have you not read in the book of Moses, in the passage about the bush, how God said to him, "I am the God of Abraham, and the God of Isaac, and the God of Jacob"? [27]He is not God of the dead, but of the living; you are quite wrong' (12:18–27).

The next question of which Mark tells us was one that the Sadducees put to Jesus. This is the first time the Sadducees have been mentioned in the Gospel. They were a party most of whose members came from high priestly families and other leading families of Jerusalem. The majority of them were rich and powerful. Mark tells us that they did not believe in a resurrection to life after death (see also Acts 4:1–2, 5:17–26 and 23:6–8). This prepares us for the question they asked Jesus.

a. Question

In order to understand their question we need to understand something of Jewish law and custom which in this case was closer to African culture than western culture. The Old Testament Mosaic Law (in Deuteronomy 25:5–6) said that if a man died leaving his wife a widow without a child, the man's brother should take the widow as his wife. She would then have the protection of a husband and, as husband, he would 'raise up children for his brother', so that there would be a succession to him in his family and his land.

In the story that the Sadducees told (verses 20–22) there were seven brothers, each of whom in turn had the one woman as his wife, but none had children by her. In the end the wife died. 'In the resurrection whose wife will she be?' they asked. To them that was a hard question. They thought it must be hard for God, too! Therefore there could not be any resurrection! People have often been foolish like that. Because there are things that they do not understand about the resurrection of Jesus, or because there are things that they cannot imagine about life after death, they say that there cannot be any resurrection.

b. Answer

Jesus told the Sadducees that they were wrong in their thinking because they knew 'neither the scriptures nor the power of God'. As far as the power of God was concerned, they needed to realize that God is able to make the future life very different from the present life. A person rises from the dead not to a body of flesh and blood as we have now, and so not to sexual relationships, marriage and giving in marriage. It is rather a life like that of 'angels in heaven'. We may not be able to say much about that life, but it will be free from sin and suffering, and (above all) will 'be with Christ', which, as the apostle Paul put it, is 'far better' than the present life (see Philippians 1:21–23).

Although there are not many things that the Old Testament says directly about life after death, there is enough for us to be sure that life does not end with the death of these earthly bodies of ours. Jesus turned the Sadducees to that passage in the Law that tells how God met with Moses in the burning bush (Exodus 3:1–6), and said to him, 'I am the God of Abraham, and the God of Isaac, and the God of Jacob.' If God calls Abraham and Isaac and Jacob His people, then He will not leave them when they come to die. They are still in His hands. This – together with the resurrection of Jesus Himself – gives us strong reason for believing in life after death. Because God has loved us, and we know through Jesus Christ that love and purpose of God, we can say that neither death nor anything else can separate us from that love (Romans 8:35–39). Or, to put it as John 17:3 puts it, to know God through Jesus *is* eternal life.

Meditation *'What no one ever saw or heard, what no one ever thought could happen, is the very thing God prepared for those who love him.'* (1 Corinthians 2:9).

For further thought and study 1. What else does the New Testament say about life beyond death, in such passages as 1 Corinthians 15:35–37, 2 Corinthians 4:16–5:5, Revelation 7:9–17 and 22:1–5? (We need to realize that the Bible can only speak of that future life in words and pictures that we can understand from this life. That life will be more wonderful than all these descriptions of it.)

2. What difference should belief in the resurrection mean to our lives? See 1 Corinthians 15 (especially the last verse of the chapter), 1 Thessalonians 4:13–14 and 1 John 3:1–3.

Notes 1. There are close parallels to these verses in Matthew 22:23–33 and Luke 20:27–40.

2. The Sadducees accepted the authority of the books of the Law but did not accept other Old Testament books in the same way. So they did not accept the clear teaching of the resurrrection in such a passage as Daniel 12:2–3. It is interesting to note that Jesus in His answer to them uses a passage from the Law.

3. With regard to the way that the Jews thought of levirate marriage (that is, marrying a brother's widow), the most important relationship was between the man and his first wife.

Study 47: A SCRIBE'S QUESTION AND A QUESTION FOR THE SCRIBES

²⁸**And one of the scribes came up and heard them disputing with one another, and seeing that he answered them well,**

asked him, 'Which commandment is the first of all?' ²⁹Jesus answered, 'The first is, "Hear O Israel: The Lord our God, the Lord is one; ³⁰and you shall love the Lord your God with all your heart, and with all your soul, and with all your mind, and with all your strength." ³¹The second is this, "You shall love your neighbour as yourself." There is no other commandment greater than these.' ³²And the scribe said to him, 'You are right, Teacher; you have truly said that he is one, and there is no other but he; ³³and to love him with all the heart, and with all the understanding, and with all the strength, and to love one's neighbour as oneself, is much more than all whole burnt offerings and sacrifices.' ³⁴And when Jesus saw that he answered wisely, he said to him, 'You are not far from the kingdom of God.' And after that no one dared to ask him any question.

³⁵And as Jesus taught in the temple, he said, 'How can the scribes say that the Christ is the son of David? ³⁶David himself, inspired by the Holy Spirit, declared,

"The Lord said to my lord,

Sit at my right hand,

till I put thy enemies under thy feet."

³⁷David himself calls him Lord; so how is he his son?' and the great throng heard him gladly   (12:28–37).

We read in the Gospels many things that the Lord said in criticism of the scribes, especially when by making many little rules they lost the main purpose and spirit of God's law. We are to read more of His criticism in verses 38–40. There were, however, good and sincere scribes. Such a man is the scribe who came to Jesus with this question here.

a. Which is the greatest commandment

The Jewish people, especially their teachers, often discussed and debated this question, 'Which commandment is the first of all?' They also asked which were greater commandments and which were less important. They said that there were 613 commandments in the Law – 365 told people what they should not do (one for each day of the year!), and 248 told people what they should do. But which of all these was the most important?

Jesus said that the first was certainly to love God with heart, soul, mind and strength. He used the words of Deuteronomy 6:4–5 which the Jews thought to be so important that they bound them on their heads and between their eyes and put them in little boxes by their door posts (following literally what Deuteronomy 6:8–9 says), and they read them at the beginning of services in their synagogues. But the Lord did not stop with this as the first and greatest commandment. He put with it the words of Leviticus 19:18, 'You shall love your neighbour as yourself.' We realize that these two together sum up all that we can say, or that the Law could say, about our duty to God and our duty to other people. We should notice from the words of Jesus that loving God stands first; we cannot rightly think of our duty to others without wanting to love and serve God above everything else. Then we have to realize that we cannot properly serve God and love Him unless we love others (see 1 John 4:20–21).

The scribe accepted the answer of Jesus, and he added what the Old Testament prophets often said, that to love God whole-heartedly was more important than all sacrifices (see Isaiah 1:11–17, Hosea 6:6, Amos 5:21–24 and Micah 6:6–8). We can say that for us it is more important than all religious observances.

b. How great is the Messiah

The Jews not only debated which was the greatest commandment in the Law, they often discussed questions about the Messiah whom they expected. It may have been in such a discussion that Jesus put the question about the teaching that the scribes gave about the Messiah. Following much that the Old Testament said, the scribes taught that the Messiah (the Christ) would be the 'son of David'. (See the prophet Nathan's words to David in 2 Samuel 7:12–16 and see Psalm 132:11–12.) That could mean that he would be a king like David, another David coming to rule his people as David had done (see Ezekiel 37:24–25). But the Messiah would be greater than that. He would do greater work, win greater victories and bring true peace to His people (see Isaiah 9:6–7 and Jeremiah 23:5–6). In Psalm 110:1 he is addressed as 'Lord'. So Jesus' question is, 'Is it enough to call the Messiah 'son of David' when he is also David's Lord?' Notice that in asking this question Jesus did not openly say that He was the Christ, as He did later in His trial (14:61–62). He simply wanted people to think, How great is the Messiah whom we hope for? What will be the work that he will do?

At the end of these two sections we see the effect of His teaching on those who listened to Him. He spoke in such a way that the ordinary people could understand and appreciate what He said, and so they 'heard him gladly' (verse 37). His wisdom was so great in His answers to questions, even questions that were meant to trap Him, that 'after that no one dared to ask him any question' (verse 34).

Prayer *Lord Almighty, the one true God over all, help us to love and to serve You with all that we have and are; and by Your Spirit fill us with love for all around us, for Your great name's sake.* AMEN.

For further thought and study 1. The words of verses 29–33 leave us with many practical questions: in our daily lives what does it mean for us to love God with all our *hearts*, with all our *minds,* with all our *strength*? How do we *link* love for God and love for other people? How do we answer the question, *Who* is my neighbour I should love as much as myself? Do I love myself – too little or too much? Am I tempted to put religious observance above love for God and for others?

2. What do you think Jesus meant when He said to the scribe, 'You are not far from the kingdom of God'?

Notes 1. Matthew 22:34–46 is parallel to this passage and Luke 20:41–44 to verses 35–37. Notice the way that these two great commandments are linked in Luke 10:25–28.

2. The most important thing abut Psalm 110 is not who the person was who wrote it, but that its words were inspired by the Spirit of God; and they speak of One who would be Priest and King, Lord and Conqueror.

Study 48: GETTING AND GIVING

[38]And in his teaching he said, 'Beware of the scribes, who like to go about in long robes, and to have salutations in the market places [39]and the best seats in the synagogues and the places of honour at feasts, [40]who devour widows' houses and for a pretence make long prayers. They will receive the greater condemnation.'

[41]And he sat down opposite the treasury, and watched the multitude putting money into the treasury. Many rich people put in large sums. [42]And a poor widow came, and put in two copper coins, which make a penny. [43]And he called his disciples to him, and said to them, 'Truly, I say to you, this poor widow has put in more than all those who are contributing to the treasury. [44]For they all contributed out of their abundance; but she out of her poverty has put in everything she had, her whole living' (12:38–44).

Often the Bible puts side by side the two different ways that we can follow in life. In this reading we have side by side the unpleasant picture of religious pride and the beautiful picture of generous, sacrificial giving.

a. Getting as much as possible

In verses 28–34 we read of the sincere question of a scribe, 'Which commandment is the first of all?' He accepted – as many of the scribes would have done – the answer that Jesus gave. 'Love God with all your heart and soul and mind and strength, and love your neighbour as yourself.' The scribes who taught such things to others should have tried most of all to live by them themselves. Many of them, however, instead of seeking to love and praise God, wanted people to praise them; instead of showing love for others, they wanted to get all that they could from other people. When Jesus said, 'beware of the scribes', He meant, 'Do not be like them'. He spoke of six things that they did.

1. They loved to walk around in long robes. Jewish priests and scribes wore long white robes. In Matthew 23:5 Jesus spoke of those who made the fringes of their robes long so that people would think them especially religious.

2. They liked people to greet them in the market place giving them titles of honour like rabbi (meaning, 'my great one'), father, master, (see Matthew 23:7–12).

3. They liked to have 'the best seats in the synagogues'; these were at the front near the great box that held the Scriptures, and faced the people so that everyone could see them.

4. They liked to have 'places of honour at feasts' when people were seated in order of importance. Read the words of Jesus about this in Luke 14:7–11.

5. When Jesus said that they 'devour widows' houses', it probably means that they accepted and encouraged gifts from widows who were much poorer than they were, although the Law said a great deal about caring for the widows and the fatherless (e.g. see Exodus 22:22–24 and Deuteronomy 24:17–22).

6. They made long prayers, not in sincerity but 'for a pretence', not to be heard by God but to be heard by other people, so that people would think them very holy.

All kinds of pride are displeasing to God and unpleasant in the eyes of other people, but religious pride most of all. All who profess to be Christians, and especially Christian ministers, need to beware of this temptation.

b. Giving as much as possible

In verses 41–44 we have a very different picture. If any one sat down, as Jesus did, by the 'treasury' with its 13 trumpet-shaped boxes for the gifts of the people, he or she would have seen the rich bringing great gifts. We are told that when people brought their gifts, they had to say to the priests the amount of their gift and what was its purpose. We can imagine some telling with a loud voice what they were giving and why they were giving it. Everyone would notice such rich people, but Jesus noticed someone else, and He called His disciples to come and see her (compare His calling His disciples aside for special teaching in 8:1 and 10:42). She was a widow who lived in great poverty. She brought to the treasury two of the smallest coins there were; 128 of these coins made up the denarius of which we read in verse 15 and which was the amount of a labourer's daily wage. She could have given just one of her two coins and kept one for her own needs, but she gave them both. That was everything that she had. 'Truly I say to you', Jesus said, 'this poor widow has put in more than all the others'. Jesus saw *how* people gave their gifts. God sees not only how much we give, but how much we keep for ourselves, and He sees the spirit of our giving.

One of the most unpleasant sights in the world is a proud person who thinks himself or herself important and wants everyone else to think so too. But one of the most beautiful sights is a generous and sacrificial gift. The Bible speaks of such a gift as being like a lovely fragrance (see Ephesians 5:2 and Philippians 4:18). Often those who are poor teach the rich a lesson in generous giving.

Meditation *Which am I more like in my character and actions – the scribes who are described in verses 38–40 or the widow who is described in verses 42–44?*

For further thought and study 1. With verses 38–40 compare the words of Jesus in Matthew 23:1–12. In what ways are Christians today tempted to make a show of their faith out of spiritual pride?

2. The scribes had special responsibility because they were religious leaders. Note the warnings to those who are religious leaders in Romans 2:1–3, James 3:1 and the end of Luke 12:48. What does 1 Peter 5:1–6 say is the way for Christian ministers to follow?

3. Along with verses 42–44, see what is said about generous giving in 2 Corinthians chapters 8 and 9 and Philippians 4:14–20.

Note   Luke 20:45—21:4 is parallel to these verses (see also Luke 11:43); Matthew 23:5–7 has teaching the same as verses 38–40.

TEACHING ABOUT THE FUTURE

Mark 13:1–37

Chapter 4 brought together a number of the parables that Jesus taught. Now this chapter brings together things that Jesus taught about the future. It might seem to cause a break in the record of the last days of the earthly life of Jesus, but in at least two ways we can see the importance of this teaching being placed where it is in the Gospel. First, you will remember that the record of the Transfiguration of Jesus came immediately after Jesus had said how He must suffer and die. Similarly, in the midst of the opposition of the Jewish leaders, there now comes the clear teaching of His triumph and the confidence the disciples could have in the face of great trials and suffering. Second, there was a connection between the rejection of Jesus by the Jewish leaders, and the judgment that would come on their city and their temple.

The Book of Daniel and other parts of the Old Testament, as well as later Jewish writings have been called 'apocalyptic' writing. In apocalyptic writing it is emphasized that God will break into our human history, show His great power, and bring an end to injustice, persecution and opposition to His rule. This chapter has been called 'the little Apocalypse'; as the Book of Revelation at the end of the New Testament has been called 'the Apocalypse'; but this chapter is not quite the same as other apocalyptic writings. The chapter has also been compared with the farewell addresses of people like Moses, Joshua, Samuel and David; it has been described as our Lord's 'farewell address' to His disciples; but that does not quite describe what it is either. So it is difficult to describe it accurately.

However, the great purpose of Jesus is to tell the disciples of the things which they must be prepared to face:

1. Fall of Jerusalem and the destruction of the temple.

2. Great troubles in the world – wars, famines, earthquakes.

3. False teachers and false Christs who will try to deceive people.

4. Suffering and persecution which will come to them as His disciples.

5. Final coming again of Jesus in great power and glory.

These things must be, but the disciples are told that they will not know the time. So they must always be watchful – the words 'watch', 'take heed', ring out often in this chapter. Disciples have work to do, to take the good news to all nations (verse 10). They have the promise of the Holy Spirit who will always help them in the trials they face (verse 11). They must watch, work on, and be ready for the Master when He comes.

We may divide this chapter into six main sections:

13:1–8	Fall of Jerusalem and future wars and troubles
13:9–13	Mission in the face of persecution
13:14–23	The 'desolating sacrilege', false prophets and false Christs
13:24–27	Son of man coming in glory
13:28–31	Parable of the fig tree
13:32–37	Most important instruction: 'Watch'.

Study 49: FUTURE TRIALS AND TROUBLES

¹And as he came out of the temple, one of his disciples said to him, 'Look, Teacher, what wonderful stones and what wonderful buildings!' ²And Jesus said to him, 'Do you see these great buildings? There will not be left here one stone upon another that will not be thrown down.'

³And as he sat on the Mount of Olives opposite the temple, Peter and James and John and Andrew asked him privately, ⁴'Tell us, when will this be, and what will be the sign when these things are all to be accomplished?' ⁵And Jesus began to say to them, 'Take heed that no one leads you astray. ⁶Many will come in my name, saying, "I am he!" and they will lead many astray. ⁷And when you hear of wars and rumours of wars, do not be alarmed; this must take place, but the end is not yet. ⁸For nation will rise against nation, and kingdom against kingdom; there will be earthquakes in various places, there will be famines; this is but the beginning of the birth-pangs.

⁹But take heed to yourselves; for they will deliver you up to councils; and you will be beaten in synagogues; and you will stand before governors and kings for my sake, to bear testimony before them. ¹⁰And the gospel must first be preached to all nations. ¹¹And when they bring you to trial and deliver you up, do not be anxious beforehand what you are to say; but say whatever is given you in that hour, for it is not you who speak, but the Holy Spirit. ¹²And brother will deliver up brother to death, and the father his child, and children will rise against parents and have them put to death; ¹³and you will be hated by all for my name's sake. But he who endures to the end will be saved' (13:1–13).

Jesus and His disciples were near the temple. 'What a wonderful building!' they exclaimed. Much of it was in white marble, decorated with gold. 'What wonderful stones!' Some of the stones were 40 feet long and 18 feet wide (12 meters by 5). Every Jew took great pride in the holy city of Jerusalem and the temple as the holy place. Yet it was only truly the holy place if people worshipped God from their hearts and served Him in their lives. As the prophets in the Old Testament had declared (see Jeremiah 7:1–15), Jesus had to warn that it was no use boasting in 'the temple of the Lord' if their hearts were far from God. So in these verses Jesus speaks about the future of the temple, the future of the world, and the future for His disciples.

a. Future of the temple

Jesus said that the beautiful buildings of the temple would be destroyed and there would not be left one stone on another (verse 2). The people had rejected the way of peace and salvation that He came to bring (see Luke 13:34–35 and 19:41–44). Jesus had more to say about Jerusalem and the temple (from verse 14), but the question in the disciples' minds was, 'When will this be?' People often ask that kind of question, but God does not set out the future for us like a map, to tell us all that will happen and when it will take place. He wants us to walk by faith and not by sight (2 Corinthians 5:7). What He does say about the future in this chapter is 'watch out', 'be careful', 'Take heed that no one leads you astray' (verse 5). People will come making great claims for themselves (verse 6). Do not be deceived. There are, however, some things that Jesus does say about the future in answer to the disciples' questions.

b. Future of the world

Christian people are in a strange position as they think about the world and about the future. We are to work to bring God's truth, God's peace, God's justice, God's righteousness, into every part of life. We are to work, hope and pray for God's rule in the world. At the same time we have to face the fact that as long as this life lasts and the world remains, until God again breaks into our history, there will be great conflict between good and evil, and wars between peoples and nations. There will also be troubles and disasters, earthquakes and famines (verse 8). Life here will never be easy. But notice that Jesus says that these troubles are like 'the beginning of the birth-pangs', like the pain a woman suffers before her child is born. Out of the troubles and suffering of the present time a new age will be born. This time of sin, injustice and persecution will not last for ever. There will be an end – but Christians must always beware of thinking that they know the time of the end. All that Jesus teaches in this chapter is that we must at all times be ready for the end and for His coming, but at all times we are to do quietly and faithfully the work that He has given us.

c. Future for disciples

It is especially important for those who are disciples to realize what they must be ready to face in the world. Although they are peacemakers and messengers of a gospel of peace, they will face opposition and persecution. Those first disciples of Jesus were Jews and they were opposed by Jewish councils and beaten in synagogues. Later Christians would be put on trial before Gentile governors. Disciples must try to live in love and harmony in their families, but sometimes (as the Old Testament said in Micah 7:6) they would face opposition from those nearest and dearest to them. It happened in the early years of the Church, and it has often happened since.

There are three positive things, however, for Christians always to remember:

1. We are called to remain faithful and to 'endure to the end' whatever happens. As someone has put it, 'the true quality of a Christian's life will be seen only at the end.'

2. The power of the Spirit of God is given to us to help us to endure; and, in particular, when we stand on trial for our faith before those who do not believe He will give us words to speak, as God has always given to those who have been His willing messengers (Jeremiah 1:9 and Ezekiel 33:22).

3. We have one great task to do, to see that His good news goes out to all nations (verse 10).

Meditation *As you have read here the disciples' question 'When?' in verse 4 and Jesus' answer, think over the question asked and the answer given in Acts 1:6–8.*

For further thought and study 1. How does the Acts of the Apostles show the fulfilment of the words of verse 9? See especially Acts 4:1–22, 5:17–33, 16:19–24 and chapters 22–26. What more recent examples of this do you know?

2. What main principles should guide Christian people in their attitude to the future?

Notes 1. See the parallels to these verses in Matthew 24:1–14 and Luke 21:5–19 and see also the similar teaching in Matthew 10:17–22 and Luke 12:11–12.

2. Verse 6 may mean that people would come claiming to be Messiah or claiming to be Jesus come again (for such claims see Acts 5:36–37, 2 Thessalonians 2:1–2 and 1 John 2:18–19).

3. When Jesus spoke about the future, as He does in these verses, He often spoke as the Old Testament prophets had spoken (e.g. about wars and troubles and comparing them to the pains of a woman giving birth to a child). Because the Old Testament had spoken in these ways, those who listened to Him would have understood well His teaching.

Study 50: DISTRESS OF JERUSALEM

[14]**"But when you see the desolating sacrilege set up where it ought not to be (let the reader understand), then let those who are in Judea flee to the mountains;** [15]**let him who is on the housetop not go down, or enter his house, to take anything away;** [16]**and let him who is in the field not turn back to take his mantle.** [17]**And alas for those who are with child and for those who give suck in those days!** [18]**Pray that it may not happen in winter.** [19]**For in those days there will be such tribulation as has not been from the beginning of the creation**

which God created until now, and never will be. [20]And if the Lord had not shortened the days, no human being would be saved; but for the sake of the elect, whom he chose, he shortened the days. [21]And then if any one says to you "Look, here is the Christ!" or "Look, there he is!" do not believe it. [22]False Christs and false prophets will arise and show signs and wonders, to lead astray, if possible, the elect. [23]But take heed; I have told you all things beforehand' (13:14–23).

The first disciples of Jesus were Jews and had to be warned of the terrible things that would happen to their temple and to their city. Such a warning of future trials and troubles can apply to all Christians whatever their race.

a. Terrible things for the temple

The words of verse 14 speak of what would happen in the temple in Jerusalem. 'Let the reader understand', that verse says. In order to understand we need to read Daniel 9:27, 11:31 and 12:11. All of these verses speak of 'the desolating sacrilege', as our translation puts it, or 'the abomination that causes desolation' (New International Bible). Any idol that took the place of God in people's lives and worship was called an 'abomination' or 'sacrilege' in the Old Testament. It was the most terrible thing for such an 'abomination' to be put in the temple of God in Jerusalem. It would make it no longer a holy place, but desolate. In the year 168 BC this happened when Antiochus Epiphanes set up a heathen altar over the altar of sacrifice in the temple. That had happened 200 years before Jesus spoke. He warned that it would happen again. In the time of the early Church, the Roman Emperor, Caligula, said he would set up his own statue in the temple, but he died in 41 AD before he could do this. The fulfilment came when the Romans fought against the Jews in the years 66 to 70 AD. The desolation of the temple was a warning of what would follow – the destruction of Jerusalem.

b. Terrible things for Jerusalem

This warning was given so that people should escape from the city before the troubles of its siege. Many of the Christians did heed this warning and went to a place called Pella on the other side of the river Jordan. It would be a time of such danger that action should be taken immediately. There would be no time to go back into one's home to take extra things or warm clothes. It would be specially hard for pregnant women or those with little children to care for, and if it were winter time when there would be no food in the fields for the people as they took flight. Terrible things did indeed happen when Jerusalem was under siege. The Jewish historian Josephus tells about the famine in the city and how people ate old hay, chewed pieces of leather and even killed and ate their own children. Great numbers of the people died before the Romans finally took the city. Many certainly felt it to be 'such tribulation as had not been from the beginning of the creation' (verse 19).

c. Warning about the future

It is hard to be sure where the words about the temple and about Jerusalem end. There are things that apply to what people later would face and to what Christians often since have experienced. Many troubles have come on the world in times of war. Many persecutions have come to Christians. We cannot expect to be free from facing great trials. But we are given the promise that such troubles will not go on and on. God has 'shortened the days'. Our troubles will never be beyond our power to endure – in His strength. But again the warning is given – in verses 21–22 as in verses 5–6 – there will be those who will try to lead us astray by making claims to be prophets or to be Christ Himself. Jesus says, 'take heed', 'be careful' (verse 23, as in verses 5 and 9). He has spoken of such things 'beforehand', not to give us a map of future events, but so that we may be ready to face whatever comes in the power of God's unfailing presence with us.

Prayer   *Pray for all those who live under conditions of war or conflict, danger or persecution.*

For further thought and study   1. With verse 20 compare what 1 Corinthians 10:13 says of the trials not being too great for us. What do Job 1:6–12 and 2:1–6 show us about human suffering?

2. Verse 22 speaks of those who are not truly God's servants and messengers yet being able to do 'signs and wonders'. What warning does this give us? See also Deuteronomy 13:1–4, 2 Thessalonians 2:8–12 and 1 Timothy 4:1–3.

Notes   1. Matthew 24:15–26 is closely parallel to these verses and Luke 21:20–24 speaks of Jerusalem 'surrounded by armies' and 'trodden down by the Gentiles'.

2. The Palestinian 'housetop' (verse 15) was the flat roof used often when a person wanted to meditate quietly alone (Acts 10:9) or when people wanted to talk together, to watch out for someone coming (Isaiah 22:1) or to announce news (Matthew 10:27). There were stairs up to it from the outside.

Study 51: CHRIST'S COMING IN POWER

²⁴'But in those days, after that tribulation, the sun will be darkened, and the moon will not give its light, ²⁵and the stars will be falling from heaven, and the powers in the heavens will be shaken. ²⁶And then they will see the Son of man coming in clouds with great power and glory. ²⁷And then he will send out the angels, and gather his elect from the four winds, from the ends of the earth to the ends of heaven.

²⁸'From the fig tree learn its lesson: as soon as its branch becomes tender and puts forth its leaves, you know that summer is near. ²⁹So also, when you see these things taking place, you know that he is near, at the very gates. ³⁰Truly, I

say to you, this generation will not pass away before all these things take place. ³¹Heaven and earth will pass away, but my words will not pass away.

³²'But of that day or that hour no one knows, not even the angels in heaven, nor the Son, but only the Father. ³³Take heed, watch; for you do not know when the time will come. ³⁴It is like a man going on a journey, when he leaves home and puts his servants in charge, each with his work, and commands the doorkeeper to be on the watch. ³⁵Watch therefore – for you do not know when the master of the house will come, in the evening, or at mid-night, or at cockcrow, or in the morning – ³⁶lest he come suddenly and find you asleep. ³⁷And what I say to you I say to all: Watch' (13:24–37).

This last part of chapter 13 leads on from the things that would happen in the years 66–70 AD, past times of war, earthquake and famine and the persecution of Christians to the great future event in the world's history – when Jesus will come again. There are many things that we cannot know about how this will be, but three things are said in these verses.

a. All creation will proclaim it

Verses 24–25 use words from the Old Testament to say that there will be signs in sun and moon and stars (see Isaiah 13:10, 34:4, Ezekiel 32:7 and Joel 2:10). When Jesus first came into our world, He came in humility and simplicity, born of a Jewish mother in a stable at Bethlehem. He will come again but 'with great power and glory'. Jesus uses the words of Daniel 7:13 (about 'one like a son of man' coming 'with the clouds of heaven') to speak of this, as He does again in His trial before the high priest (in 14:62). All will see and know His coming – there will be no mistaking it (see Matthew 24:27 and Revelation 1:7). It will be a time of judgment for all the world. Jesus also speaks of it as a time of the gathering together of His people from all races and nations, from north and south and east and west (verse 27), all who have sought to live for Him. It will mean the end of suffering and persecution – the final victory of good over evil, of the kingdom of God triumphant over all the forces of wrong and injustice, oppression and violence.

b. We do not know the time

Jesus makes it clear that we do not know the time of His coming 'with great power and glory'. Even He in His life on earth, when He limited Himself to our humanity, did not know the time (verse 32). We are, therefore, wrong if we think we can know, or if we follow the teaching of those who make confident predictions about the future. Jesus' warning was that He would come as suddenly and unexpectedly as a thief in the night (Matthew 24:42–44 and see 1 Thessalonians 5:1–5). We do not know the *time*, but the *fact* that He will come is certain. God Himself never changes, and when we have His word and His promise, that is one unchanging, unfailing thing that we can hold on to; Jesus could say, 'Heaven and earth will pass away, but my words will not pass away' (verse 31).

There are signs of His coming, just as there are signs of the seasons (verses 28–29). When we face great troubles and disasters, suffering and persecution in the world, we are to realize that these will only be for a time – God's victory is sure and there will be a final coming of His kingdom. But we do not know the time. Our attitude must be, 'It may be today' – but God's time is not our time; 'with the Lord one day is as a thousand years, and a thousand years as one day' (2 Peter 3:8). So we are to go on quietly, faithfully, with the work God gives us to do, realizing that the time we have may be short, prepared to lay foundations on which others after us may build.

c. Call to watch

The word 'watch' (used four times in verses 33–37) tells us how we should live our life in preparation for Christ's coming. Jesus made His meaning clear with a parable. He said a man had to go on a journey and he left his servants in charge of his house, each with their work to do. The important thing was that in whatever hour of day or night he returned, they should be ready for him. They would be ready if they had been faithfully doing the work he had given them. That is what matters to us. It is not helpful when some Christians spend a lot of time and trouble trying to tell others of the details of the future. They only become excited and neglect their real work. Be watchful, not too excited to work, nor yet spiritually asleep and inactive (see Romans 13:11–14 and 1 Thessalonians 5:1–8).

Meditation   *Meditate on 1 John 3:1–3, especially thinking of what it says should be the effect on our lives of the hope that we have for the future.*

For further thought and study   1.   What other passages in the Bible speak, as verse 31 does, about things that change and things that do not change? How should this affect the way that we think and the way that we live? See, for example, Psalm 102:25–28 quoted in Hebrews 1:10–12; see also Hebrews 12:25–29 and 1 Peter 1:23–25.

2.   What other New Testament teaching enlarges on what verses 33–36 say about the work God entrusts us to do and the gifts that He gives us to use for Him? See, for example, Matthew 25:14–30, Luke 19:11–27, Romans 12:3–8 and 1 Corinthians 12.

Notes   1. There are parallels to these verses in Matthew 24:29–36 and Luke 21:25–33; see also Matthew 24:42–51 and Luke 12:35–48 and 21:34–36.

2. Verse 30 is a difficult verse. There were things that Jesus predicted that came true in the 'generation' of those alive at the time when He spoke: His own resurrection, the witness and the persecution of Christians, wars and troubles and in particular the fall of Jerusalem. But the 'generation' may mean the human race or this age in which we live – that will not cease to be until Christ comes 'with great power and glory' (see Matthew 28:20).

DEATH AND RESURRECTION OF JESUS

Mark 14:1—16:8

The second half of the Gospel (from 8:31 in particular) has been leading to Jesus' rejection and His death. Most of what chapters 14 and 15 tell us took place in fact in 24 hours. The events which led to the death of Jesus – and to His resurrection – were of the greatest importance for Christians. The account told here was probably recorded before the other events in the Gospels were written down. The details of these events are important for Christians for four main reasons.

1. From the earliest days of the Church Christians met together to worship their Lord and especially for the 'breaking of bread' (see Acts 2:42, 46). This meant that, as Jesus had told them at the Last Supper, they met to share the bread and the wine in remembrance of His death, His body broken and His blood outpoured as a sacrifice for the sins of the world (see 1 Corinthians 10:16–17 and 11:23–26).

2. The death and resurrection of Jesus were central in the preaching of the Church as is seen in the records that we have in the Acts of the Apostles (e.g. Acts 2:22–24, 10:36–40 and 13:26–39) and in the way Paul sums up that preaching: 'I delivered to you as of first importance what I also received, that Christ died for our sins in accordance

211

with the scriptures, that he was buried, that he was raised on the third day in accordance with the scriptures' (1 Corinthians 15:3–4).

3. It was no easy task for missionaries – in the earliest days and since – to call people to believe in and to follow a crucified Jew and accept Him as Saviour and Lord of their lives. It was necessary to show why He was put to death on the cross and to tell of the events that led to His death and how He faced His sufferings, trials, and crucifixion.

4. Christian people need to be taught the meaning of the death of Jesus in the purpose of God. Although these chapters for the most part tell just what happened, they sometimes indicate why it happened.

The chapters may be divided as follows:

14:1–2	Plan of the chief priests to kill Jesus
14:3–9	Anointing of Jesus at Bethany
14:10–11	Judas' offer to betray Jesus
14:12–16	Preparations for the Passover
14:17–21	Warning for the traitor
14:22–25	Institution of the Lord's Supper
14:26–31	Warning of the disciples' failure and of Peter's denial
14:32–42	Jesus' agony on Gethsemane
14:43–50	Betrayal and arrest
14:51–52	Young man who followed
14:53–65	Trial before Caiaphas
14:66–72	Peter's denial
15:1–5	Trial before Pilate
15:6–15	Death sentence
15:16–20	Mockery by the soldiers
15:21–32	Crucifixion
15:33–39	Death of Jesus
15:40–41	Women witnesses
15:42–47	Burial
16:1–8	Risen from the dead

Study 52: PLANS OF HATRED AND OF LOVE

[1]It was now two days before the Passover and the feast of Unleavened Bread. And the chief priests and the scribes were seeking how to arrest him by stealth, and kill him; [2]for they said, 'Not during the feast, lest there be a tumult of the people.'

[3]And while he was at Bethany in the house of Simon the leper, as he sat at table, a woman came with an alabaster flask of ointment of pure nard, very costly, and she broke the flask and poured it over his head. [4]But there were some who said to themselves indignantly, 'Why was the ointment thus wasted? [5]For this ointment might have been sold for more than three hundred denarii, and given to the poor.' And they reproached her. [6]But Jesus said, 'Let her alone; why do you trouble her? She has done a beautiful thing to me. [7]For you will always have the poor with you, and whenever you will, you can do good to them; but you will not always have me. [8]She has done what she could; she has anointed my body beforehand for burying. [9]And truly, I say to you, wherever the gospel is preached in the whole world, what she has done will be told in memory of her.'

[10]Then Judas Iscariot, who was one of the twelve, went to the chief priests in order to betray him to them. [11]And when they heard it they were glad, and promised to give him money. And he sought an opportunity to betray him (14:1-11).

Several times in his Gospel Mark places one event beside another, each to show up the other more clearly. Here hatred shows up love more strongly, love shows up hatred. We see the Jewish leaders wanting to kill Jesus, and a disciple willing to receive money to betray Him; and we see a woman pouring out her costly perfume in love and thankfulness to Jesus.

Each of the Gospels tell us that this was the time of the Passover and the Festival of Unleavened Bread. That was the time each year when the Jewish people remembered how God had brought them out of slavery in Egypt. The Passover lamb reminded them how God had saved them from death; the unleavened bread reminded them how they escaped in haste from Egypt (see Exodus 12:1–13:10). At Passover time the people looked back on what God had done in the past and they looked forward to a new and greater deliverance. Although they did not realize it, Jesus, by His death as a sacrifice ('the Lamb of God'), was bringing them that salvation – freedom from sin and evil. It was fitting that it was Passover time. Later the apostle Paul would explain it by saying, 'Christ, our Passover lamb, has been sacrificed' (1 Corinthians 5:7, Good News Bible). Now we see what people chose to do to Him – in their love or in their hatred.

a. Acts of hatred

We have seen already how the Jewish leaders wanted to silence the voice of Jesus and to get rid of Him by putting Him to death (see 3:6 and 12:12). They were afraid to act openly. Ordinary people could see the good in what He said and did. So the chief priests and scribes knew that they must find a way to arrest Him secretly, or there might be a riot of the people. Their plans of jealousy and hatred were helped forward when Judas, 'one of the twelve', went to them offering to betray his Master and to lead them to the place where Jesus might be found during the hours of darkness when the crowds would not be there. They 'promised to give him money', and so 'he sought an opportunity to betray him' (verse 11).

b. An act of love

Verses 3–9 tell a different story, of a woman whose heart was full of love. No gift was too costly for her to bring. She had an alabaster flask of precious perfume, perhaps handed down from her mother and grandmother, perfume worth as much as a labouring man might earn in a year ('three hundred denarii' – verse 5). She would no longer save for herself this precious possession, but 'broke the flask and poured it over his head'. People criticized what she did. John (12:4) says it was Judas who led the criticism. '*Why* this waste?', they asked. Jesus said, '*Why* do you trouble her?' Notice three things that Jesus said:

1. He accepted what the woman did as something 'beautiful' (verse 6). Love that is willing to give costly gifts is always beautiful. Such love is itself like a fragrant perfume. Ephesians 5:2 says this of the sacrificial love of Christ. Philippians 4:18 says it of the sacrificial gifts of Christians. The love of Christ in Christian people's words and actions 'spreads the fragrance of the knowledge of him everywhere' (2 Corinthians 2:14.) It is those who have love in their hearts – love for God and for people – who give to the poor.

2. Jesus said that the woman had anointed His body in preparation for burial. Perhaps she sensed that Jesus would soon die and this was the last opportunity to show her love and to show that she honoured Him as Master and Lord. (In Luke 7:37–38 we read of one who anointed the feet of Jesus; this woman anointed His head, as in the Old Testament kings and prophets were anointed with oil on the head.)

3. What she did would be told wherever the good news of Jesus was told. This story has been read by millions of people, and it has inspired many to actions of love and sacrifice.

Prayer *Lord God, take from our hearts all jealousy and bitterness that leads to hatred and seeks to do harm to others. By Your Spirit fill us with love that seeks only good, especially for those in need, and fill us with the desire to honour and glorify Your name.* AMEN.

For further thought and study 1. In the light of verse 7 consider passages in the New Testament that speak of the Lord's concern for the poor and the concern of the early

Christian church for those in need. See Mark 10:21, Luke 4:18, 14:12–14, 21–23, John 13:29, Acts 2:44–45, 4:32–37 and Galatians 2:10.

2. How should Christian people link together love for God and meeting the needs of the poor and the oppressed? See James 1:27, 2:1–17 and 1 John 3:17 and 4:20–21.

Notes 1. In the other Gospels, Matthew 26:1–16, Luke 22:1–6 and John 12:1–8 are parallel to these verses. We read of an anointing of Jesus in Luke 7:36–50 in the house of 'Simon the Pharisee'. When we compare the passages, it is clear that Jesus was anointed more than once.

2. 'Alabaster' was the kind of finely-ground limestone of which the jar or flask was made; 'nard' was the plant used in making the perfume.

Study 53: AT TABLE IN THE UPPER ROOM

[12]And on the first day of Unleavened Bread, when they sacrificed the passover lamb, his disciples said to him, 'Where will you have us go and prepare for you to eat the passover?' [13]And he sent two of his disciples, and said to them, 'Go into the city, and a man carrying a jar of water will meet you; follow him, [14]and wherever he enters, say to the householder, ''The Teacher says, Where is my guest room, where I am to eat the passover with my disciples?'' [15]And he will show you a large upper room furnished and ready; there prepare for us.' [16]And the disciples set out and went to the city, and found it as he had told them; and they prepared the passover.

[17]And when it was evening he came with the twelve. [18]And as they were at the table eating, Jesus said, 'Truly, I say to you, one of you will betray me, one who is eating with me.' [19]They began to be sorrowful, and to say to him one after the other, 'Is it I?' [20]He said to them, 'It is one of the twelve, one

who is dipping bread into the dish with me. ²¹For the Son of man goes as it is written of him, but woe to that man by whom the Son of man is betrayed! It would have been better for that man if he had not been born.'

²²And as they were eating, he took bread, and blessed, and broke it, and gave it to them, and said, 'Take; this is my body.' ²³And he took a cup, and when he had given thanks he gave it to them, and they all drank of it. ²⁴And he said to them, 'This is my blood of the covenant, which is poured out for many. ²⁵Truly, I say to you, I shall not drink again of the fruit of the vine until that day when I drink it new in the kingdom of God.'

²⁶And when they had sung a hymn, they went out to the Mount of Olives (14:12–26).

Three things were in the heart and mind of Jesus as the time moved forward towards that last evening that He would spend with His disciples before He went out to His death: the celebration of the Passover, His concern for the one who would betray Him, and the desire to show His disciples in a special way the meaning of His death.

a. Celebration of the Passover

In Jerusalem at that time the minds of all the Jews turned to the Passover. His disciples, as well as Jesus Himself, were thinking of this and so they asked their Master, 'Where will you have us go and prepare for you to eat the Passover?' He had His answer ready, because He had made His plans, as He had before for His entry into Jerusalem (11:1–6). Some have understood Jesus' words in verses 13–14 as showing a miraculous knowledge that others could not have; but it may simply be that He had arranged things before. 'A man carrying a jar of water' would be an unusual sight. Usually women in Palestine carried the water, and if men did it they carried the water in leather bottles rather than jars. This man whom the two disciples met would be able to answer Jesus' question, 'Where is my guest room, where I am to eat the Passover with my disciples?' So the disciples went, found the man, came to the upper room, and there they prepared for the celebration of the Passover.

b. Warning about His betrayal

As Jesus sat at table in that upper room, He must have been thinking a great deal of what He soon must suffer. He was also thinking of His disciples. They were His friends whom He loved, had taught, had prayed for, and had led in His ways. Soon they would run away in fear when He was arrested. Worse still, one of them would betray Him and hand Him over to His enemies. John (13:21) says that 'He was troubled in spirit', in sorrow, not for Himself, but for Judas. He gave Judas a warning and made His last appeal to him – 'One who is eating with me', 'one of the twelve', 'one who is dipping bread in the dish with me' – 'one of you will betray me'. Jesus knew that for Him the way of arrest, trial, suffering, death 'must be'. The purpose of the Father, foretold in the Scriptures, had to be fulfilled. But the traitor must bear the responsibility for what he did. 'Woe to that man by whom the Son of man is betrayed!' Judas knew what Jesus meant. The others, fearing for themselves, asked, 'Is it I?'. A disciple can become a traitor. People can turn from the light they know to the darkness. A person can know and follow Jesus but then turn away, oppose Him, and take the side of His enemies.

c. Meaning of His death

The Lord's Supper, the Holy Communion, the Breaking of Bread – we call it by many names. It has meant so much to Christians down the ages that it is hard to write of it in a few words. With the bread and the cup of wine at that supper Jesus told simply the meaning of His death. At that time the disciples would hardly understand. Soon they would understand, and the Lord's Supper would become the most important act of Christian worship. Every time it would be celebrated, it would be the reminder of Jesus' death and what that meant. The broken bread given to them – His body broken on the cross for the life of the world. The cup of wine of which they would all drink – His blood poured out. That spoke of His death as a sacrifice, fulfilling and bringing to an end all the old sacrifices for people's sins. In the Old Testament there had been a covenant between the people and God. Now there was a new covenant made by His death. The broken relationship with God was restored by His forgiveness. There was new life, a new relationship with God, and fellowship for the people of God. New life now is His gift and the promise of fulness of life, eternal life, for the disciples of Jesus 'in the kingdom of God'.

Meditation *'As often as you eat this bread and drink the cup, you proclaim the Lord's death until he comes'* (1 Corinthians 11:26).

For further thought and study With these verses read the parallels in Matthew 26:17–30, Luke 22:7–23 and John 13:1–30. In particular note what things are said in Matthew and Luke and by Paul in 1 Corinthians 10:14–22 and 11:23–32 about the Lord's Supper. Read also Luke 24:28–35 and Acts 2:42–47, 20:7 and 27:35. It is helpful to make a list of the different things that are shown us about the Holy Communion, such as the meaning of Christ's death for us, the fellowship of those who eat of the 'one loaf' and drink of the one cup, the feeding of our spiritual lives on Christ, the loyalty that we owe to Him, the hope that we have.

Notes 1. As we read the four Gospels carefully, there are some puzzling things about the celebration of the Passover by Jesus with His disciples. John (18:28) writes as if at the time of Jesus' trial the Passover celebration had not yet taken place, and as if He died at the time when they were killing the lambs for the Passover. In the Gospel records we do not read about the details of the lamb, the bitter herbs, the telling of the story of Exodus, but only about the breaking of bread and the sharing of the cup of wine. Some ask,

Could the meeting of the Sanhedrin and the trial of Christ have taken place on Passover night? Yet here in Mark, verses 12–16 seem to say that this was an actual Passover meal that the disciples prepared. One suggestion is that different groups of Jews may have kept the Passover on different days. Another is that the Last Supper may not have been the full Passover meal. Or perhaps Jesus, for His own special reasons, kept the Passover a day before the normal time. At least that 'Last Supper' was a meal with all the meaning of the Passover strongly in the minds of Jesus and His disciples.

2. Old Testament passages that help us to understand verses 22–25 are Exodus 24:1–8 (telling of the old covenant and its sacrifices), Jeremiah 31:31–34 (foretelling the new covenant) and Isaiah 53:12 (the sacrifice for 'the sin of many').

3. It was the custom to sing Psalms 116–118 at the end of the Passover. It is good to read these Psalms, therefore, knowing that they may have been in the thoughts of Jesus and His disciples as they went out from the Upper Room to the Mount of Olives (verse 26).

Study 54: HOUR OF TESTING – FOR JESUS, FOR THE DISCIPLES

[27]And Jesus said to them, 'You will all fall away; for it is written, "I will strike the shepherd, and the sheep will be scattered." [28]But after I am raised up, I will go before you to Galilee.' [29]Peter said to him, 'Even though they all fall away, I will not.' [30]And Jesus said to him, 'Truly, I say to you, this very night, before the cock crows twice, you will deny me three times.' [31]But he said vehemently, 'If I must die with you I will not deny you.' And they all said the same.

[32]And they went to a place which was called Gethsemane; and he said to his disciples, 'Sit here, while I pray.' [33]And he took with him Peter and James and John, and began to be greatly distressed and troubled. [34]And he said to them, 'My soul is very sorrowful, even to death; remain here, and

watch.' ³⁵And going a little farther, he fell on the ground and prayed that, if it were possible, the hour might pass from him. ³⁶And he said, 'Abba, Father, all things are possible to thee; remove this cup from me; yet not what I will, but what thou wilt.' ³⁷And he came and found them sleeping, and he said to Peter, 'Simon, are you asleep? Could you not watch one hour? ³⁸Watch and pray that you may not enter into temptation; the spirit indeed is willing, but the flesh is weak.' ³⁹And again he went away and prayed, saying the same words. ⁴⁰And again he came and found them sleeping, for their eyes were very heavy; and they did not know what to answer him. ⁴¹And he came the third time, and said to them, 'Are you still sleeping and taking your rest? It is enough; the hour has come; the Son of man is betrayed into the hands of sinners. ⁴²Rise, let us be going; see, my betrayer is at hand'   (14:27–42).

Verse 26 has said that from the Last Supper Jesus and His disciples 'went out to the Mount of Olives'. There in the darkness of the night was the supreme test for Him and for the disciples, which way they would take in the hours ahead. A great weight hung over the Lord as He faced death, but His constant thought was for His disciples, that they should realize their weakness and be kept from failing the test that would come to them.

a. False confidence of the disciples

As Jesus had warned Judas and made a final appeal to him, so now He warned the other disciples, 'You will all fall away.' True to the words of Scripture (in Zechariah 13:7), their Good Shepherd would be taken and the sheep would be scattered. As Jesus put it (in the words of John 16:32), 'you will be scattered, every man to his home, and will leave me alone.' The disciples were confident, however, that that would never happen to them. They all felt the same way (verse 31) but it was Peter who spoke, 'Even though they all fall away, I will not.' 'If I must die with you,

I will not deny you.' It was false confidence, and Jesus said that before the cock crowed in the morning, Peter would have denied his Master three times. It was false confidence, because it was based on Peter, on his desire and determination. He had to learn that he was weaker than he thought, and that in his weakness he needed God's power if he was to stand firm and remain faithful. Notice, however, that Jesus gave them encouragement and hope for their hour of failure. He was able to look beyond the cross and the failure of the disciples. There would be a new beginning in the place where they had first begun to follow Jesus; 'after I am raised up, I will go before you to Galilee' (verse 28).

b. True confidence of Jesus

'They went to a place which was called Gethsemane.' The name meant 'oil press', and ancient olive trees (such as were used for producing oil) are there today in that 'garden' (see John 18:1) on the slopes of the Mount of Olives. Luke 22:39 tells us that in these days Jesus had been coming regularly to that place. He knew that what He needed most was to be alone with the Father. 'Sit here, while I pray,' He said to the disciples. He took with Him the three who had been closest to Him on special occasions before, Peter and James and John (see 5:37–42 and 9:2–8). He asked them to 'watch' while He went ahead to pray. It says of Him that He was then 'greatly distressed and troubled', 'sorrowful, even to death'. This was the 'hour' to which all His life and work had been moving. Because He was truly human, He wished that it might 'pass from him' (verse 35). This was the 'cup' that He knew He must drink (see Study 40 on 10:38).

We can only begin to understand His agony in Gethsemane when we realize there was something more than the physical suffering of crucifixion, more than the deep disappointment in His disciples, more even than rejection by His people whom He had come to save. He was to be 'betrayed into the hands of sinners' (verse 41). He was to die for sinners, bearing the sin of the world. Jesus' words about His death, spoken at the Last Supper, help us to understand the prospect that He faced as He prayed in Gethsemane. His body was to be broken, His blood poured out, to make a new covenant. We can have forgiveness because He bore our sins (as 1 Peter 2:24 puts it) 'in his body on the tree'.

He prayed, and prayed, and prayed again. He prayed with true confidence, 'Abba, Father'. He wished that the hour might pass and the cup be taken away, but He gave Himself to do His Father's will.

c. Opportunity – lost and gained

The time in Gethsemane should have been an opportunity for the disciples to prepare for the tests that would soon face them. 'Watch,' Jesus said to them. 'Watch and pray that you may not enter into temptation.' They had a willing spirit but their human strength was small (verse 38). 'Their eyes were very heavy'. For them also the past days had been a great strain. Luke (22:45) says that they slept 'for sorrow'. Yet there are times when, if we are to be faithful as disciples, prayer is more important than everything else.

Jesus Himself took that opportunity for prayer while there was time. He found strength to do the Father's will, costly though that was. From that hour of agony and prayer He could go forward with confidence – to betrayal, arrest, trial, mockery, crucifixion, death. 'Rise, let us be going; see, my betrayer is at hand.'

Meditation *Sin and evil came into the world when man and woman said to God, 'Not Your will, but mine be done.' The power of sin and evil is overcome by the prayer and the dedication of life. 'Not my will, but Yours, be done.'*

For further thought and study 1. What does it mean to disciples today to 'watch'? How are 'watching' and 'praying' linked? With verses 34, 37 and 38 see 13:33–37 and also

Ephesians 6:18.

2. For the meaning of 'the hour' that Jesus knew to be approaching as He prayed in Gethsemane (verses 35 and 41) see John's Gospel 8:20, 12:23–32 and 13:1–3.

3. The Aramaic word 'Abba' was the word children used when coming to their 'Daddy'. It had never been used by Jewish people in coming to God in prayer, but it was used by Jesus, and Christians are taught to come to God in such an intimate way, saying, 'Abba, Father.' See Romans 8:15 and Galatians 4:6.

Study 55: JESUS' ARREST

[43]And immediately, while he was still speaking, Judas came, one of the twelve, and with him a crowd with swords and clubs, from the chief priests and the scribes and the elders. [44]Now the betrayer had given them a sign, saying, 'The one I shall kiss is the man; seize him and lead him away under guard.' [45]And when he came, he went up to him at once, and said, 'Master!' And he kissed him. [46]And they laid hands on him and seized him. [47]But one of those who stood by drew his sword, and struck the slave of the high priest and cut off his ear. [48]And Jesus said to them, 'Have you come out as against a robber, with swords and clubs to capture me? [49]Day after day I was with you in the temple teaching, and you did not seize me. But let the scriptures be fulfilled.' [50]And they all forsook him, and fled.

[51]And a young man followed him, with nothing but a linen cloth about his body; and they seized him, [52]but he left the linen cloth and ran away naked (14:43–52).

Jesus had just said, 'The hour has come; the Son of man is betrayed into the hands of sinners' (verse 41). In one way it was the 'hour', as Luke 22:53 puts it, of the victory of 'the power of darkness'. In a deeper way it was the hour of Jesus' victory, as He went forward to give His life for others. We can best understand these verses as we watch those who were involved in what is described.

a. Traitor

Judas is described as 'the betrayer', the one who handed Jesus over to His enemies. 'Judas came, one of the twelve...'. That fact could never be forgotten, that it was 'one of the twelve' who acted as traitor. The sign that he gave was a 'kiss', which should have been a sign of love and loyalty. He said 'Master', but Jesus was no longer Judas' Master. Whatever reasons we may give for it, Judas little by little had turned away from Jesus, so that in the end he was willing to join His enemies and hand Jesus over to them.

b. Arrest party

Those who came with Judas are described as 'a crowd with swords and clubs, from the chief priests and the scribes and the elders'. Did they think, Jesus asked them, that they needed to 'come out as against a robber, with swords and clubs'? Had He ever threatened to act violently against any one? And why in the darkness of the night, when day by day He was with them openly teaching in the temple? They knew the answer to these questions. At least the Jewish leaders did. They were afraid to act openly for fear of the people supporting Jesus (verses 1, 2). Perhaps these people in the 'crowd' who came with swords and clubs had a secret fear of Jesus, too, because He had shown such power to heal the sick, to make the lame walk and the blind see. (Notice in John 18:4–6 how they acted when they came face to face with Jesus.)

c. Disciples

The disciples were there with Jesus when the 'crowd with swords and clubs' came to arrest Him; but what could they do? 'One of those who stood by' – John (18:10) says it was Peter – was determined to do something. He lashed out with his sword and 'struck the slave of the high priest and cut off his ear'. The way of the sword was never Jesus' way.

Violence feeds violence. Matthew 26:52 gives His words at this attempt to defend Him with the sword, 'Put your sword back into its place; for all who take the sword will perish by the sword.' John (18:11) adds that Jesus said, 'Shall I not drink the cup which the Father has given me?' So He gave Himself up to those who came to arrest Him. What then would the disciples do? Peter had said, 'If I must die with you, I will not deny you.' 'And they all said the same' (verse 31). But now the story is told simply and sadly, 'They all forsook Him and fled.' The opportunity for them to prepare for that hour of testing had not been taken. How often, later in life, when they had learnt from their failure, the words of Jesus must have come back to their minds, 'Watch and pray that you may not enter into temptation' (verse 38).

d. Young man who followed

There was one person who did not immediately run away with the others. All that is said of him is that he was a 'young man' who 'followed him, with nothing but a linen cloth about his body'. The words used may suggest that he was a young disciple who was in bed when he heard or realized what was happening. He threw a cloth about him and ran out to Gethsemane. Some think that the young disciple was Mark, and that his home in Jerusalem (see Acts 12:12) may have been used for the Last Supper. We cannot tell who he was, nor why the Gospel gives this particular detail. All that we can say is that the young man had the courage to try to follow – but then courage failed him. He ran away like the others and Jesus was left alone with His enemies.

Prayer *Lord, help me when I am in danger of running away and of failing to keep my promise to serve You. I am weak, but You are strong to help, and You have promised to be with me always.* AMEN.

For further thought and study 1. Having reached this

point in the study of the Gospel, consider why people turned against One who had done nothing but good to others and spoken only words of love and truth. Are people different today in their attitudes and actions?

2. Having in mind the attitude of Jesus here, do you think there are times when it is right for Christians to use violence in serving the Lord, and in the cause of those who are oppressed or unjustly held by others?

Note   The parallels to this section in other Gospels are Matthew 26:47–56, Luke 22:47–53 and John 18:1–12.

Study 56: THREE TRIALS

[53] And they led Jesus to the high priest; and all the chief priests and the elders and the scribes were assembled. [54] And Peter had followed him at a distance, right into the courtyard of the high priest; and he was sitting with the guards, and warming himself at the fire. [55] Now the chief priests and the whole council sought testimony against Jesus to put him to death; but they found none. [56] For many bore false witness against him, and their witness did not agree. [57] And some stood up and bore false witness against him, saying, [58] 'We heard him say, "I will destroy this temple that is made with hands, and in three days I will build another, not made with hands."' [59] Yet not even so did their testimony agree. [60] And the high priest stood up in the midst, and asked Jesus, 'Have you no answer to make? What is it that these men testify against you?' [61] But he was silent and made no answer. Again the high priest asked him, 'Are you the Christ, the Son of the Blessed?' [62] And Jesus said, 'I am; and you will see the Son of man seated at the right hand of Power, and coming with the clouds of heaven.' [63] And the high priest tore his garments, and said, 'Why do we still need witnesses? [64] You have heard his blasphemy. What is your decision?' And they all con-

demned him as deserving death. ⁶⁵And some began to spit on him, and to cover his face, and to strike him, saying to him, 'Prophesy!' And the guards received him with blows.

⁶⁶And as Peter was below in the courtyard, one of the maids of the high priest came; ⁴¹and seeing Peter warming himself, she looked at him, and said, 'You also were with the Nazarene, Jesus.' ⁶⁸But he denied it, saying, 'I neither know nor understand what you mean.' And he went out into the gateway. ⁶⁹And the maid saw him, and began again to say to the bystanders, 'This man is one of them.'

⁷⁰But again he denied it. And after a little while again the bystanders said to Peter, 'Certainly you are one of them; for you are a Galilean.' ⁷¹But he began to invoke a curse on himself and to swear, 'I do not know this man of whom you speak.' ⁷²And immediately the cock crowed a second time. And Peter remembered how Jesus had said to him, 'Before the cock crows twice, you will deny me three times.' And he broke down and wept   (14:53–72).

This section begins by telling us what happened after Jesus' arrest in Gethsemane. First, it tells what happened to Jesus. He was brought before the high priest; 'and all the chief priests and the elders and the scribes were assembled'. That probably means that during the night the Jewish Council, the Sanhedrin, was gathered together. They held an inquiry about Jesus, and then about daybreak (see 15:1) they condemned Jesus as deserving to die, and sent Him to Pilate, the Roman governor. Second, we read what happened to Peter. Mark purposely tells of the trial of Jesus between the two parts that speak of Peter (verse 54 and verses 66–72). Jesus was on trial. So was Peter. So were the Jewish leaders. There were three trials taking place that night.

a. Trial of Jesus
In any trial witnesses are called. Jewish law said that there should be the agreement of at least two witnesses (see

Deuteronomy 19:15). They had special rules about witness when a person was to be condemned to death, so that the judges might be completely sure that the person deserved to die. The Jewish leaders broke all their own laws and rules. They 'sought testimony against Jesus to put him to death' – they did not seek testimony that was in favour of Him. 'Many bore false witness against him, and their witness did not agree.' They twisted his words. Still they could find no reason to condemn Him. So the high priest asked if Jesus claimed to be the Christ, the Son of God. When he was asked that question, Jesus could not be silent. They might use the word 'Christ' in a different way from Him, but He had come to be the Messiah. He had been sent as God's Son into the world. He could only say, 'I am', and use the words taken from the Old Testament to tell the truth about Himself. From the point of view of the Jewish leaders that was the end of the trial. It was 'blasphemy' to speak like that; 'they all condemned him as deserving death.'

b. Trial of the Jewish leaders

The Jewish leaders thought that Jesus was on trial before them. Yet really they were on trial before Jesus – and they were condemned by what they said and did. They were condemned by the silence of Jesus (verse 61). There was no truth or justice in what the witnesses were saying. There was nothing that He needed to answer. They were on trial because they had before them One who had always spoken and acted in love, truth and justice, the One sent by God to be their Messiah and their Saviour. What would they do with Him? They made their decision. But they needed to know that one day they would stand before Him. They would see the One whom they condemned to die 'at the right hand of Power'; that is, in the place of highest honour with God the Father, 'and coming with the clouds of heaven.' As they knew the words from Daniel 7:13–14 (referred to also in 13:26) and Psalm 110:1, they would know the meaning of this. Still they would not listen. They not only condemned Him, they laughed at Him, spat on Him and struck Him (verse 65). They were the ones who were condemned by what they said and did that day – not Jesus.

c. Trial of Peter

Although Peter had run away when the other disciples did (verse 50), he turned round and 'followed...at a distance'. He wanted to see what would happen to his Master. So he went 'right into the courtyard of the high priest; and he was sitting with the guards and warming himself at the fire'. This was his test, his trial. Would he be true to his promise, 'Even though they all fall away, I will not...If I must die with you, I will not deny you' (verses 29 and 31)? Perhaps it would have been easier for Peter if he had had to stand before the high priest. It was a servant girl who accused him of being a disciple of the despised 'Nazarene', Jesus (verse 67). Peter denied it. 'He went out into the gateway' – it was a dangerous position in the courtyard of the high priest by the fire where people could see him clearly. Again he was challenged as the servant girl said to the others, 'This man is one of them.' Either Peter had to go back on his words, confess that he had not spoken the truth – or deny Jesus again. He denied Him the second time. A third time he denied, even with a 'curse on himself'. 'And immediately the cock crowed a second time.' 'And Peter remembered' the warning that Jesus had given him. 'And he broke down and wept.'

What verdicts would we give in the three trials that took place that night? Jesus – not guilty and innocent of every charge against Him. The Jewish leaders – guilty, of injustice, violence, false witness and murder. They were unrepentant in their trial. Peter – guilty of failing to keep his promise, guilty of denying his Master, but repentant and able to be pardoned.

Meditation *Jesus is still on trial in the world – all who see His love and truth and kingship must choose to accept or reject: but all of us who see His love and truth and kingship are on trial by our response to Him.*

For further thought and study 1. With verse 58 read Mark 13:1–2 and John 2:19–22. What did Jesus actually say and what do you think He meant about the destroying and building of the temple?

2. List the things that were unjust and unfair in the trial of Jesus before the high priest.

Notes 1. We have the record of the trial of Jesus before the Jewish leaders in Matthew 26:57–68, Luke 22:63–71 and John 18:12–14, 19–24. John tells us of a trial before the high priest, Annas, as well as before Caiaphas. The Jews accepted Annas as high priest till he died, but the Romans had removed him from his office and put Caiaphas in his place.

2. The story of Peter's denial is told in Matthew 26:69–75, Luke 22:54–62 and John 18:15–18, 25–27. There are small differences, but in each case there are three denials and the cock crows at the end.

3. In verse 61 'the Son of the Blessed' means the Son of God, and in verse 62 'the right hand of Power' means the right hand of God. Out of reverence, Jewish people often avoided saying the name of God.

4. The tearing of the clothes, as in verse 63, was a way of expressing horror, as it also often expressed sorrow and grief. 'Blasphemy' (verse 64) was usually speaking against God, but Jesus' claims could be said to be 'blasphemy' by those who were unwilling to accept their truth.

5. When it says in verse 71 that Peter 'invoked a curse on himself', that meant that he called on God to bring some judgment on him if he was not speaking the truth.

6. The term 'Nazarene' (verse 67) was used by those who looked down on and despised Jesus, because Nazareth where He was brought up was a town in the half-Gentile area of Galilee; it had no importance in history and was not mentioned in Old Testament prophecy. See John 1:46 and 7:41 and 52.

7. Recalling that early Christian writers indicate that Mark's Gospel comes especially from the writer's knowledge of the preaching and teaching of Peter (see page 8), we can appreciate how Mark must often have heard Peter tell of his sad failure in his denying his Master, but also of the Master's willingness to forgive and restore him.

Study 57: HANDED OVER

¹And as soon as it was morning the chief priests, with the elders and scribes, and the whole council held a consultation; and they bound Jesus and led him away and delivered him to Pilate. ²And Pilate asked him, 'Are you the King of the Jews?' And he answered him, 'You have said so.' ³And the chief priests accused him of many things. ⁴And Pilate again asked him, 'Have you no answer to make? See how many charges they bring against you.' ⁵But Jesus made no further answer, so that Pilate wondered.

⁶Now at the feast he used to release for them one prisoner for whom they asked. ⁷And among the rebels in prison, who had committed murder in the insurrection, there was a man called Barabbas. ⁸And the crowd came up and began to ask Pilate to do as he was wont to do for them. ⁹And he answered them, 'Do you want me to release for you the King of the Jews?' ¹⁰For he perceived that it was out of envy that the chief priests had delivered him up. ¹¹But the chief priests stirred up the crowd to have him release for them Barabbas instead. ¹²And Pilate again said to them, 'Then what shall I do with the man whom you call the King of the Jews?' ¹³And they cried out again, 'Crucify him.' ¹⁴And Pilate said to them, 'Why, what evil has he done?' But they shouted all the more, 'Crucify him.' ¹⁵So Pilate, wishing to satisfy the crowd, released for them Barabbas; and having scourged Jesus, he delivered him to be crucified   (15:1–15).

In 14:41 we read how the hour of Jesus' arrest meant He was 'betrayed into the hands of sinners', handed over to sinners for them to do with Him what they wished. (See Study 36 for the way that the Gospel constantly speaks of Jesus being 'handed over'.) Now we see further the results of this.

a. Handed over to Pilate

The trial of Jesus before the Jewish leaders had been taking place during the hours of darkness. It may have been that, because such a trial at night-time was illegal, 'as soon as it was morning' there was an official meeting of the 'whole council' (the Sanhedrin). Then the decision was made. Jesus was 'handed over' to Pilate, the Roman Governor. John 18:31 makes clear that, because Palestine was under Roman rule, it was not lawful for the Jews to put anyone to death. Perhaps in some cases – like that of Stephen in Acts 7 – they took the law into their own hands and put a person to death. They certainly could not do this with Jesus, especially when such crowds were in Jerusalem at Passover time. The Jewish leaders, as we have seen in 14:1–2, were afraid to do such a thing, as Jesus had such a great following with the people. So they handed Him over to Pilate. It seems clear that they prepared the way during the night by telling Pilate that their prisoner was politically dangerous. He must carry out the trial at daybreak. Jesus' claim to be Messiah was made to sound political. 'King of the Jews' was the way that it was put to Pilate (verse 2 and Luke 23:1–5). As in the trial before the Jewish leaders, so now before Pilate, Jesus gave no answer to the false accusations. Only one question He would answer. 'Jesus...in his testimony before Pontius Pilate made the good confession' (1 Timothy 6:13). He could not deny that He was the true 'King of the Jews', but He answered in such a way as to show that His kingship was a different kind of kingship from what Pilate would think of (verse 2, and see John 18:33–37). His kingdom was the kingdom of God, the rule of God in the hearts and lives of men and women.

b. Handed over in place of Barabbas

Verse 6 speaks of a custom of the Roman governor to release a prisoner at Passover time. At the time of this trial, Pilate seems to have had two crowds coming to him. As well as the crowd interested in the trial of Jesus, there was also a crowd who came to ask for the release of Barabbas (verse 8), 'a well-known prisoner', Matthew (27:16) says, who 'was in prison with the rebels who had committed murder in the riot' (verse 7, Good News Bible). When people asked Pilate to release a prisoner, he saw his opportunity to release Jesus. He could see the Jewish leaders were insincere in what they said about Jesus being politically dangerous. He saw that out of envy and jealousy they had handed Him over (verse 10). Perhaps they would be satisfied if Pilate condemned Jesus, but then released Him. 'But the chief priests stirred up the crowd to have him release for them Barabbas instead.' That was their choice. As the hymn puts it, 'A murderer they save, the Prince of life they slay.' It was also Jesus' own choice. He remained silent in the face of all the accusations against Him. He could have been free, but He was willing to go to the cross and for Barabbas to go free. Christians have always seen this as showing the meaning of Jesus' death. The sinless Son of God dies – the sinner is pardoned and goes free.

c. Handed over to be crucified

In our last study we thought of the trial of Jesus before the Jewish leaders as being also a trial of the Jewish leaders. So this trial before Pilate was a trial of Pilate. Would he stand for justice or act to please the people and make life easier for himself? He could see that Jesus had done no wrong (verse 5). But he faced the pressure of the crowds, stirred up by the chief priests to shout, 'Crucify him!' 'So Pilate, wishing to satisfy the crowd, released for them Barabbas; and having scourged Jesus, he delivered Him over to be crucified.'

'Scourged' and 'to be crucified'. Mark, and the other Gospels say little about the physical sufferings of Jesus. Crucifixion was the most terrible death possible. Scourging meant that a person was stripped of his clothes, tied to a post and beaten with a leather whip which had pieces of bone or lead in the leather. Yet the Gospels all show that the deepest and most awful suffering of Jesus was spiritual rather than physical. He was giving Himself to bear the sins of the world – and we can only begin to realize what that meant.

Meditation *'Christ... died for sins once for all, the righteous for the unrighteous, that he might bring us to God'* (1 Peter 3:18).

For further thought and study 1. Compare the account of this trial before Pilate with the accounts of it in Matthew 27:1–26, Luke 23:1–25 and John 18:18–19:16. In what ways do the other Gospels fill out the picture Mark gives?

2. How far do you think envy and jealousy of Jesus (verse 10) led the Jewish leaders to their actions against Jesus? See also John 11:45–48 and 12:19. To what sins do envy and jealousy lead people, even 'religious people', today? See Proverbs 6:34 and 27:4.

Notes 1. We have no record other than in the Gospels of the custom of releasing a prisoner at the time of the Passover festival. There are parallels, however, in Roman authorities granting pardons; and often Roman governors used such means to please the people whom they governed.

2. From some early manuscripts of Matthew 27:16 it seems that Barabbas may also have had the name Jesus. The choice then was between Jesus Barabbas and Jesus the Christ. It is interesting that Barabbas means, 'son of the father'.

Study 58: CRUCIFIED

¹⁶And the soldiers led him away inside the palace (that is, the praetorium); and they called together the whole batallion. ¹⁷And they clothed him in a purple cloak, and plaiting a crown of thorns they put it on him. ¹⁸And they began to salute him, 'Hail, King of the Jews!' ¹⁹And they struck his head with a reed, and spat upon him, and they knelt down in homage to him. ²⁰And when they had mocked him, they stripped him of the purple cloak, and put his own clothes on him. And they led him out to crucify him.

²¹And they compelled a passer-by, Simon of Cyrene, who was coming in from the country, the father of Alexander and Rufus, to carry his cross. ²²And they brought him to the place called Golgotha (which means the place of a skull). ²³And they offered him wine mingled with myrrh; but he did not take it. ²⁴And they crucified him, and divided his garments among them, casting lots for them, to decide what each should take. ²⁵And it was the third hour, when they crucified him. ²⁶And the inscription of the charge against him read, 'The King of the Jews'. ²⁷And with him they crucified two robbers, one on his right and one on his left. ²⁹And those who passed by derided him, wagging their heads, and saying, 'Aha! You who would destroy the temple and build it in three days, ³⁰save yourself, and come down from the cross!' ³¹So also the chief priests mocked him to one another with the scribes, saying, 'He saved others; he cannot save himself. ³²Let the Christ, the King of Israel, come down now from the cross, that we may see and believe.' Those who were crucified with him also reviled him (15:16–32).

The Roman writer, Cicero, called crucifixion the most cruel and terrible punishment a person could face. The hands were nailed to the cross-bar, the feet nailed or tied. The pain, the thirst, the strain of the body being fixed and unable to move however troubled by heat or insects – all of these made it an awful death. Yet, as we have seen, Mark, like the other Gospels, says little of the physical sufferings of Jesus. Jesus accepted those sufferings. He refused the drugged wine that would reduce the pain (verse 23), because that would have prevented Him realizing fully all that was happening. What Mark tells us here helps us to see the deeper meaning of the Lord's suffering and dying.

a. Mocked by the soldiers

The soldiers who had the job of scourging and then crucifying Jesus, led him to the place where all Pilate's soldiers were gathered. The crime of a person crucified was written down and put on the cross. For Jesus that was, 'The King of the Jews'. So the soldiers treated Him as a king – in mockery. A soldier's red cloak was put on Him and a crown of thorns was thrust on His head. As soldiers would prostrate themselves before the emperor, so in mockery they 'knelt down in homage to him' and said, 'Hail, King of the Jews'. He was no king to them. They struck Him and spat on Him. Later they put His own clothes back on Him, but before He was crucified they took these clothes, the only earthly possessions that he had, divided them among them and, as John 19:23–24 says, they gambled for His seamless robe.

b. Set between two robbers

There were three men crucified that day. Two were robbers, one on either side of Jesus. They were guilty of crimes. He was guilty of none. Verse 32 says, 'Those who were crucified with him also reviled him.' Luke (23:39–43) tells how one of the two came to confess his sin, to recognize that Jesus had done no wrong, and to pray to Him, 'Jesus, remember me when you come into your kingdom.' The Lord could respond to that prayer because on the cross He was giving himself to die in the midst of sinners for sinners.

c. Despised and rejected by the chief priests

The Jewish leaders stayed to see to the end what they had planned and brought to pass. They 'derided him' (verse 29) and mocked Him, but, as 1 Peter 2:23 says, 'When he was reviled he did not revile in return.' All that they said, in fact, had a deeper and truer meaning than they knew. As in His trial (in 14:58), they talked about His threat to destroy the temple and to build another in three days. Indeed in three days the temple of His body would be raised up. 'He saved others; he cannot save himself,' they cried. How true – for Him to save others He had to give Himself and not to try to save His life, even though He might have called for legions of angels to rescue Him (Matthew 26:53). They said, 'Let the Christ, the King of Israel, come down from the cross, that we may see and believe' (verse 32). Instead of this, countless men and women of almost every tribe and nation on earth have believed because He did not come down from the cross, but died there that we might have life.

d. The one who carried the cross

The upright post of the cross was put in the ground in the place where the crucifixion would take place. The one to be crucified had to carry the crossbar there. It seems that Jesus began to carry his (John 19:17), but collapsed under its weight. An African from Cyrene in North Africa, perhaps an African Jew, was compelled by the soldiers to carry Jesus' cross. Perhaps he had not known Jesus before that day. We know nothing more about him, but since Mark speaks of him as the father of Alexander and Rufus, people known to his readers, we can only imagine what happened. The one who that day was compelled to bear the cross of Jesus later, together with his sons, came to believe in the One who was crucified and voluntarily took up his cross and followed Him.

Meditation *Mocked by Gentile soldiers, despised and rejected by Jewish priests, but even as He was crucified, His love began to draw people to Him in repentance and faith.*

For further thought and study 1. How many of the things

that are written in Isaiah 50:4–9 and 53:1–12 do you think found a deep meaning in the sufferings of Jesus?

2. 'The sacrifice of one means life for many.' How is that illustrated by the death of Jesus? How should it be illustrated in the lives of Christians?

Notes. 1. The parallels to these verses in the other Gospels, with some different details added, are in Matthew 27:27–44, Luke 23:26–43 and John 19:17–24.

2. We saw in the Introduction to the Gospel how Mark probably wrote his Gospel first for Christians in Rome, and so it would have been there that Alexander and Rufus were known; perhaps Rufus is the one mentioned in Romans 16:13.

3. The name Golgotha may have been given because it was a hill shaped like a skull (although none of the Gospels speak of it as a hill), or because it was a place of execution.

4. Various explanations have been given of the apparent difference between verse 25 and John 19:14 in the time of the crucifixion. Some think that the number 6 was originally written and not 3 (in Greek the two are similar).

5. In most modern versions of the Bible there is no verse 28. Some manuscripts had the words, 'And the scripture was fulfilled which says, "He was reckoned with the transgressors".' This was probably a later addition. This quotation of Isaiah 53:12 is in Luke 22:37.

Study 59: DEATH OF THE SON OF GOD

[33] And when the sixth hour had come, there was darkness over the whole land until the ninth hour. [34] And at the ninth hour Jesus cried with a loud voice, 'Elo-i, Elo-i, lama sabachthani?' which means, 'My God, my God, why hast thou forsaken me?' [35] And some of the bystanders hearing it said, 'Behold he is calling Elijah.' [36] And one ran and, filling a sponge full of vinegar, put it on a reed and gave it to him to drink, saying, 'Wait, let us see whether Elijah will come to

take him down.' ³⁷And Jesus uttered a loud cry, and breathed his last. ³⁸And the curtain of the temple was torn in two, from top to bottom. ³⁹And when the centurion, who stood facing him, saw that he thus breathed his last, he said, 'Truly this man was the Son of God!' (15:33–39).

These verses again give no details of the terrible physical sufferings of our Lord as He was crucified. They tell us of the last hours before He died so that we can see something of the meaning of His death.

a. Darkness over the land

It was as if all nature was mourning because of what the world was doing to Jesus. Human sinfulness is seen at its worst. The Son of God had come and lived a human life, doing only good, giving Himself in love and care for all in need, showing the blessings that follow when God rules in the lives of men and women. But those who had the greatest opportunity to understand what He was doing rejected Him and demanded that He should be crucified. It was humanity's darkest hour. Yet it is said that the darkest hour is just before the dawn. What follows in these verses shows that because of His great love in giving Himself to die, the darkness was passing away (see 1 John 2:8). Light and blessing were to come to the world through His death.

b. His cry from the cross

Mark tells us that some of those who heard Jesus' cry from the cross misunderstood it. They thought that He was calling out for Elijah whom the Hebrew people believed would come to those in great distress. It was not a cry for Elijah, but 'Eloi' or 'Eli' in Aramaic or Hebrew, meaning, 'my God'. It was a mysterious cry, but to begin to understand it we need to notice three things:

1. The words are the words that begin Psalm 22, and perhaps the whole of the Psalm was in the thoughts of Jesus as He suffered on the cross.

2. They are the words of faith; in spite of the deep darkness of His suffering He still turns to His Father and says, 'My God, my God'.

3. Yet they are words of desolation, 'why hast thou forsaken me?'. We cannot say that He was actually forsaken. What Jesus did for us on the cross was the Father's purpose and the Father's work also. As the apostle Paul puts it (in 2 Corinthians 5:19), 'God was in Christ reconciling the world to Himself.' Perhaps we may understand it best in this way. What is the result of sin in our lives? We cannot take ourselves out of the presence of God. Psalm 139 describes most powerfully how we can never escape from God's presence. Yet when we consciously sin against God we lose our peace and joy and the sense of His presence. When the Lord Jesus bore in Himself the sins of the world, when He took on Himself our sins, that meant that He must lose at that time the sense of the Father's presence, which before had been the constant experience of his life. From that awful loss He had shrunk in Gethsemane. But the loud cry that came from His lips was a cry of victory, and then He 'breathed his last' (verse 37).

c. Torn curtain in the temple

Another sign of the meaning of the death of Christ is given in verse 38 where it says, 'the curtain of the temple was torn in two, from top to bottom.' In the temple the Holy Place, where the priests burnt incense in their worship of God, was separated from the Holy of Holies by a heavy curtain. Into that Holy of Holies only the high priest went, and that only once a year, on the Day of Atonement when sacrifice was offered for the sins of all the people. (See Leviticus 16.) Hebrews 9:8 says that the Holy Spirit in this way indicated that the way into the holiest place of the presence of God was not yet open. Now the curtain was torn in two from top to bottom. The way was open. The one perfect sacrifice for the sins of the world had been offered. Through Jesus Christ and because of His dying for us, we can come freely to God and find His forgiveness and acceptance of us.

d. Centurion's confession

The centurion was the Roman army officer in charge of the crucifixion. He had watched all that had happened. He had never seen any person suffer and die like this. In his amazement he was moved to say, 'Truly this man was the Son of God!' He could not understand all that Christians mean when they confess Jesus as Son of God. Some would therefore translate his words as 'a son of God'. Mark saw that his confession had at least some understanding of the great fact that he had expressed in the first verse of his Gospel that it was about the good news of 'Jesus Christ the Son of God.' Many Romans, like those for whom Mark first wrote his Gospel, were to make the confession that this Roman centurion made at the foot of the cross. They would make it with fuller understanding. Countless people all over the world have come to believe in the Crucified One as 'truly... the Son of God.'

Prayer   *All glory and thanksgiving to You, Holy Father, because You gave Your only Son Jesus Christ to be the one perfect sacrifice for the sin of the world, that all who believe in Him might have eternal life.*   AMEN.

For further thought and study   1. Psalm 22 was written by one who suffered much evil at the hands of others and yet he kept his faith in God. How much of that Psalm can you apply to the sufferings of Jesus?

2. How does Hebrews 9 help us to understand more the words of verse 38?

3. The Acts of the Apostles shows us how Christian preaching centred on the death (and resurrection) of Jesus. How far does Mark tell us the meaning of His death? In what ways do the Epistles express this more fully? See such passages as Romans 3:21–26, 2 Corinthians 5:17–21, Gala-

tians 2:20, 1 Peter 2:21–25, 3:18 and 1 John 1:5–2:2.

Notes 1. The parallels in the other Gospels give us details of Jesus' sufferings and more of His words from the cross. See Matthew 27:45–54, Luke 23:34–49 and John 19:18–30.

2. Some have suggested the physical cause of the 'darkness over the whole land' (verse 33) was a 'black sirocco', that is the dust-laden wind which blows in from the desert, and known from time to time in Palestine.

3. Another explanation of verse 38 is that the curtain was the large heavy curtain at the entrance to the Holy Place (rather than that between the Holy Place and the Holy of Holies). The tearing of this other curtain could be seen by worshippers in the temple. It would be a sign that the worship of the temple had come to an end. There need be no more sacrifices. Jesus had fulfilled the meaning of the temple and had offered the one perfect Sacrifice for sin. A few years later, the temple was destroyed, in 70 AD. This explanation of verse 38 is possible, but it is more likely that the curtain that shut off the Holy of Holies is meant.

Study 60: BURIAL OF JESUS

40There were also women looking on from afar, among whom were Mary Magdalene, and Mary the mother of James the younger and of Joses, and Salome, 41who, when he was in Galilee, followed him, and ministered to him; and also many other women who came up with him to Jerusalem.

42And when the evening had come, since it was the day or Preparation, that is, the day before the sabbath, 43Joseph of Arimathea, a respected member of the council, who was also himself looking for the kingdom of God, took courage and went to Pilate, and asked for the body of Jesus. 44And Pilate wondered if he were already dead; and, summoning the centurion, he asked him whether he was already dead. 45And when he learned from the centurion that he was dead, he granted the body to Joseph. 46And he bought a linen

shroud and, taking him down, wrapped him in the linen shroud, and laid him in a tomb which had been hewn out of the rock; and he rolled a stone against the door of the tomb. [47]**Mary Magdalene and Mary the mother of Joses saw where he was laid**   (15:40–47).

It was important that the Gospels should tell of the burial of Jesus. It made clear that His death was a fact that people could not dispute. The apostle Paul said that the good news that he preached was that 'Christ died for our sins in accordance with the scriptures, that he was buried' (1 Corinthians 15:3–4). From the earliest centuries of the Church Christians have confessed in their Creed that Jesus 'suffered under Pontius Pilate, was crucified, dead and buried.' In spite of what some people have tried to say at times in history, Jesus truly died and was buried. There were plenty of witnesses. Mark speaks here of a few of them.

a. The women

When all of the disciples had run away, some of the women who had followed Jesus stood by the cross to the end. They were women who had helped Jesus and His band of disciples in Galilee. Luke 8:3 says that they gave of their possessions to support the Lord and the twelve with Him. When verse 41 says that these women 'followed him, and ministered to him', we can imagine what their practical help and service meant. Now they were with Him till they saw Him die and His body placed in the tomb. Some of them are named. There was 'Mary Magdalene' – we can understand her gratitude to Jesus as before she met Him she had been a demon-possessed woman (Luke 8:2). There was 'Mary the mother of James the younger and of Joses' – James and Joses must have been known to Mark's readers and perhaps James was the one of the twelve mentioned in 3:18. There was Salome, and when we read verse 40 here with Matthew 27:56, we may be right to say that Salome was the mother of James and John and the sons of Zebedee.

Verse 41 says there were 'many other women'.

b. Joseph of Arimathea

The person who did the work of burying Jesus was Joseph of Arimathea (according to John 19:39 Nicodemus helped him). Verse 43 describes him in two ways:

1. He was 'a respected member of the council'. That seems to mean that he was a member of the Sanhedrin, the Jewish council who handed Jesus over to Pilate (verse 1); but Luke 23:51 says that he 'had not consented to their purpose and deed'.

2. He was 'looking for the kingdom of God'. Luke 2:25 and 38 tell us of people like that at the time when Jesus was born. It is in Matthew (27:57) and John (19:38) that he is called a 'disciple', 'but secretly for fear of the Jews'.

Jewish law did not allow the dead body of a crucified person to remain all night unburied (see Deuteronomy 21:23). But because of what Jesus had come to mean to him, Joseph 'took courage' and asked Pilate for permission to bury the body of Jesus. Since death often came slowly to people who were crucified, Pilate was surprised that Jesus was already dead; but 'when he learned from the centurion that he was dead, he granted the body to Joseph'.

The Jewish leaders had done the work that they had wanted to do – they had condemned Jesus and handed Him over to Pilate. Pilate had done his work – he had condemned Jesus to death, and handed Him over to the soldiers. The soldiers had done their work – they had nailed Jesus to the cross and now reported to Pilate that he was dead. Now Joseph does his work – he buries the body of Jesus in his tomb in the rock. As with tombs that can be seen in Jerusalem today, a great round stone was rolled into place at the entrance to the tomb. The sorrowing women watched all that happened and they 'saw where he was laid'. To everyone concerned that seemed to be the end of the story of Jesus of Nazareth.

Meditation   *'Low in the grave He lay,*
            Jesus, my Saviour,
            Waiting the coming day,
            Jesus my Lord.'
            (R. Lawry)

For further thought and study   1. For what reasons do
you think it is important that the Gospels tell us that the
women followers of Jesus stayed with Him to the end and
witnessed His burial?

2. What further details are there about Joseph of
Arimathea and what he did for the burial of Jesus (see
Matthew 27:55–66; Luke 23:49–56 and John 19:31–42)?

Study 61: 'HE HAS RISEN'

[1]And when the sabbath was past, Mary Magdalene and
Mary the mother of James, and Salome, bought spices, so
that they might go and anoint him. [2]And very early on the
first day of the week they went to the tomb when the sun had
risen. [3]And they were saying to one another, 'Who will roll
away the stone for us from the door of the tomb?' [4]And
looking up, they saw that the stone was rolled back – it was
very large. [5]And entering the tomb, they saw a young man
sitting on the right side, dressed in a white robe; and they
were amazed. [6]And he said to them, 'Do not be amazed; you
seek Jesus of Nazareth, who was crucified. He has risen, he
is not here; see the place where they laid him. [7]But go, tell his
disciples and Peter that he is going before you to Galilee;
there you will see him, as he told you.' [8]And they went out
and fled from the tomb; for trembling and astonishment had
come upon them; and they said nothing to anyone, for they
were afraid   (16:1–8).

It must have seemed that the story of Jesus of Nazareth

was at an end on the Friday of His crucifixion. He was dead and buried. The hopes of his disciples were dashed to the ground. 'We had hoped that he was the one to redeem Israel', one disciple said (Luke 24:21). But death was not the end. Vividly Mark tells us of those who on the Sunday morning came to realize that He was no longer in the tomb. He was risen. There was good news to tell, good news of a living Lord, good news that has since been taken to all the world. Notice three things that Mark says about those to whom this good news first came.

a. Surprised

The same women (at least some of them) who saw Jesus die (15:40), and saw Him buried (15:47), came to the tomb in the morning after the Jewish sabbath was over. They had brought spices, and their thought was to carry out the last possible act of love and devotion, and anoint the body of Jesus. The problem that concerned them as they made their way to the tomb was how they could move the great stone rolled into the entrance of the tomb. They were utterly surprised at what they found. 'The stone was rolled back.' The tomb was empty except for 'a young man...dressed in a white robe', who had a message for them.

b. Amazed

They understood quickly that it was no ordinary young man whom they saw. 'They were amazed' as they saw him. They were more amazed at his message: 'You seek Jesus of Nazareth, who was crucified. He has risen, he is not here; see the place where they laid him.' They were overcome by the sense of the mighty power and majesty of God. God had been at work in a way that was beyond their thought and understanding. The crucified Jesus had been raised from the dead. They had a message to pass on (verse 7), but in the first place they could do nothing but run away from the tomb – trembling, amazed, astonished, saying nothing to anyone, 'for they were afraid.'

c. Comforted

Mark does not tell us what the women did later, but they had a message of great joy to pass on. The angel's presence and message were awe-inspiring, but of wonderful comfort too. It was for all the disciples; and the women were to pass it on to them. Peter was mentioned specially. We can imagine how he must have felt since Friday – not only because his Master was crucified, but also because he had failed and denied Him, two things he had promised so confidently that he would never do. Peter needed to know now that his Master would welcome him back as a disciple. Jesus, risen from the dead, wanted to see him again, even though he had failed Him so badly.

In every part of the New Testament *the resurrection* stands at the *centre of the Christian good news*. If it were not for the resurrection there would have been no good news, no church, no power to transform lives.

But people have questioned it, challenged it, and given reasons why they find it hard to believe. We must be prepared to face the challenges and to find the answers to them. Here are some of the things that have been said.

1. Jesus did not really rise from the dead. His disciples came and stole the body and said He was risen. We find this said in Matthew 28:13. But could His disciples, if they had done such a thing, go out with such confidence and love and risk their lives for what they knew was untrue?

2. There are differences in the reports that we have in the four Gospels. Yes, there are differences of detail – as there can be today in the witness of those who tell of the same event. The differences show that the reports are independent one of another. They agree in the basic things – the time, the place, the empty tomb, the risen Lord.

3. The Gospels were written at least 30 years after Jesus had died and so some say that they are not accurate. Perhaps it was just that the disciples felt that Jesus was alive,

not that the tomb was empty and His body raised from death. In many parts of Africa, and amongst other peoples in the world, there are those who can speak confidently of seeing a loved one who has died. Perhaps it was like that with the disciples who saw Jesus. There are some important things to say against such a view. The apostle Paul said how he passed on to others the good news that he received 'that Christ died for our sins...that he was buried, that he was raised on the third day' (1 Corinthians 15:3–4). He must have received this information at the time of his conversion to Christ a very few years after Jesus died. He says clearly that Jesus was dead, buried, raised. That must mean raised from the grave. Jewish people (unlike Greeks) could not think or speak of resurrection unless it was the raising of the body from death. Moreover, there was a time when the experience of the risen Jesus began – the third day. This led Christians from earliest times to change the day of weekly celebration from the seventh day, the Sabbath, to the Lord's Day, the first day of the week.

4. People are sometimes perplexed by the question, How could the physical body of Jesus be raised from the dead and then return as a physical body to a heavenly life? There are many things that are beyond our human understanding, but when we read the Gospel records (Matthew 28, Luke 24 and John 20–21 with this chapter in Mark) we find that they indicate that the body of Jesus was raised from the tomb and then transformed into a spiritual body (as Paul speaks of resurrection and the life to come in 1 Corinthians 15:42–54). The Sadducees, as Jesus said in 12:24, questioned the resurrection because they did not know the power of God. Ephesians 1:19–20 speaks of the 'immeasurable greatness' of God's power that was shown when He raised Christ from the dead. He is the Creator of the universe and the source of all life and of every kind of life. He has power to raise the physical body and transform it to a spiritual body.

Meditation   *Jesus said, 'Fear not; I am the first and the last, and the living one; I died, and behold I am alive for evermore'* (Revelation 1:17–18).

For further thought and study   1. Study the importance the Resurrection had in the preaching of the early Church. See Acts 2:22–36, 3:13–16, 5:30–32, 10:36–43, 13:26–39 and 17:24–31.

2. What should the resurrection of Christ mean for the Christian today, especially in what it means to serve a living Master, to be called to live a new life in Christ and to have hope for the future? See, for example, Romans 8:31–39, 1 Corinthians 15, Colossians 3:1–4 and 1 Peter 1:3–9.

Note   Verse 7, like 14:28, speaks of the risen Lord going before His disciples to meet them in Galilee. According to Luke and John He met them first in Jerusalem. Perhaps what this means is that as He first called them to be disciples in Galilee, so He would gather them together again there, and send them out from there to their work for Him. Matthew 28:16–20 tells how on a mountain in Galilee He told them to go out to 'make disciples of all nations' and promised to be with them always.

Ending of the Gospel

There is something strange about the close of this Gospel. Verses 9–20 are not found in some of the oldest copies of Mark. A few ancient copies have a different ending. As we read verses 9–20 we can see that they do not really follow on from verse 8. They give us brief accounts of some of the things that happened after Jesus rose from the dead. (Some of these are told in more detail in Luke 24 and John 20.) They are in a different style of writing from verses 1–8. It seems certain that verses 9–20 were not in the Gospel as Mark originally wrote it. Did the Gospel end with verse 8, telling how the women at the tomb went out in fear and said nothing to anyone? Some people think that Mark purposely ended his Gospel at this point. Yet that is hardly likely.

Verse 7, in particular, leads us to expect a record of Jesus meeting with His disciples (including Peter) in Galilee. If verse 8 was not the end, what happened? Perhaps something caused Mark to stop his writing suddenly, never to finish it off. That is unlikely. More probably, the end of the scroll on which the Gospel was written was damaged and so the ending has been lost.

This remains a mystery, but it seems that another writer in the early years of the Church added verses 9–20 to round off the Gospel with details of the appearances of the risen Lord. Because of this, translators of the Bible have not been sure whether to have verses 9–20 as part of the Gospel or not. The Revised Standard Version has sometimes printed these verses as part of the Gospel and sometimes put them in small print at the bottom of the page. Probably we are wisest to conclude that these verses which have come down to us from so early in the life of the Church should be treated as part of our Scriptures, and we will study them for the sake of the things that they tell us of Jesus after His resurrection.

Study 62: CLOSING OFF THE GOSPEL

⁹**Now when he rose early on the first day of the week, he appeared first to Mary Magdalene, from whom he had cast out seven demons. ¹⁰She went out and told those who had been with him, as they mourned and wept. ¹¹But when they heard that he was alive and had been seen by her, they would not believe it.**

¹²**After this he appeared in another form to two of them as they were walking in the country. ¹³And they went back and told the rest, but they did not believe them.**

¹⁴**Afterward he appeared to the eleven themselves as they sat at table; and he upbraided them for their unbelief and hardness of heart, because they had not believed those who**

saw him after he had risen. ¹⁵And he said to them, 'Go into all the world and preach the gospel to the whole creation. ¹⁶He who believes and is baptized will be saved; but he who does not believe will be condemned. ¹⁷And these signs will accompany those who believe: in my name they will cast out demons; they will speak in new tongues; ¹⁸they will pick up serpents, and if they drink any deadly thing it will not hurt them; they will lay their hands on the sick, and they will recover.'

¹⁹So then the Lord Jesus, after he had spoken to them, was taken up into heaven, and sat down at the right hand of God. ²⁰And they went forth and preached everywhere, while the Lord worked with them and confirmed the message by the signs that attended it. Amen (16:9–20).

These verses which round off the Gospel – probably after the original ending was lost – tell us briefly five things that happened after the Lord's resurrection.

a. He appeared to Mary Magdalene
We read the fuller account of this in John 20:1–2, 11–18. She was one of the women who was by the cross when Jesus died and witnessed His burial (15:40–47). She was with those who were first at the tomb on Sunday morning (verse 1). How true to the ways of God that Jesus 'appeared first to Mary Magdalene', not first to the great and powerful, not even to 'the eleven' special disciples, but to a woman whose life had once been dominated by the powers of evil and whom Jesus had set free. We can understand how with great joy she ran to tell the good news to others. 'I have seen the Lord!' she said to them in her excitement. (John 20:18). But, burdened with their sorrow and disappointment and sense of failure, 'they would not believe it' (verse 11).

b. He appeared to two disciples on the road
What we read in verses 12–13 is told more fully in Luke

24:13–33. The two were talking on the road to Emmaus 11 kilometres (7 miles) from Jerusalem. They did not recognize the form of Jesus at first. He helped them to understand from the Scriptures that the Christ had to suffer and die and then 'enter into his glory'. At their journey's end, He made Himself known in the way He broke the bread among them. Again we read that those who heard their report 'did not believe them'. Soon they would be convinced; and down through history the risen Lord, though now unseen, has made His presence known to His people in word and sacrament.

c. He appeared to the eleven

Verse 14 tells us of an appearance of Jesus 'to the eleven themselves as they sat at table'. Luke (24:36–49) tells us of such an appearance. John (20:19–23) tells of Jesus coming to the disciples that Sunday night when they were behind closed doors for fear. Thomas was not with them then, but he was there when Jesus came to them again a week later (John 20:26–29). Unbelief, hardness of heart, slowness to accept the good news – these things Jesus rebuked in His disciples. He had told them to expect the resurrection, but it had been hard for them to understand and to believe.

d. He sends them to preach the good news in all the world

One of the most important things that happened after Jesus' resurrection is told in verses 15–18. The Lord gave to His disciples what was to be their work – and the work of the whole Church – in the days and years ahead. They had good news to tell, and to tell to all the world. It was good news of life and salvation, the good news of what Jesus had come to do, by His life, His death, his resurrection. From the earliest days of the Church believers (often with their families) were baptized in water as an outward sign of faith and also of the cleansing work of God, setting free from sin those who turn to Him (see Acts 2:37–41; 8:12 and 36–38; 10:44–48; 16:14, 15 and 30–34). The truth and power of the gospel would be seen by the signs that the Lord would do through His messengers and often by His protecting of them. God works in power as His gospel is preached. He has done so again and again; but He works as He chooses, and we have no right to demand, for ourselves or for others, any miracle that we would choose. As we read a passage like Hebrews 11:32–38 we realize that while God sometimes delivers His servants from danger and death, sometimes He allows them to suffer even martyrdom for His sake. Like verse 17 here the Acts of the Apostles sometimes speaks of the gift of tongues – in Acts chapter 2 it is the means of the gospel being understood by those who spoke different languages, while in Acts 10:44–48 and 19:1–7 it is a sign of the presence and the power of the Spirit. It is helpful to read what the apostle Paul says in 1 Corinthians chapters 12–14 about 'tongues' as one of the gifts of the Spirit, not necessarily for all and to be related rightly to the gift of 'prophecy' and above all to the most important gift of 'love'.

e. Jesus' ascension

Verse 19 tells us, as Acts 1:9–11 does also, that when His work on earth was at an end, Jesus returned to the Father. When it says that He 'sat down on the right hand of God', it uses our human language to speak of His place with the Father and His authority. So His disciples 'went forth and preached everywhere'. Wherever they went 'the Lord worked with them', showing the gospel was not just the thoughts of the people who preached it, but His own message of truth and salvation for all the world. Verse 20 closes the Gospel for us, but it describes the work which is also our work to do, and the work of the Church 'to the close of the age' (Matthew 28:20).

For further thought and study 1. Compare the way that the mission of Christ's disciples is given in verses 15–18 with what is said in Matthew 28:18–20, Luke 24:44–49, John

20:21–23 and Acts 1:6–8. How do those other passages add to what is said in this ending of Mark?

2. How does the Acts of the Apostles illustrate what is said in verses 17–18 and 20 about the signs that take place when the gospel is preached? See Acts 2:1–18, 43; 3:1–16; 4:16, 22, 29–30; 5:12–16; 6:8; 8:4–8, 13; 9:32–43; 10:44–46; 14:8–10; 16:16–18; 19:5–6, 11:12; 28:1–6. Do you think that such signs are given especially when the gospel is first preached in a place, and later the quality of Christian people's lives becomes the greatest sign to others of the truth and power of the gospel? See John 13:35.

Prayer *Lord God Almighty, we praise and thank You for this record in the Gospel of Your Son Jesus Christ and of His coming to us. May we continue to learn from it so that we may know Him more truly, love Him more dearly, obey Him more fully, and in the power of the Holy Spirit share the good news of Him, to the blessing of others and to the glory of Your great Name.*   AMEN.